BYRON
A Critical Study

BYRON

A Critical Study

ANDREW RUTHERFORD

OLIVER AND BOYD

EDINBURGH AND LONDON

1961

OLIVER AND BOYD LTD
Tweeddale Court
Edinburgh 1

39A Welbeck Street
London W 1

First Published 1961

To my Wife

Preface

M ANY people have helped me in the preparation of this book, but I wish in particular to thank Professor W. L. Renwick for his encouragement throughout, Dr Ian Jack for his advice (especially in the early stages), Miss Helen Gardner for her stimulating criticisms of my argument, Mr John P. Mackintosh for his comments on the political material, Professor A. Norman Jeffares for his suggestions on revising the MS for publication, and finally my friend and colleague Mark Kinkead-Weekes, for whose sympathetic and perceptive criticism I am deeply grateful.

My indebtedness to other writers on Byron is considerable, but instead of attempting to acknowledge it in detail in this preface, I have listed in the bibliography the books and articles that I found most useful. Special mention must be made, however, of the essays by Dr F. R. Leavis and the late Professor Grierson—essays which rank, in my opinion, with the best Byron criticism of this century, and which have provided me with starting points for many fruitful lines of inquiry.

My thanks are due to the Carnegie Trust for the Universities of Scotland, for the scholarship which first enabled me to undertake research on Byron's poetry ; to Sir John Murray, for his kindness in allowing me to examine, and in one case to quote from, Byron MSS in his collection; and to the following publishers for permission to quote from the works indicated: Edward Arnold Ltd (Oliver Elton, *A Survey of English Literature 1780-1830*); Bowes and Bowes Ltd (E. M. Butler, *Byron and Goethe*); Chatto and Windus Ltd (H. J. C. Grierson, *The Background of English Literature*; F. R. Leavis, *The Common Pursuit*; Ralph Milbanke, Lord Lovelace, *Astarte*); the Clarendon Press (*Wordsworth's "Prelude"*, ed. E. de Selincourt, rev. Helen Darbishire); Constable and Co. Ltd (E. C. Mayne, *The Life and Letters of Anne Isabella, Lady Noel Byron; The Letters of Sir Walter Scott*, ed. H. J. C. Grierson, D. Cook, W. M. Parker and others); Faber and Faber Ltd (T. S. Eliot, *On Poetry and Poets*);

Rupert Hart-Davis, Ltd (Humphry House, *Coleridge*); Harvard University Press (*The Keats Circle: Letters and Papers 1816-1878*, ed. H. E. Rollins); Manchester University Press (J. H. Frere, *The Monks and the Giants*, ed. R. D. Waller); Methuen and Co. Ltd (*The Poems of Alexander Pope*, Twickenham edn); John Murray Ltd (Lord Broughton, *Recollections of a Long Life*, ed. Lady Dorchester; *Lord Byron's Correspondence*, ed. John Murray; *Byron. A Self-Portrait. Letters and Diaries, 1798 to 1824*, ed. Peter Quennell; L. A. Marchand, *Byron. A Biography*); Thomas Nelson and Sons Ltd, and the University of Texas Press (*Byron's "Don Juan"*, ed. T. G. Steffan and W. W. Pratt); Putnam and Co. Ltd (Charles du Bos, *Byron and the Need of Fatality*, tr. E. C. Mayne); University of North Carolina Press (W. J. Calvert, *Byron: Romantic Paradox*); Vandenhoeck und Ruprecht (S. C. Chew, *The Dramas of Lord Byron*); Yale University Press (*Unpublished Letters of Matthew Arnold*, ed. Arnold Whitridge).

All quotations from Byron's poems are from E. H. Coleridge's edition, but in a few cases where there is a significant variation in the readings preferred by Steffan and Pratt in their edition of *Don Juan*, I have cited these in footnotes.

Contents

Introduction

THE object of this book is to offer an account of Byron's career and achievement as a poet.

His life and personality have always fascinated readers, and today (as in the past) there is no shortage of biography or psychological analysis to satisfy their curiosity. But this perennial interest in "Byron the man" has led all too often to a neglect of Byron the poet; and although his works have never gone completely out of fashion—although they are indeed the subject of some valuable modern studies—they cannot be said to have received their due of critical attention. I propose, therefore, to concentrate on them, assuming that the main facts of his life are well-known, and presenting only such biographical material as seems directly useful to the critic.

There is, however, a good deal of this: his literary work was only one of Byron's interests, and in my first chapter I attempt to place it in the context of his other main ambitions, showing how they affected his whole attitude to poetry. Then again, his work varies remarkably in character and content, and to explain these variations one must frequently refer to aspects of his mind and personality (as well as to his fluctuating literary tastes), for many of the poems derive directly from his own experience, or reflect his changing and contrasting moods, his psychological and mental conflicts. Biography and criticism, in Byron's case at any rate, are not opposed but complementary approaches.

His career as poet divides itself into two major phases. In the first of these (from 1805 or so to the summer of 1817) he wrote his early satires, some comparatively unimportant minor verse, and the long series of romantic works that made him famous. Throughout this period, which covers almost two-thirds of his entire creative life, he was trying his hand at different types of poetry and expressing certain of his moods and feelings, without ever finding a poetic manner wholly suited to his personality and genius. One studies the results as one does the juvenilia and subsequent experiments of any author: they reveal his early motives and intentions, his false starts and misconceptions of his talent, his peculiar dangers and temptations, his technical problems, his first presentation of recurring themes, and his anticipation of some features, good or bad, of his great poetry. Yet one is also conscious of the need for a more sustained critique of works like the verse tales and *Childe Harold's Pilgrimage*, which are in a sense important facts of literary history; a critique too of "Byronism" as it figures in these poems seems essential in any serious assessment of this kind. And what is really being examined here (in Chapters Two to Six) is not just the early stages of Byron's development, but his claim to be considered great as a romantic poet.

His main achievement lies, however, in his satires in *ottava rima*, for his discovery of the *Beppo* style transformed him, almost overnight, into a major poet, and he retains this status only so long as he confines himself to that style—it was an essential condition of his greatness, the one medium that allowed his genius its full scope. Yet this discovery did not mean (as is frequently supposed) that Byron's difficulties were all over—that from now on masterpieces would flow easily or inevitably from his pen. Although he could now write superbly he was still faced with artistic and personal problems, his solutions to which vary in effectiveness from poem to poem; so that important discriminations must be made even within this group of satires which are superficially so much alike. Chapters Seven to Thirteen, then, are concerned almost entirely with the *ottava rima* poems. They were not the only works that Byron wrote in these years, but they were the best: apart from them the period 1817-24 was one of largely misguided experiment on his part, and the plays which were his other main concern are far inferior in quality. Once he has found his true poetic *métier*, therefore, I prefer to concentrate on it, referring to his other writings only in so far as they affect or throw light on the greater work. And while this obviously makes my survey less complete than it would otherwise have been, it allows fuller consideration of the poems that really merit it—the *ottava rima* satires on which Byron's lasting fame depends.

ABBREVIATIONS

Corr.   *Lord Byron's Correspondence*, ed. John Murray, London 1922.

L.J.   *The Works of Lord Byron : Letters and Journals*, ed R. E. Prothero, London 1898-1901.

P.M.L.A.   Publications of the Modern Language Association of America.

P.W.   *The Works of Lord Byron : Poetry*, ed. E. H. Coleridge, 2nd edn, London 1904-5.

Self-Portrait Byron. *A Self-Portrait. Letters and Diaries, 1798 to 1824,* ed. Peter Quennell, London 1950.

I

The Poet Aristocrat

BYRON was not a dedicated poet like Wordsworth, Keats, or Shelley, but a gentleman amateur; and though poetry was one of his chief interests and activities throughout his life, his attitude towards it was peculiarly ambivalent. From an early age he felt the urge to write, and he developed an intense desire for literary fame. He wanted to be hailed by everyone as a great poet, and his claim that he had never courted popularity[1] was rather disingenuous, for on several occasions he had based new projects or experiments on his estimate of the public's taste, and he tried almost every *genre* in his endeavours to establish, maintain and extend his reputation. "A successful work," he once told Lady Blessington, "makes a man a wretch for life: it engenders in him a thirst for notoriety and praise, that precludes the possibility of repose; this spurs him on to attempt others, which are always expected to be superior to the first";[2] and he himself felt this compulsion very strongly. But in spite of his ambition and the efforts which he made to satisfy it, Byron seldom rated poetry very highly among human activities. He would speak disparagingly about authors as a class, and he refused to be regarded as a mere poet or man of letters: always conscious of his rank, he prided himself more on being a man of fashion and of noble birth, while he also liked to think of himself as a leader, politician, and man of action. These conceptions co-existed rather uneasily in his mind, often in a state of tension, and sometimes in open conflict. A Renaissance gentleman could be a soldier, athlete, traveller-explorer, man of fashion, poet, lover, and administrator, and feel no incompatibility between these roles since they were unified and integrated for him in the ideal of

---

[1] *The Works of Lord Byron* : *Letters and Journals*, ed. R. E. Prothero, London 1898-1901, (henceforth cited as *L.J.*), VI. 138.

[2] Lady Blessington, *Conversations of Lord Byron with the Countess of Blessington*, London 1834, (henceforth cited as Lady Blessington, *Conversations*), p. 273.

the Courtier. Byron, with a comparable range of interests, found it very difficult to reconcile his various ambitions and ideals of personality.

His earliest dreams, he tells us, had been martial[3]—as a boy he longed to raise a troop of horse (to be called "Byron's Blacks"), which he said would perform "prodigies of valour."[4] This was only a boy's daydream, and his lameness forbade serious consideration of the Army or the Navy as careers, in spite of his family connexions with both services. Yet he spent a lot of time on fencing, boxing, swimming, and pistol-practice, while his travels and adventures in the East enabled him to sneer at "homekeeping bards,"[5] and to think of himself as having led an active life instead of just a literary one. He also had some oratorical ability, which showed itself when he was still at school; and in February 1812, with his speech on the Framebreakers Bill, he embarked on the parliamentary career to which he had looked forward before leaving England in 1809. His success on this occasion was soon over-shadowed by the greater triumph of *Childe Harold*, but even so, he did not immediately abandon his political ambitions: for some months he continued to attend the House (though less assiduously than before), and in April 1812 he spoke again, on the issue of Catholic Emancipation. This speech, however, seems to have been less well received, and although Byron rose again in June 1813 to present Major Cartwright's petition on Reform, he had by then conceived a distaste for the whole business,[6] and in November he declared himself "sick of parliamentary mummeries."[7] He continued to write verses—often highly provocative—on events of the day, but once his *liaison* with Lady Oxford had come to an end, he soon ceased to take any active part in political affairs.[8]

---

[3] *L.J.*, v. 426.

[4] Thomas Moore, *The Life, Letters and Journals of Lord Byron*, new and complete edn, repr., London 1932, (henceforth cited as Moore, *Life*), p. 46.

[5] *L.J.*, III. 117 (cp. 119-20).

[6] *L.J.*, II. 197-8.

[7] *L.J.*, II. 318.

[8] For an account of Lady Oxford's encouragement of Byron in his political career, see D. V. Erdman, "Lord Byron and the Genteel Reformers," in *P.M.L.A.*, LVI. (1941), pp. 1065 ff., and "Lord Byron as Rinaldo," in *P.M.L.A.*, LVII. (1942), pp. 189 ff.

Nevertheless, he still professed to regard such activities as more important than mere literary work. "I by no means rank poetry or poets high in the scale of intellect," he wrote to Annabella Milbanke in November 1813:

> This may look like affectation, but it is my real opinion.
> . . . I prefer the talents of action—of war, or the senate, or even of science,—to all the speculations of those mere dreamers of another existence (I don't mean religiously but fancifully) and spectators of this apathy. Disgust and perhaps incapacity have rendered me now a mere spectator ; but I have occasionally mixed in the active and tumultuous departments of existence, and in these alone my recollection rests with any satisfaction, though not the best parts of it.[9]

In his journal for that winter he was even more emphatic, saying that he no longer attaches

> that importance to authorship which many do, and which, when young, I did also. . . . I do think the preference of *writers* to *agents*—the mighty stir made about scribbling and scribes, by themselves and others—a sign of effeminacy, degeneracy, and weakness. Who would write, who had any thing better to do ? 'Action—action—action' said Demosthenes : 'Action*s*—action*s*,' I say, and not writing,—least of all, rhyme. Look at the querulous and monotonous lives of the 'genus ;'—except Cervantes, Tasso, Dante, Ariosto, Kleist (who were brave and active citizens), Æschylus, Sophocles, and some other of the antiques also—what a worthless, idle brood it is![10]

This attitude appears again and again throughout his life, and is of course associated with his own hopes of excelling in some other field. In March 1807, for example, he had declared that poetic fame was by no means the acme of his wishes,[11] and in February 1817 he told Moore that if he lived another ten years he would do something great, but not in literature— "for that is nothing; and it may seem odd enough to say, I do not think it my vocation."[12]

In such outbursts Byron's low opinion of poetry is obvious. He had given practically no thought to the justification or to

[9] *L.J.*, III. 405.　　[10] *L.J.*, II. 345 (cp. 338, 342-3, 351).
[11] *L.J.*, I. 122.　　[12] *L.J.*, IV. 62: cp. V. 453.

the defence of literature, and for much of his career he stood alone among the great Romantics in not holding any "theory of poetry," any high—or clear—conception of its nature, functions, and value. A note jotted down in January 1821 suggests a visionary notion: "What is Poetry?—The feeling of a Former world and Future"[13]; but this was not at all characteristic of him, and in general he was unaffected by, or hostile to, current romantic theories. Nor had he gleaned from neoclassicism any adequate alternative. In *English Bards*, indeed, he appears to hold the conventional view of satire as a corrective to vice, folly, and bad taste, but he soon abandoned this position: "The end of all scribblement," he wrote in October 1810, "is to amuse";[14] and the conception of poets as mere entertainers lies behind many of his subsequent pronouncements. He knew from his own experience that writers often feel deeper compulsions, yet this knowledge made him look on poetry simply as a mechanism of escape—"To withdraw *myself* from *myself* . . . has ever been my sole, my entire, my sincere motive in scribbling at all"[15]—or as the safety-valve for an unbalanced mind—"It is the lava of the imagination whose eruption prevents an earthquake."[16] None of these accounts of the matter made literature seem important for mankind, and Byron valued it accordingly: "As to defining what a poet *should* be," he wrote contemptuously in 1821, "it is not worth while, for what are *they* worth? what have they done?"[17]

Versifying for him was, as it were, a natural activity, and he wrote a great deal without bothering to justify it or to think about his final purpose. When he wanted to defend Pope publicly, however, he was forced to reconsider this whole question, for on entering the Bowles controversy he had to challenge the assumptions of Pope's critics and define his own; and the result was that he now took up a very different critical position, asserting that "the highest of all poetry is ethical poetry, as the highest of all earthly objects must be moral truth."[18] "He who can reconcile poetry with truth and wisdom," he goes on to say in this first Bowles pamphlet, "is the

[13] *L.J.*, v. 189.   [14] *L.J.*, i. 299.   [15] *L.J.*, ii. 351.

[16] *L.J.*, iii. 405.   [17] *L.J.*, v. 196.   [18] *L.J.*, v. 554.

only true '*poet*' in its real sense, 'the *maker*,' 'the *creator*,'—why must this mean the 'liar,' the 'feigner,' the 'tale-teller'? A man may make and create better things than these."[19] He later praised Pope as the greatest moral poet of any age,[20] and his whole panegyric implies a changed and more traditional view of the writer's function: "Without canting, and yet without neglecting religion, he has assembled all that a good and great man can gather together of moral wisdom cloathed in consummate beauty."[21]

These revised opinions are reflected in his own poetic practice. In *Don Juan*, for example, Byron was trying to create a better thing than the poems which had made him famous—it is an attempt to reconcile poetry with truth and wisdom (even if his truth and wisdom are occasionally limited in nature). He is telling an amusing tale, but amusement is not its sole end: all the cantos—even the most flippant—show his desire to influence the reader's mind by challenging and deflating false emotions and beliefs; and as time went on he often thought of his satires as *weapons* with which he could strike blows at tyranny, war, social hypocrisy, and other evils.[22] Poetry, in fact, had become for him another form of action, not to be despised or undervalued.

Even in these later years, however, Byron was not wholly consistent in his theory or practice. In defending *Don Juan* and *Cain* against outraged reviewers he sometimes denied that poems could have any effect on a reader's behaviour or morality;[23] sometimes, too, he reverted to more trivial kinds of writing; and when faced with situations in which he could help the cause of liberty by action in real life, even his most "engaged" and influential poetry seemed unimportant. He admired great liberators such as Washington and Bolivar, and hoped to emulate their deeds, compared with which mere versifying was a slight achievement in his eyes. Thus in April 1821, soon after writing the Bowles letters with their praise of

---

[19] *L.J.*, v. 559-60.   [20] *L.J.*, v. 568, 590.   [21] *L.J.*, v. 590.

[22] *The Works of Lord Byron : Poetry*, ed. E. H. Coleridge, 2nd edn, London 1904-5, (henceforth cited as *P.W.*), vi. 294, 329, 370-1 ; *L.J.*, vi. 101 ; Lady Blessington, *Conversations*, p. 12.

[23] E.g., *Byron. A Self-Portrait. Letters and Diaries, 1798 to 1824*, ed. P. Quennell, London 1950, (henceforth cited as *Self-Portrait*), ii. 493 ; *L.J.*, v. 469-70.

Pope, he described the collapse of the Italian revolutionary movement and went on to say:

> And now let us be literary ;—a sad falling off, but it is always a consolation. If 'Othello's occupation be gone', let us take to the next best ; and, if we cannot contribute to make mankind more free and wise, we may amuse ourselves and those who like it. What are you writing ? . . .[24]

Or again, when the Greek expedition was being planned he put *Don Juan* aside, telling Lady Blessington that he hoped to "return . . . with something better and higher than the reputation or glory of a poet."[25] Once he had begun the great task of freeing Greece from her oppressors, "scribbling" seemed a trivial unworthy pastime: "Poetry," he said to Gamba when they were in Cephalonia, "should only occupy the idle. In more serious affairs it would be ridiculous."[26]

In this mood Byron tended to despise not only poetry-writing but the idle useless life of men of fashion. The "Corinthian" was far from being effete, and the sporting accomplishments expected of him formed a common ground between the dandy and the man of action, but Byron had a recurrent sense of the futility of fashionable life. In England this led him at times to long for the East again; in Italy he was often disgusted with his role of "*cavalier' servente*"; and on the eve of his thirty-third birthday he felt "a heaviness of heart at having lived so long, and to so little purpose."[27] On going to Greece he felt at last that he had dedicated himself to a great heroic enterprise which would justify or redeem his wasted years, and he contrasted his activities there with those of men in Society: ". . . after all," he reflected when considering his expenditure, "it is better playing at nations than gaming at Almack's or Newmarket or piecing or dinnering."[28] And Stanhope told

---

[24] *L.J.*, v. 272.

[25] Lady Blessington, *Conversations*, p. 402. Cp. *The Idler in Italy* (by the same author), London 1839-40, II. 22 : "He asserts that he who is only a poet has done little for mankind, and that *he* will endeavour to prove in his own person that a poet may be a soldier."

[26] Pietro Gamba, *A Narrative of Lord Byron's Last Journey to Greece*, London 1825, (henceforth cited as Gamba, *Narrative*), p. 48.

[27] *L.J.*, v. 181 (cp. 182).

[28] *Self-Portrait*, II. 754 : "piecing" means wenching.

Hobhouse that Byron "would say that it was better being at Missolonghi than going about talking and singing at parties in London, at past forty, like Tom Moore."[29] Yet Byron to the very last retained some qualities of the man-about-town, and his companions in Greece were struck by the extent to which his conversation and behaviour were still coloured by his life in London. He remained extremely conscious of his rank, and proud of the position he had once enjoyed; and even though he satirised Society in these later years, the ideal of the aristocrat —even of the dandy—is perhaps the one he aimed at most consistently throughout his life, trying however to combine it with those of the man of action and the poet.

As I have tried to show, he found it hard to reconcile these last two roles, and the attempt to be both poet and dandy faced him with more complex difficulties still. In Byron's "years of fame" he owed his position to his poetry, for it was the success of *Childe Harold's Pilgrimage* that gave him the *entrée* to Society, which otherwise he might never have achieved. Lord Holland once made this point most emphatically, when Moore mentioned Byron's favourite claim that he had held his place by virtue of his rank:

> Lord Holland said it was not so ; it was *not* from his birth that Lord Byron had taken the station he held in society, for till his talents became known, he was, in spite of his birth, in any thing but good society, and *but* for his talents would never, perhaps, have been in any better.[30]

Once he became known, however, Byron was accepted for his rank and personality—in some circles it was in spite of his poetry; and he liked to think that it had been so all along.[31]

[29] Lord Broughton (John Cam Hobhouse), *Recollections of a Long Life*, ed. Lady Dorchester, London 1909-11, (henceforth cited as Hobhouse, *Recollections*), III. 60.

[30] *Memoirs, Journal and Correspondence of Thomas Moore*, ed. Lord John Russell, London 1853-6, (henceforth cited as Moore, *Memoirs*), V. 284-5.

[31] "I liked the Dandies ; they were always very civil to *me*, though in general they disliked literary people, and persecuted and mystified M[m]e. de Staël, Lewis, Horace Twiss, and the like, damnably . . . . The truth is, that, though I gave up the business early, I had a tinge of Dandyism in my minority, and probably retained enough of it, to conciliate the great ones ; at four and twenty. I had gamed, and drank, and taken my degrees in most dissipations ; and having

He chose to forget his loneliness and isolation prior to the spring of 1812, and he preferred to regard himself as primarily a member of the *beau monde*, rather than as a purveyor of its entertainment. He was always ready to act as patron and help other writers with both money and encouragement, but he often professed an aristocratic disdain for full-time authors:

> [Scott], and Gifford, and Moore, [he wrote in March 1817] are the only *regulars* I ever knew who had nothing of the *Garrison* about their manner : no nonsense, nor affectations, look you ! As for the rest whom I have known, there was always more or less of the author about them—the pen peeping from behind the ear, and the thumbs a little inky, or so.[32]

And again in 1821 :

> In general, I do not draw well with literary men : not that I dislike them, but I never know what to say to them after I have praised their last publication. There are several exceptions, to be sure ; but then they have either been men of the world, such as Scott, and Moore, etc., or visionaries out of it, such as Shelley, etc. : but your literary every day man and I never went well in company—especially your foreigner, whom I never could abide.[33]

For years Byron refused to accept money on his own behalf in payment for his works, and even after he had given up this practice and taken to haggling over prices, he regarded himself not as a professional poet, but as a gentleman who happened to write verses. ("Of nothing was he more indignant," says Trelawny, "than of being treated as a man of letters, instead of as a Lord and a man of fashion."[34]) In spite of this he

no pedantry, and not being overbearing, we ran quietly together. I knew them all more or less, and they made me a Member of Watier's (a superb Club at that time), being, I take it, the only literary man (except *two others*), both men of the world, M. and S.) in it." *Detached Thoughts*, 1821. (*L.J.*, v. 423 : cp. v. 456 ; vi. 189).

[32] *L.J.*, iv. 85 : cp. Moore, *Memoirs*, v. 285.

[33] *L.J.*, v. 435.

[34] E. J. Trelawny, *Recollections of the Last Days of Shelley and Byron*, ed. E. Dowden, London 1923, (henceforth cited as Trelawny, *Recollections*), p. 24. Another account of this dualism is given by Lady Blessington (*Conversations*, pp. 158-60) : "Byron had two points of ambition,—the one to be thought the greatest poet of his day, and the other a nobleman and man of fashion, who could have

continued to write and to delight in his successes, but he was
often casual about his work, even when he had really taken
pains with it; and the impression that he liked to give is
perfectly described by Scott when he refers to Byron's "man-
aging his pen with the careless and negligent ease of a man of
quality."[35]

Partly as a result of this ambition, he often repudiated the
personality which he created and the feelings he expressed in
his own poems. There was a fundamental opposition between
what might be called his "romantic" and "aristocratic",
attitudes to life, for while the passion, melancholy and misanthropy of the Byronic hero pleased and satisfied him in
some ways, they were directly contrary to his social ideal and
alien to his normal self. This conflict in his own mind is
reflected in his works: *Childe Harold* and *Don Juan*, for example,
are so different in their modes of feeling and expression that
they seem almost irreconcilable, and some readers have indeed
condemned his more romantic poetry as mere posing. "The
whole of your misanthropy . . . is humbug," Lockhart told
him bluntly in "John Bull's" *Letter to Lord Byron:*

> You do not hate men, 'no, nor woman neither,' but you
> thought it would be a fine, interesting thing for a handsome
> young Lord to depict himself as a dark-souled, melancholy,
> morbid being, and you have done so, it must be admitted, with
> exceeding cleverness. In spite of all your pranks, (Beppo, &c.
> Don Juan included,) every boarding-school in the empire
> still contains many devout believers in the amazing misery
> of the black-haired, high-browed, blue-eyed, bare-throated,

---

arrived at distinction without the aid of his poetical genius. This often produced
curious anomalies in his conduct and sentiments, and a sort of jealousy of himself
in each separate character, that was highly amusing to an observant spectator.
If poets were talked of or eulogized, he referred to the advantages of rank and
station as commanding that place in society by right, which was only accorded to
genius by sufferance . . . . If men of fashion were praised, Byron dwelt on the
futility of their pursuits, their ignorance *en masse*, and the necessity of talents to
give lustre to rank and station . . . . I recollect once laughingly telling him that
he was fortunate in being able to consider himself a poet amongst lords, and a
lord amongst poets." Cp. Stendhal on Byron, *L.J.*, III. 442 ; and Thomas Medwin,
*Conversations of Lord Byron : Noted during a Residence with His Lordship at Pisa, in the
Years 1821 and 1822*, 2nd edn, London 1824, (henceforth cited as Medwin,
Conversations), p. 420.
[35] *Quarterly Review*, XVI. (Oct. 1816), 186.

Lord Byron. . . . Stick to Don Juan : it is the only sincere thing you have ever written ; and it will live many years after all your humbug Harolds have ceased to be, in your own words,
'A school-*girl's* tale—the wonder of an hour.' [36]

This advice is admirable. Yet the diagnosis seems inadequate and superficial in dismissing Byron's melancholy as a pose.[37] His character was complex, and Spurzheim the craniologist came nearer to the truth in telling him that his faculties and dispositions were all "strongly marked—but very antithetical; for every thing developed in & on this same skull . . . has its *opposite* in great force. . . . "[38] Gloom and gaiety were both recurrent moods throughout his life. Thus Dallas tells of Byron's loneliness and melancholy before leaving England in 1809, yet the verses sent to Hodgson from Falmouth are light-hearted and exuberant.[39] John Galt describes how Byron changed on board ship from dark solitary musing to playful activity,[40] and though his account may have been influenced by the poet's works, it is corroborated by Lady Hester Stanhope, who met Byron in September 1810: "One time he was mopish, and nobody was to speak to him; another he was for being jocular with everybody."[41] At Malta in 1811 he had an attack of morbid melancholy, though a few days later he was writing some amusing verses; and after his return to England the death of his mother and of several friends left him very

[36] *John Bull's "Letter to Lord Byron,"* ed. A. L. Strout, Norman (Oklahoma) 1947, pp. 80, 82.

[37] In any case the term is psychologically crude. As Charles du Bos says (*Byron and the Need of Fatality,* tr. E. C. Mayne, London 1932, pp. 17-18) : "there can be, even in their extremest puerilities, poses which are sincere, poses which are so much the appurtenances of the essential being that there is a sense in which his very sincerity itself demands their presence." Du Bos, however, does not consider the question of whether such "poses" ought to be indulged in or restrained by the mature intelligence.

[38] E. C. Mayne, *The Life and Letters of Anne Isabella, Lady Noel Byron,* London 1929, p. 447.

[39] R. C. Dallas, *Recollections of the Life of Lord Byron, From the Year 1808 to the End of 1814 . . .*, London 1824, (henceforth cited as Dallas, *Recollections*), pp. 61-5 ; *L.J.,* I. 230, n. 2.

[40] John Galt, *The Life of Lord Byron,* 3rd edn, London 1830, (henceforth cited as Galt, *Life*), pp. 59-61.

[41] Dr. C. L. Meryon, *Memoirs of Lady Hester Stanhope,* London 1845, III. 218.

wretched.[42] These fits of depression did not disappear when he was famous and successful: Moore observed them, and came to see that they were genuine, in spite of Byron's usual high spirits; Scott noted that although Byron was animated, "he was often melancholy,—almost gloomy"; and Lady Byron thought of his merriment and levity "only as the foam that might float on the waters of bitterness."[43] Nor would it be true to say that such emotions were confined to his adolescence and young manhood, his maturity being one of common sense, good-humour and light-heartedness. One mood was dominant in the summer of 1816, and the other in his early years in Italy, but the alternation was to continue till his death. Stanhope says that he has "often observed Lord Byron, in the midst of a humourous conversation, to pause, meditate, and his eyes become suffused with tears."[44] Dr Kennedy had noted similar lapses into melancholy,[45] while Lady Blessington in Italy thought Byron's nervous system was deranged—"a fact," she wrote, "which is evinced by the frequency of his rapid transitions from deep depression to a reckless gaiety, which as quickly subsides into sadness."[46] Even Teresa Guiccioli, when attacking the idea that Byron resembled his own early heroes, does not deny his fits of despondency—she merely argues that they were due to particular events and griefs, not to hereditary or constitutional causes.[47] There can be no doubt then that such melancholy was a fact of his experience.

The critic's primary concern, however, is not with this question of sincerity, nor with the problem of explaining

[42] L. A. Marchand, *Byron. A Biography*, London 1957, (henceforth cited as Marchand, *Byron*), I. 272-4 ; *P.W.*, III. 24-7 ; *Lord Byron's Correspondence*, ed. John Murray, London 1922, (henceforth cited as *Corr.*), I. 43-5.

[43] Moore, *Life*, p. 163 ; *L.J.*, III. 415 (cp. IV. 73, n. 1) ; R. Milbanke (Lord Lovelace), *Astarte. A Fragment of Truth Concerning . . . Lord Byron*, rev. edn, London 1921, (henceforth cited as Milbanke, *Astarte*), p. 1, n. 2 (cp. *L.J.*, V. 446).

[44] Leicester Stanhope, *Greece, in 1823, 1824, & 1825 ; Being Documents on the Greek Revolution . . . To which are added Reminiscences of Lord Byron*, London 1828, (henceforth cited as Stanhope, *Greece*), p. 504, n. (cp. pp. 504-5).

[45] James Kennedy, *Conversations on Religion, with Lord Byron and Others, held in Cephalonia . . .*, London 1830. (henceforth cited as Kennedy, *Conversations on Religion*), p. 319.

[46] *The Idler in Italy*, II. 88.

[47] Teresa Guiccioli, *My Recollections of Lord Byron ; and Those of Eye-witnesses of his Life*, London 1869, II. 301 ff.

psychologically Byron's contradictory and changing moods, but with the quality of the works themselves; and the poetry which he based on these darker emotions rarely satisfies us. There is nearly always a factitious element in his expression—and indeed in his experience—of melancholy and the associated feelings of pride, remorse, misanthropy, and loneliness. Byron's imagination was saturated in the second and third-rate romantic literature of the period, and he loved to dramatise his personality and situation in terms suggested by this reading. The result varies from poem to poem, but for the most part his romantic works never attain "the firm, sad honesty of self-analysis"[48] which we find, for example, in Coleridge's *Dejection*. Byron makes no genuine, sustained attempt to examine and evaluate his own thoughts and feelings, or to give them un-exaggerated and precise expression. Instead he presents us with highly-coloured, wrought-up versions of his mood, which act as barriers to full self-knowledge, to the understanding of himself and his predicaments; and although there are good things in these poems, they are usually incidental, while the central theme or figure is nearly always marred by this flat-tering, uncritical self-dramatisation, which was to Byron what self-pity was to Coleridge—a moral failing that he had to overcome in order to write his best poetry.

For some years, however, it was primarily in his poetry that he indulged this tendency. He projected into fictitious or semi-fictitious heroes his idealised self-portraits, his fantasies of adventure and escape, his picture of himself as a gloomy, isolated, wronged, misunderstood, evil, and suffering creature; and having put all this into poetry, he was for the most part free of it in his everyday life. He might occasionally like to pose as one of his own heroes—the painter West says that when Byron was sitting for his portrait "he assumed a countenance that did not belong to him, as though he were thinking of a frontispiece for Childe Harold."[49] But Moore tells how readily Byron would abandon his "romantic mystification" if he felt a breath of ridicule;[50] and he often spoke with amusement

[48] Humphry House, *Coleridge*, London 1953, p. 134.
[49] Quoted by Moore, *Life*, p. 562 : cp. *L.J.*, IV. 130, n.2.
[50] Moore, *op. cit.*, pp. 647-8.

and extreme detachment of his "Harrys and Larrys, Pilgrims and Pirates."[51] Whatever place they may have held in his private dream-world, and however satisfying they may have been to him in certain moods, they were not the essential Byron, and he did not hesitate to say so: "The reputation of 'gloom'," he told Moore in 1813, "if one's friends are not included in the *reputants*, is of great service; as it saves one from a legion of impertinents, in the shape of common-place acquaintance. But thou know'st I can be a right merry and conceited fellow, and rarely *larmoyant*."[52] He continued to have fits of melancholy and depression, which he exploited in his poetry, but for most of the time he was gay, sociable, and loquacious; and this side of his character, which dominates his letters and conversations, was for years excluded from his published works, so that there was a sharp division between his normal and his poetic personalities. This was modified in 1816, by his coming closer in real life to the emotions and the attitudes he had presented in his verse-tales; but the divergence became marked again in later years, when he delighted in repudiating or deflating the Byronic hero and the Poet figure of *Childe Harold*, Canto III: "Now, confess," he once said to Trelawny, "you expected to find me a 'Timon of Athens', or a 'Timur the Tartar'; or did you think I was a mere sing-song driveller of poesy, full of what I heard Braham at a rehearsal call '*Entusamusy*'; and are you not mystified at finding me what I am,— a man of the world— never in earnest—laughing at all things mundane?"[53]

This was essentially a conflict between Byron the poet and Byron the aristocrat—a conflict which was fully resolved only in his *ottava rima* satires: there and there alone he found a form and style which enabled him to write like a man of the world, with gay witty astringency, and to avoid the attitudinising and

---

[51] *L.J.*, III. 169 : cp. III. 101 and *Corr.* I. 244.

[52] *L.J.*, II. 273 : cp. III. 399, 405.

[53] Trelawny, *Recollections*, p. 25. Cp. *L.J.*, v. 318 : "I have had a friend of your Mr. Irving's—a very pretty lad—a Mr. Coolidge, of Boston—only somewhat too full of poesy and 'entusymusy' . . . . I suspect that he did not take quite so much to me, from his having expected to meet a misanthropical gentleman, in wolf-skin breeches, and answering in fierce monosyllables, instead of a man of this world."

emotional exaggeration which made him ashamed of his own earlier verses. Sometimes, indeed, this new poetic personality might issue in mere cynicism or frivolity, so that it seems a limiting as well as liberating agent: at other times, however, he uses it to express his deepest feelings, though these are now controlled by his intelligence and social sense, which prevent them from degenerating into sentimentality or self-dramatisation. As we have seen, too, he had now more definite ideas about the value of poetry for mankind, and his conception of it as a vehicle for truth and wisdom influenced these satires very strongly. So that while it is always dangerous to seek neat formulations in the case of a man so complex (or confused) as Byron, he might be regarded as achieving in some of these works the synthesis he aimed at less successfully in his own life—the union of the poet with the man of fashion and the benefactor of humanity. And certainly many of the strengths and limitations of his greatest poetry are the result of his being primarily no mere man of letters and romantic poet, but a sophisticated man of the world, a Regency aristocrat.

II

Early Works

(i) *Juvenilia*

BYRON'S MUSE was Janus-faced, and his poetry oscillates between the poles of sentiment and satire. This duality appears in his earliest work, and is even indicated by the rival accounts of what induced him to write poetry in the first place—his old nurse said it was his resentment at the "insults" of an elderly lady who used to visit his mother, while he himself maintained it was his boyhood love for Margaret Parker, or his grief at her death.[1] Whatever his original motive, Byron continued to write verses when he was at Harrow, Cambridge, and Southwell, and the idea of publishing occurred to him in 1806, when he was discussing some of these poems with Miss Pigot. He thought first of printing a small volume for private circulation, and *Fugitive Pieces* appeared accordingly in November. It was suppressed almost immediately on the advice of the Reverend J. C. Becher, who objected to the immodesty of certain stanzas, but a revised and enlarged collection, *Poems on Various Occasions*, was soon put in hand. This was published in January 1807, in a limited edition of one hundred copies, and it met with such approval that Byron now decided to prepare a volume "for the public at large,"[2] although he quailed at the thought of critical, unsympathetic readers, and his preface shows the diffidence and apprehension that he felt on this occasion. This third collection, *Hours of Idleness*, was the first to bear his name on the title-page (though he had signed two single poems in *Fugitive Pieces*), and its publication marks the real beginning of his career as a man of letters.

Byron's genius, however, was not lyrical—even in his later years his short poems seldom escape the metrical banality and

---

[1] Moore, *Life*, p. 14 ; *L.J.*, v. 449 ; *P.W.*, I. 5, n. 1.
[2] *L.J.*, I. 123 (cp. 125).

sentimentalism which Moore's works encouraged[3]—and the level of accomplishment in these early verses is too low to warrant detailed critical attention. Yet they do provide us with evidence of his taste in poetry at this period; they also show his tendency to exaggerate or romanticise his own emotions and experiences; and they display an interesting range of attitudes and feelings. One of Byron's greatest problems was to be that of selecting, discovering or creating his own best poetic personality, and perhaps (in view of this) the most significant feature of these early poems is the variety of roles in which he chooses to present himself. Sometimes he writes as the proud scion of a noble house, hoping to emulate the glory of his ancestors:

> Of the mail-cover'd Barons, who, proudly, to battle,
>   Led their vassals from Europe to Palestine's plain,
> The escutcheon and shield, which with ev'ry blast rattle,
>   Are the only sad vestiges now that remain. . . .
>
> Paul and Hubert too sleep in the valley of Cressy ;
>   For the safety of Edward and England they fell :
> My Fathers ! the tears of your country redress ye :
>   How you fought ! how you died ! still her annals can tell.
>
> On Marston, with Rupert, 'gainst traitors contending,
>   Four brothers enrich'd, with their blood, the bleak field ;
> For the rights of a monarch their country defending,
>   Till death their attachment to royalty seal'd.
>
> Shades of heroes, farewell ! your descendant departing
>   From the seat of his ancestors, bids you adieu !
> Abroad, or at home, your remembrance imparting
>   New courage, he'll think upon glory and you.[4]

At other times he prefers to think of his idealised childhood in Aberdeenshire, and to suggest that at heart he is still a young

---

[3] "So we'll go no more a-roving" is one of the very rare exceptions, and the best of Byron's handful of great lyrics.

[4] *P.W.*, I. 2-3.

Highlander, uncorrupted by the delights and privileges of his present life:

> Away, ye gay landscapes, ye gardens of roses !
>> In you let the minions of luxury rove ;
> Restore me the rocks, where the snow-flake reposes,
>> Though still they are sacred to freedom and love. . . .
>
> Years have roll'd on, Loch na Garr, since I left you,
>> Years must elapse, ere I tread you again :
> Nature of verdure and flowers has bereft you,
>> Yet still are you dearer than Albion's plain :
> England ! thy beauties are tame and domestic,
>> To one who has rov'd on the mountains afar :
> Oh ! for the crags that are wild and majestic,
>> The steep, frowning glories of dark Loch na Garr.[5]

Or, less impressively:

> Fortune ! take back these cultur'd lands,
>> Take back this name of splendid sound !
> I hate the touch of servile hands,
>> I hate the slaves that cringe around :
> Place me among the rocks I love,
>> Which sound to Ocean's wildest roar ;
> I ask but this—again to rove
>> Through scenes my youth hath known before.[6]

While rejections and nostalgias like these can also modulate to a melancholy longing for solitude and escape:

> Fain would I fly the haunts of men—
>> I seek to shun, not hate mankind ;
> My breast requires the sullen glen,
>> Whose gloom may suit a darken'd mind.
> Oh ! that to me the wings were given,
>> Which bear the turtle to her nest !
> Then would I cleave the vault of Heaven,
>> To flee away, and be at rest.[7]

---

[5] *P.W.*, I. 171, 173.

[6] *P.W.*, I. 206. This stanza and the next are from a poem which appeared for the first time in Byron's fourth collection, *Poems Original and Translated.*

[7] *P.W.*, I. 207-8.

B

In his imitations of Augustan satire, on the other hand, the personality implied by his poetic manner is quite different—Byron aims now at an effect of intense but controlled indignation, of mature judicial poise. This intention—not of course fully achieved—can be seen in his lines on a change of headmasters at Harrow:

> Where are those honours, IDA ! once your own,
> When Probus fill'd your magisterial throne ?
> As ancient Rome, fast falling to disgrace,
> Hail'd a Barbarian in her Caesar's place,
> So you, degenerate, share as hard a fate,
> And seat *Pomposus* where your *Probus* sate.
> Of narrow brain, yet of a narrower soul,
> Pomposus holds you in his harsh controul ;
> Pomposus, by no social virtue sway'd,
> With florid jargon, and with vain parade ;
> With noisy nonsense, and new-fangled rules,
> (Such as were ne'er before enforc'd in schools.)
> Mistaking *pedantry* for *learning's* laws,
> He governs, sanction'd but by self-applause ;
> With him the same dire fate, attending Rome,
> Ill-fated Ida ! soon must stamp your doom :
> Like her o'erthrown, for ever lost to fame,
> No trace of science left you, but the name.[8]

His tone changes again when he attempts to speak with the accents of passion (or of pathos), though the deep feeling he professes in these poems of sentiment is continually belied by their stylistic triviality:

> Though my vows I can pour,
> To my Mary no more,
> My Mary, to Love once so dear,
> In the shade of her bow'r,
> I remember the hour,
> She rewarded those vows with a *Tear*.[9]

Side by side with this youthful sentimentality, however,

---

[8] *P.W.*, I. 16-17.
[9] *P.W.*, I. 52.

there is a youthful cynicism. Byron writes with flippant worldly wisdom on the way to treat a cruel mistress:

> Would you teach her to love ?
> For a time seem to rove ;
> At first she may *frown* in a *pet* ;
> But leave her awhile,
> She shortly will smile,
> And then you may *kiss* your *coquette*.[10]

And he shows an aggressive common sense when he refuses a *rendezvous* in a garden on a December night, rebuking the young lady in question for her romantic silliness:

> Why should you weep like *Lydia Languish*,
> And fret with self-created anguish ?
> Or doom the lover you have chosen,
> On winter nights to sigh half frozen ;
> In leafless shades, to sue for pardon,
> Only because the scene's a garden ?
> For gardens seem, by one consent,
> (Since Shakespeare set the precedent ;
> Since Juliet first declar'd her passion)
> To form the place of assignation.
> Oh ! would some modern muse inspire,
> And seat her by a *sea-coal* fire ;
> Or had the bard at Christmas written,
> And laid the scene of love in Britain ;
> He surely, in commiseration,
> Had chang'd the place of declaration.
> In Italy, I've no objection,
> Warm nights are proper for reflection ;
> But here our climate is so rigid,
> That love itself is rather frigid. . . .[11]

And he suggests that their passion would run a more satisfactory course in the comfort of her home. This poem is far from satisfactory—longwinded, repetitive, loosely strung together, it shows Byron's characteristic inability to make his points succinctly; but for all its laboured clumsiness of wit and technique, it already shows his inclination, so important for

[10] *P.W.*, I. 54. [11] *P.W.*, I. 36-7.

Don Juan, to deflate and ridicule false sentiment. And indeed
many of the attitudes he was to strike in later works appear in
embryonic form in these early collections, which suggest at
once the catholicity of his taste and the many-sidedness of his
own personality.

(*ii*) *Experiments in satire*

In spite of its obvious weaknesses *Hours of Idleness* sold readily,
and was well received by most reviewers. Very naturally
Byron was exhilarated by this moderate success, and forgetting
his premature renunciation of the Muse[12] he now turned to a
variety of literary projects, the most important of which was a
satire on contemporary poetry. This work, *The British Bards*,
was ready in January 1808, but its appearance was delayed,
and Byron's growing self-satisfaction shattered, by the *Edinburgh's* article on *Hours of Idleness*. He had borne some other
adverse criticisms with at least a pretence of equanimity, noting
like a seasoned author that abuse might help his sales,[13] but
this attack was a different matter altogether. The *Edinburgh*
enjoyed a unique prestige—it was the only literary periodical
with high intellectual standards, the as-yet-unrivalled arbiter
of taste; and politically it was the semi-official organ of the
party Byron meant to join in Parliament; so that its hostility
seemed doubly disastrous to his hopes. Yet this public humili-
ation, painful as it was, did him good by checking his facility
and over-confidence, and forcing him to realise (for a time at
least) that he must take more pains with his productions.
Instead of rushing into print now he rewrote his whole poem
in the course of 1808, relieving his wounded feelings by incor-
porating an attack on Jeffrey and his colleagues, and after
further detailed revisions the work was published in March
1809 as *English Bards and Scotch Reviewers*.

Satire on contemporary poetry and drama was a well-
established "kind," which looked back to Pope and Churchill

---

[12] "It is highly improbable," he had written in the preface to *Hours of Idleness*,
"from my situation, and pursuits hereafter, that I should ever obtrude myself a
second time on the Public ; nor even, in the very doubtful event of present
indulgence, shall I be tempted to commit a future trespass of the same nature."
(*Hours of Idleness*, Newark 1807, p. ix : cp. *P.W.*, I. 254-6).

[13] *L.J.*, I. 147 (cp. 148, 171).

as its main exponents. About the turn of the century it enjoyed an increased vogue, occasioned by conservative reactions to the new movements and fashions,[14] and this fact was probably responsible for Byron's choice of *genre* and subject in his second bid for literary fame. His knowledge of such works, moreover, influenced the treatment of his own poem. Anxious to succeed in this field, he paid close attention to existing models, imitating their style, conventions, and techniques, assuming their customary attitudes and tone, and adopting the traditional *persona* of this kind of satirist: like Gifford, Pope himself, and many minor writers, Byron speaks as a man of common sense and sound morality, a patriot, and an upholder of established literary standards.

This role, however, was not wholly congenial, and the manner he was aiming at did not come easily or naturally to him—it called for a maturity of mind and brilliance of technique which he did not possess at this stage. In Augustan satire at its best the form and style are perfectly adapted to the writer's quality of mind, his social poise, his fine perceptions, lively wit, and subtle discriminations. As Dr Leavis puts it,

> . . . "versification" here involves more than the term is generally felt to convey. When Pope is preoccupied with the metrical structure, the weight, and the pattern of his couplets, he is bringing to bear on his "materials" habits of thought and feeling, and habits of ordering thought and feeling. The habits are those of a great and ardent representative of Augustan civilization.[15]

Byron (like so many of Pope's followers) admired the resulting style without sharing the emotional and mental qualities of which it is the expression: he imitates the surface, the idiom,

---

[14] Gifford's *Baviad* (1794) and *Maeviad* (1795) were satires on the Della Cruscan school of poetry, and on the theatre of the seventeen-nineties. T. J. Mathias, in his *Pursuits of Literature* (1794-7) had surveyed contemporary letters from the viewpoint of a moralist and a political conservative. *The Anti-Jacobin* (1797-8), with similar beliefs, had ridiculed the style and sentiments of much romantic poetry, though it relied for the most part on parody and direct abuse instead of formal satire. Further attacks on the Romantics are to be found in the opening lines of Lady Anne Hamilton's *Epics of the Ton* (1807), and in Richard Mant's *Simpliciad* (1808).

[15] F. R. Leavis, *The Common Pursuit*, London 1952, p. 90.

the rhetorical devices of Augustan satire, but fails to experience or reproduce its essence; and so one finds in *English Bards* a coarsening of the traditional techniques—clumsy attempts at bathos, for example, commonplace antitheses, crude ridicule, lame epigrams, and heavy-handed irony:

> Next comes the dull disciple of thy school,
> That mild apostate from poetic rule,
> The simple WORDSWORTH, framer of a lay
> As soft as evening in his favourite May,
> Who warns his friend 'to shake off toil and trouble,
> And quit his books, for fear of growing double ;'
> Who, both by precept and example, shows
> That prose is verse, and verse is merely prose ;
> Convincing all, by demonstration plain,
> Poetic souls delight in prose insane ;
> And Christmas stories tortured into rhyme
> Contain the essence of the true sublime.
> Thus, when he tells the tale of Betty Foy,
> The idiot mother of 'an idiot Boy ;'
> A moon-struck, silly lad, who lost his way,
> And, like his bard, confounded night with day ;
> So close on each pathetic part he dwells,
> And each adventure so sublimely tells,
> That all who view the 'idiot in his glory'
> Conceive the Bard the hero of the story.
>
> Shall gentle COLERIDGE pass unnoticed here,
> To turgid ode and tumid stanza dear ?
> Though themes of innocence amuse him best,
> Yet still Obscurity's a welcome guest.
> If inspiration should her aid refuse
> To him who takes a Pixy for a muse,
> Yet none in lofty numbers can surpass
> The bard who soars to elegize an ass :
> How well the subject suits his noble mind,
> He brays, the Laureate of the long-eared kind.[16]

This is mere slovenly butchering, to borrow Dryden's phrase. The imperceptiveness of the actual judgments does not matter— who cares about Theobald's merits as an editor?—but Byron

[16] *P.W.*, I. 315-17.

fails to give us the peculiar pleasure we expect from a satirical attack. Instead of "fine raillery" and incisive polished wit he can offer us only a kind of schoolboy humour, boisterous, abusive, heavily sarcastic, nearly always crude both in conception and in execution. Hence he usually fails to engage our sympathies, to carry us along with him in his condemnation, to convince us by the way he makes his points that they have any real validity; and although his hectoring ridicule may often amuse us, the amusement is of rather a low order. There are, however, notable exceptions, when Byron strikes out forceful, witty couplets like the best of those on Wordsworth—

> Who, both by precept and example, shows
> That prose is verse, and verse is merely prose. . . .

And in fairness one must recognise that *English Bards* is better than some comparable works of its own day: it is, for example, far more vigorous and pointed than the wearisome satires of Mathias, which still enjoyed great popularity; and though it is very much a young man's poem, brash, rudely assertive, technically crude, it does not lack vitality and interest of a kind. Yet taken as a whole this work is disappointing, even by the standards of its age. Gifford, Byron's own immediate model, shows in *The Baviad* and *Maeviad* a limited mastery of the heroic couplet, a skilful control of language, a formal and verbal precision even in violent attacks,[17] which Byron failed to achieve in his imitation of these poems; and when he is compared with Crabbe, whose Augustan sensibility is

---

[17] See, for example, these random samples of his style :

    (a) "Lost in amaze at language so divine,
        The audience hiccup, and exclaim, 'Damn'd fine !' "

    (b) "Happy the soil, where bards like mushrooms rise,
        And ask no culture but what Byshe supplies !
        Happier the bards, who, write whate'er they will,
        Find gentle readers to admire them still !"

    (c) "Now—But I sing in vain ; from first to last,
        Your joy is fustian, and your grief bombast :
        Rhetoric has banish'd reason ; kings and queens,
        Vent in hyperboles their royal spleens ;
        Guardsmen in metaphors express their hopes,
        And 'maidens, in white linen,' howl in tropes."
        (*The Baviad, and Maeviad*, 8th edn, London 1811, pp. 21, 30, 75).

everywhere apparent in his style, his limitations become still more obvious.[18]

English Bards suggests then that this kind of satire was not Byron's *forte*; but the work had an immediate success and ran through four editions, and when Byron returned to England in 1811 he was eager to extend his reputation by another poem in the same vein—*Hints from Horace*, which he had written in Athens, was "intended as a sequel to 'English Bards and Scotch Reviewers',"[19] just as *The Maeviad* had been a sequel to *The Baviad*. While it was in the printer's hands (along with *The Curse of Minerva*), Byron busied himself with preparing a fifth edition of *English Bards*; and though Dallas persuaded him to have *Childe Harold* published in the meantime, it seems clear that he had pinned his main hopes on these satires—especially on *Hints from Horace*.

This "paraphrastic imitation" of the *De arte poetica* shows considerable ingenuity in the substitution of English equivalents for characters and authors named by Horace, and it contains occasional felicities—some mediocre lines, for example, can culminate unexpectedly in an admirable couplet:

> But every thing has faults, nor is't unknown
> That harps and fiddles often lose their tone,
> And wayward voices, at their owner's call,
> With all his best endeavours, only squall ;
> Dogs blink their covey, flints withhold the spark,
> And double-barrels (damn them !) miss their mark.[20]

Yet on the whole this satire misses its mark too. It commits the unpardonable sin of being dull, while technically it often falls short even of the level Byron had achieved in *English Bards*. He was never very happy in translation, for the need to adhere closely to a given text interfered with his normal improvising mode of composition; and it is only here and there in *Hints*

[18] Cp. F. R. Leavis, *Revaluation*, London 1936, pp. 124-9.

[19] *P.W.*, I. 385. See also Dallas, *Recollections*, p. 103.

[20] *P.W.*, I. 427. Moore's interesting comment on these lines points to the relation between Byron's poetic wit and his conversational modes : "The concluding couplet . . . is amusingly characteristic of that mixture of fun and bitterness with which their author sometimes spoke in conversation ;—so much so, that those who knew him might almost fancy they hear him utter the words." (*Life*, p. 124).

from Horace that he escapes from stilted laboured paraphrase to
develop his own satiric rhetoric. He seems, too, to have had
some difficulty with his verse form—syntax and word-order
are often racked to make his sentences fall into couplets, or to
make his lines and passages correspond to Horace's, while
sometimes the alliteration is mechanical, excessive, and non-
functional. This stylistic awkwardness can be seen in the very
opening lines:

> Who would not laugh, if Lawrence, hired to grace
> His costly canvas with each flattered face,
> Abused his art, till Nature, with a blush,
> Saw cits grow Centaurs underneath his brush ?
> Or should some limner join, for show or sale,
> A Maid of Honour to a Mermaid's tail ?
> Or low Dubost—as once the world has seen—
> Degrade God's creatures in his graphic spleen ?
> Not all that forced politeness, which defends
> Fools in their faults, could gag his grinning friends.
> Believe me, Moschus, like that picture seems
> The book which, sillier than a sick man's dreams,
> Displays a crowd of figures incomplete,
> Poetic Nightmares, without head or feet.[21]

And the faults are just as marked in his digressions, where he
is not following the Latin but composing freely:

> Yes, Friend ! for thee I'll quit my cynic cell,
> And bear Swift's motto, 'Vive la bagatelle !'
> Which charmed our days in each Ægean clime,
> As oft at home, with revelry and rhyme.
> Then may Euphrosyne, who sped the past,
> Soothe thy Life's scenes, nor leave thee in the last ;
> But find in thine—like pagan Plato's bed,
> Some merry Manuscript of Mimes, when dead.[22]

It is not perhaps without some reference to his own difficulties
that Byron chose the second epigraph to *Hints from Horace*:
"Rhymes are difficult things—they are stubborn things, Sir";[23]
and he came to realise that this verse form was not really congenial—he needed more elbow-room, more freedom, than the

[21] *P.W.*, I. 389-91.   [22] *P.W.*, I. 414.   [23] *P.W.*, I. 385.

couplet could provide, and in September 1812, when he was struggling with the *Drury Lane Address,* he admitted to Lord Holland that "latterly, I can weave a nine-line stanza faster than a couplet, *for which measure I have not the cunning.*"[24]

By this time the first cantos of *Childe Harold* had been published, and Byron was basking in the fame that they had brought him. *English Bards* had been suppressed at the request of Lord and Lady Holland, in whose circle he now moved, and *The Curse of Minerva* at the request of Lord Elgin or his friends, for in his hour of triumph Byron could well afford to be magnanimous. *Hints from Horace* shared the fate of its companions, and he now began to think of writing something more in his new romantic style, yet he had not given up all hope of a further success in his early manner: the *Drury Lane Address* kept him busy for nearly a month, but soon after its completion he presented Murray with *The Waltz,* which he described as being "in the old style of *English Bards, and Scotch Reviewers.*"[25] When this work appeared anonymously, however, it seems to have met with a cool reception, for Byron tried to disown it;[26] and now, turning to the composition of his verse-tales, he abandoned his attempts at satire in favour of the romantic vein he had already begun to work so profitably in *Childe Harold's Pilgrimage.*

(iii) Romantic travelogue

Childe Harold was begun at Janina in October 1809, and Cantos I and II were written in the East, with a freedom that came from Byron's having no thoughts of immediate publication, or of studying the public's taste. Nor was he concerned here with "decorum" (as in *English Bards*),[27] for the new poem did not

---

[24] *L.J.,* II. 150 (my italics).   [25] *L.J.,* II. 176.   [26] *L.J.,* II. 202.

[27] Such a concern appears only in the archaisms, which show the traces of a decadent and lifeless theory of decorum. Byron seems to see the medievalism of this poem as a necessary consequence of his stanza form : "the appellation 'Childe'," he says in the Preface, "as in 'Childe Waters', 'Childe Childers', etc., is used as more consonant with the old structure of versification which I have adopted" (*P.W.,* II. 4) ; and the archaisms of diction are presumably to be attributed to the same cause—to the fact that he was imitating Spenser and the eighteenth century Spenserians. It is, however, a curiously debased conception of decorum that makes the choice of stanza determine both the poet's style and his treatment of the hero. And Byron cannot justify his archaisms as Beattie does

really fall into any existing *genre*. It had been suggested by conversations with John Galt on board ship;[28] it owed something to the eighteenth-century Spenserians, and to landscape and travel poets—one can trace debts to James Beattie's *Minstrel* and to Goldsmith's *Traveller*; but Byron himself (and his readers) saw it as a new departure: "If ever I did any thing original," he wrote in 1814, "it was in *Childe Harold*."[29] In this work, therefore, he had no firmly established convention to guide or restrict him in his choice of tone and sentiments, for although he imitated the "Spenserian" style, he thought of this mode as allowing considerable freedom; and he now proceeded to give much fuller expression to his own moods, thoughts and personality.

The poem is based on Byron's travels, and keeps closely to his own experiences: there are very few modifications of his actual itinerary (whether in the interests of clarity or of rhetorical effectiveness), the development and structure of the poem being determined primarily by the order of events as they occurred. It should not, however, be regarded as the mere "rhymed diary of two years' travel,"[30] for a comparison of these two cantos with prose records of the tour reveals some important differences. A great deal of good-fellowship, high spirits and buffoonery, which figures in the travellers' letters and diaries, is never mentioned in the poem; and most striking of all is the absence of Byron's friend Hobhouse or of any character to fill his role—a change closely connected with the introduction of the pilgrim hero. Childe Harold was essentially a solitary figure, and a travelling companion other than his "little page" and "staunch yeoman" would have destroyed, or at least greatly reduced, the imaginative appeal he had for Byron and his public.

Harold was the first of a long series of "Byronic heroes," who resemble him in varying degrees, but he does not dominate

---

his occasional use of "old words" in *The Minstrel*, by saying they are appropriate to his subject, for Childe Harold, though referred to as a pilgrim, is a contemporary figure, and there is no point in using pseudo-medieval jargon to describe his actions.

[28] Galt, *Life*, pp. 180-1.

[29] *L.J.*, III. 77 : cp. *Corr.*, II. 44.

[30] It is so described by Oliver Elton (*A Survey of English Literature 1780-1830*, London 1912, II. 141.

this poem as Selim, Conrad and the others do the works in which they figure. He was introduced (partly at least) "for the sake of giving some connection to the piece,"[31] and his actions and surroundings provide the occasion for the narrator's comments and reflexions. There are thus two central characters instead of one, and they are for the most part clearly differentiated: "My readers will observe," wrote Byron in an early draft of the Preface, "that where the author speaks in his own person he assumes a very different tone from that of

> 'The cheerless thing, the man without a friend,'

at least, till death had deprived him of his nearest connections."[32] Sometimes he may fail to preserve an adequate distinction: we are occasionally left uncertain whether Harold or the poet-protagonist is the holder of particular opinions, and once Byron ascribes to the hero views on the Convention of Cintra which seem more in keeping with the character of the narrator;[33] but he did correct such blunders when he noticed them. (Thus on revising the poem he saw the incongruity of making Harold sing a gay ditty like "The Girl of Cadiz," and by substituting the doleful song "To Inez" he at once restored the pilgrim's proper character.[34])

This hero was originally called Childe Burun (an old form of the name Byron), and he is obviously based on aspects of the poet himself. Byron later denied emphatically that the Childe was meant as a self-portrait:

> I by no means intend to identify myself with *Harold*, but to *deny* all connection with him. If in parts I may be thought to have drawn from myself, believe me it is but in parts, and I shall not own even to that. . . . I would not be such a fellow as I have made my hero for all the world.[35]

Yet in spite of this final protestation he derived considerable satisfaction from imagining himself as a sated, melancholy, lonely wanderer, and the result is that his treatment of Childe

---

[31] *P.W.*, II. 3.
[32] *P.W.*, II. 4 : cp. Dallas, *Recollections*, pp. 155-6.
[33] *P.W.*, II. 38-42.
[34] See *P.W.*, III. 1-3 ; II. 75-7.
[35] *L.J.*, II. 66 : cp. *P.W.*, II. 3-4.

Harold is extremely sympathetic.[36] He expects the reader to
accept in all seriousness his exaggerated unconvincing portrait
of a *blasé* and remorseful sinner, and Harold's faults—his facile
cynicism and self-pity, for example—are presented without any
hint of condemnation or detachment:

> And none did love him !—though to hall and bower
>   He gathered revellers from far and near,
>   He knew them flatterers of the festal hour,
>   The heartless Parasites of present cheer.
> Yea ! none did love him—not his lemans dear—
>   But pomp and power alone are Woman's care,
>   And where these are light Eros finds a feere ;
>   Maidens, like moths, are ever caught by glare,
> And Mammon wins his way where Seraphs might despair.[37]

The narrator, it is true, makes occasional disapproving comments on the hero's life:

> Ah me ! in sooth he was a shameless wight,
>   Sore given to revel and ungodly glee ;
>   Few earthly things found favour in his sight
>   Save concubines and carnal companie,
> And flaunting wassailers of high and low degree.[38]

But this kind of head-shaking does not really convey moral
censure—it tends rather to suggest that Harold's wickedness is
somehow fascinating, and thus contributes to a paradoxical
idealisation of the hero, who is presented as interesting because
of his very vices. "I knew two old maids in Buckinghamshire,"
says Rogers, "who used to cry over the passage about Harold's

[36] One may compare his unmistakable self-satisfaction in portraying himself
as a melancholy misanthrope in some of his early verses :

> "Weary of love, of life, devour'd with spleen,
>   I rest a perfect Timon, not nineteen ;
>   World ! I renounce thee ! all my hope's o'ercast !
>   One sigh I give thee, but that sigh's the last."

> "Mix'd in the concourse of a thoughtless throng,
>   A mourner, midst of mirth, I glide along ;
>   A wretched, isolated, gloomy thing,
>   Curst by reflection's deep corroding sting . . ."
>
> (*P.W.*, I. 84, 104).

[37] *P.W.*, II. 21-2.   [38] *P.W.*, II. 16.

'laughing dames' that 'long had fed his youthful appetite',"[39]
and this sentimental wallowing was only an exaggeration of
the actual response invited by this section of the poem. In
practice, therefore, it is difficult for us to take much interest
in Childe Harold: he is so slightly sketched, so unconvincing
as a character, while the gloom and *ennui* which he parades
complacently seem superficial, boring, rather silly affectations.

The narrator, on the other hand, is much more worthy of
attention. Often, admittedly, he writes extremely badly, with
a disconcerting awkwardness of style and an uncertainty of
tone which appear in his comments on the port of Lisbon:

> But whoso entereth within this town,
>> That sheening far, celestial seems to be,
>> Disconsolate will wander up and down,
>> 'Mid many things unsightly to strange ee ;
>> For hut and palace show like filthily :
>> The dingy denizens are reared in dirt ;
>> Ne personage of high or mean degree
>> Doth care for cleanness of surtout or shirt,
> Though shent with Egypt's plague, unkempt, unwashed,
> unhurt.[40]

He can escape, however, from this feeble humour and barbarity
of diction, to write rather pleasing stanzas of description or of
landscape poetry, and he shows a new ability to soliloquise in
verse—to meditate with simple but effective rhetoric on topics,
often commonplace enough, to which he brings some freshness
of response and power of feeling:

> To sit on rocks—to muse o'er flood and fell—
>> To slowly trace the forest's shady scene,
>> Where things that own not Man's dominion dwell,
>> And mortal foot hath ne'er or rarely been ;
>> To climb the trackless mountain all unseen,
>> With the wild flock that never needs a fold ;
>> Alone o'er steeps and foaming falls to lean ;
>> This is not Solitude—'tis but to hold
> Converse with Nature's charms, and view her stores unrolled.

[39] *Recollections of the Table-Talk of Samuel Rogers*, ed. A. Dyce, London 1887
(henceforth cited as Rogers, *Table-Talk*), p. 232.
[40] *P.W.*, II. 33.

> But midst the crowd, the hum, the shock of men,
>> To hear, to see, to feel, and to possess,
>> And roam along, the World's tired denizen,
>> With none who bless us, none whom we can bless ;
>> Minions of Splendour shrinking from distress !
>> None that, with kindred consciousness endued,
>> If we were not, would seem to smile the less,
>> Of all that flattered—followed—sought, and sued ;
> This is to be alone—This, This is Solitude !⁴¹

In spite of these sentiments, the narrator is not flying from humanity—he is always aware of Nature and fine prospects, but he is just as much concerned with the life and activities going on around him—with a bull-fight in Spain, with the habits and appearance of Albanian warriors, or with his impressions on board a British frigate. And this interest in his surroundings issues not only in detailed observation of men and manners, but also in more general reflexions on the nations and events which he describes—on the war in Spain, for example, and the predicament of Greece.

We may say then that Childe Harold, the *blasé* Cain-like Wanderer, is a projection of the author's moods of melancholy, loneliness, boredom, and disillusion, and that the narrator mirrors his more normal and attractive personality. Their co-existence in this one poem is a result of Byron's trying here to express and organise a wide range of responses to experience. His friends all comment on the contradictions in his character —the alternations between gloom and gaiety, misanthropy and sociability, enthusiasm and *ennui* or cynicism; and his early poems had shown something of this variety. In *Childe Harold* he attempted to include a similar diversity of mood and sentiment within the framework of a single poem. He was searching for a medium—a verse form and a convention—which would enable him to give complete expression to his own complex nature, and the experiment, however unsuccessful, does point forward to the freedom that he found in the *ottava rima* style. This unexpected link between *Childe Harold* and *Don Juan* is made clear in Byron's own account of his intentions:

> The stanza of Spenser, [he writes in his Preface] according

---

⁴¹ *P.W.*, II. 115-16.

to one of our most successful poets, admits of every variety. Dr. Beattie makes the following observation :—'Not long ago I began a poem in the style and stanza of Spenser, in which I propose to give full scope to my inclination, and be either droll or pathetic, descriptive or sentimental, tender or satirical, as the humour strikes me ; for, if I mistake not, the measure which I have adopted, admits equally of all these kinds of composition.' Strengthened in my opinion by such authority, and by the example of some in the highest order of Italian poets, I shall make no apology for attempts at similar variations in the following composition ; satisfied that, if they are unsuccessful, their failure must be in the execution, rather than in the design sanctioned by the practice of Ariosto, Thomson, and Beattie.[42]

The different moods distinguishable in the poem are a result of this plan, but it had an even stronger influence on the first draft, which contained a number of satirical or humorous stanzas on several topics. Byron's friends persuaded him to cancel most of these, thinking that they were blemishes; and certainly his wit tended to be ponderously ineffective in such passages:

> But when Convention sent his handy work
>> Pens, tongues, feet, hands combined in wild uproar ;
>> Mayor, Aldermen, laid down the uplifted fork ;
>> The Bench of Bishops half forgot to snore ;
>> Stern Cobbett, who for one whole week forbore
>> To question aught, once more with transport leapt,
>> And bit his devilish quill agen, and swore
>> With foes such treaty never should be kept,
> While roared the Blatant Beast, and roared, and raged, and—
> slept ! ! [43]

Apart from their own weaknesses, such stanzas were insufficiently related to the more serious parts of the poem; and even in the final version the abrupt changes of tone sometimes seem awkward and arbitrary. In passing from one extreme to another we are usually passing from Harold's viewpoint to the narrator's (or *vice versa*); and it looks as if Byron, by thus isolating his more "romantic" from his "normal" states of

[42] *P.W.*, II. 4-5.   [43] *P.W.*, II. 39-40.

mind and feeling, is attempting to analyse and understand himself more fully. The attempt is, however, rudimentary in the extreme: the two characters of hero and narrator might have been used to give a unified though complex picture of his own varied responses, but he never seems to realise their potential importance. The central weakness of the poem, indeed, lies in his failure to establish any significant relationship between them. They co-exist but do not interact. The one is not observed and criticised by the other (as in *Don Juan*); and the alternation of their different moods seems curiously haphazard: instead of being deliberately played off against each other they seem simply to reflect the fluctuations in Byron's own mood as he writes. So that although he does succeed in presenting different aspects of his personality in this poem, he fails to unite them into a coherent artistic whole—a failure which must be attributed in part to careless workmanship and lack of planning, but also to his inability at this stage to resolve the conflicts in his nature, to develop a consistent attitude to life, to reject or come to terms with the "Childe Harold" elements in his own personality.

Then again, the cantos fall uncomfortably between fiction and autobiography. Having invented Harold, Byron is at a loss to know what to do with him, and even the simple structural idea is obscured by the narrator's himself appearing as a traveller in Greece. By this intrusion he usurps or duplicates one of the hero's chief functions, for Harold was supposed to thread together the description and reflexions, and may seem superfluous if this is done by someone else. Indeed at one point Byron has even to remind himself of the pilgrim's existence,[44] only to forget it for the last long section of the poem; and the effect of this is not like that of the digressions in *Don Juan*— they are entertaining in themselves, but the plot holds our attention too and we return to it with pleasure, whereas here the plot is virtually non-existent. Harold is conceived of as a character, or as a set of attitudes, not as the hero of a story; and Byron's close adherence to the facts of his own tour limits the actions which he can attribute to his central character.

[44] "But where is Harold? shall I then forget/To urge the gloomy Wanderer o'er the wave?" (*P.W.*, II. 110).

C

The narrative is weak simply because Byron's experiences did not fall naturally into a significant pattern: unlike a real pilgrim, he had had no one objective to determine the plan of his journey (and hence of his poem); nor did the value of these years lie in any particular achievement or event—no spiritual revelation, for example, came to him from classical antiquities or scenes, or from the noble savages of Albania. What he got from his "pilgrimage" was simply a wealth of new experiences, and he put most of them into his poem, regardless of its consequent looseness of structure: ". . . it was intended," he wrote defensively, "to be a poem on *Ariosto's plan*, that *is to say* on *no plan* at all."[45] He does not, then, impose on his material an interpretative pattern which would falsify his own experience, but this means that the plot is really functionless, for no significance emerges from the hero's wanderings or from the work as a whole. And indeed, in spite of claims which Byron sometimes made for it, it is impossible to find a theme or "moral" in *Childe Harold's Pilgrimage*, because he had no clearly-conceived purpose in writing it, and his experiences are only half-digested, half-transformed into a work of art.

Or one might say that Byron had two separate intentions: to embody certain of his moods in Harold, displaying the gloomy Wanderer in situations he has known; and, writing more *in propria persona*, to give his impressions of the countries, peoples, scenes and incidents of his own tour. Most of his contemporaries liked both aspects of the work, but to us the second seems much more successful, for whatever faults one has to find with Byron's presentation of Childe Harold, the travelogue itself is good. There is a certain charm in the narrator's lively, fresh responses, even though they do not find expression in great poetry; his individual experiences are often well described; and in spite of the stylistic defects—pointless archaisms, pseudo-literary words and phrases, imprecision in the use of language, uncertainties of tone, and awkward padding-out of lines and stanzas—one is conscious of an interesting mind and personality at work here.

For some years, however, Byron chose to concentrate on the other line he had struck out in this poem: he went on

[45] *L.J.*, I, 320.

portraying Byronic heroes, though instead of letting them wander aimlessly like Harold, he invented plots to show them to advantage, and to hold the reader's interest. The verse tales therefore show a marked improvement in his narrative technique, but on the whole he seems to have taken the wrong course, for he was turning his back on the most promising features of *Childe Harold*. In considering the difference between his romantic and satiric writings, Charles du Bos suggests that Byron had two main poetic talents—that he was a maker of myths and an acute observer of human life.[46] In these early cantos he had written in both modes, but he made no attempt to reconcile them; and he was soon to relegate the more interesting one to a subordinate role, for in his verse tales the observer with his great potentialities yields to the myth-maker —whose myths we now see to have no enduring value.

(iv) Romantic fantasy

The Giaour, The Bride of Abydos, The Corsair, Lara, Parisina and *The Siege of Corinth*, were all written and published between the spring of 1813 and February 1816. In these years Byron was living as a man of fashion, and poetry was only one of his pursuits—one to which he did not choose to give a great deal of care and attention. When the "scribbling mood"[47] was on him he would write with great rapidity, but his interest "went off," he told John Murray, at the end of a week.[48] The first draft of *The Giaour* was dashed off in this way; *The Bride of Abydos* he "scribbled *stans pede in uno*"[49] in the same time or less, and *The Corsair* in ten days; while *Lara* was "written amidst balls and fooleries, and after coming home from masquerades and routs."[50] He returned to each of these poems, but his revisions were often as casual as his original composition: they frequently consisted of extensions rather than of changes, and although he made many minor alterations, these are usually of doubtful value. On the other hand, he sometimes strove to improve key passages, like the meditation

---

[46] *Byron and the Need of Fatality*, pp. 159-60.
[47] *L.J.*, III. 16.   [48] *L.J.*, III. 76.
[49] *L.J.*, II. 279.   [50] *L.J.*, VI. 81 (cp. 77).

on Greece in *The Giaour*; but in general it is true to say that at this period he had little trace of an artistic conscience, and that his way of writing (on which he prided himself) made for occasional shoddy workmanship—for carelessness in style and structure. He showed an interest in some points of metrical technique, and the tales are on the whole well told in vigorous and competent though far from subtle verse, but there are bad lapses where he seems totally insensitive to the effects of rhyme and rhythm. His planning too is often faulty or haphazard. *The Giaour* was expanded from 407 lines to 1334, in a series of additions made over a number of months with little regard to the poem's plot or coherence; and though Byron felt uneasy about these extensions, professing a new concern for structure in his next work, he cannot be said to have developed a real sense of form. He inserted in *The Corsair* a long extract from *The Curse of Minerva*, simply because he was eager to publish it in one way or another,[51] and he began *Lara* without even having decided on the catastrophe.[52] Byron was writing popular romances, and writing them quite well, but he did not pretend to be a dedicated artist or skilled craftsman, and he showed no concern for perfection. On the contrary, he realised himself that he was not producing works of a high quality, for he thought his poems had been "strangely over-rated," and spoke of his "own want of judgment in publishing, and the public's in reading things, which cannot have stamina for permanent attention."[53] This curious combination of carelessness in writing and an awareness of at least some of the faults it brings can be explained only by his rather contemptuous attitude to poetry, and his pride in being considered not a professional author but a gentleman-amateur, writing with negligent ease.[54]

[51] *P.W.*, III. 270, n.l. : cp. *L.J.*, II. 176-7, 179.

[52] Dallas, *Recollections*, p. 284.

[53] *L.J.*, III. 56 (cp. 64). Cp. also Hobhouse, *Recollections*, I. 100.

[54] Cp. Matthew Arnold, *Essays in Criticism, Second Series*, London 1888, pp. 175-6 : "Byron is so negligent in his poetical style, he is often, to say the truth, so slovenly, slipshod, and infelicitous, he is so little haunted by the true artist's fine passion for the correct use and consummate management of words, that he may be described as having for this artistic gift the insensibility of the barbarian ; —which is perhaps only another and a less flattering way of saying, with Scott, that he 'manages his pen with the careless and negligent ease of a man of quality.' "

For all their faults, these poems were received with quite remarkable enthusiasm—ten thousand copies of *The Corsair*, for example, were sold on the day of publication; and though Byron might say that his reputation was only a temporary one,[55] he was delighted by his repeated triumphs. He seems indeed to have deliberately aimed at this effect: the verse tale had achieved great popularity in Scott's hands; Byron now adapted it to present his favourite hero-type in the Eastern settings which he knew so well; and in doing this he was consciously exploiting a new field of literary subjects and of public interest:

> Stick to the East [he wrote to Moore in August 1813] ;— the oracle, Stael, told me it was the only poetical policy. The North, South, and West, have all been exhausted ; but from the East, we have nothing but Southey's unsaleables,—and these he has contrived to spoil, by adopting only their most outrageous fictions.[56]

His own interest, as this last remark suggests, was not in Oriental tales of fantasy and wonders: he knew *The Arabian Nights* and admired Beckford's *Vathek*, but neither of these works had much influence on his poetry. For him, unlike both Moore and Southey, the Near East was not a land of peris and enchanters, but of pashas, pirates and banditti; and it was the passion and adventure to be met with in real life there that he drew on in his Turkish tales. His plots are to a large extent fictitious, but they are founded in varying degrees on fact, history, or legend, and except for the supernatural episode in *The Siege of Corinth* they do not go beyond the bounds of possibility; while he prided himself on authenticity of detail in his presentation of Moslem life: "As to poesy," he wrote to Professor Clarke, "that is, as 'men, gods, and columns,' please to decide upon it; but I am sure that I am anxious to have an observer's, particularly a famous observer's, testimony on the fidelity of my manners and dresses. . . ."[57] Byron's own experience and observations were thus the source of much of his material, and indeed his recollections of Albania, Greece, and Asia Minor were the soil from which the verse tales sprang. ("With those countries, and events connected with them," he

[55] *L.J.*, III. 25, 64.   [56] *L.J.*, II. 255.   [57] *L.J.*, II. 309 (cp. 283).

told Moore, "all my really poetical feelings begin and end."[58])
From 1811 to 1814 he kept planning to return to the Levant—
partly because of his debts, for he could live more cheaply in
Greece than in England, but also because he loved the East,
and when he felt disgusted with life as a man of fashion, he
would think with longing of his former travels and adventures.
"Why should I remain or care?" he wrote to Lady Melbourne
early in 1814. ". . . My life here is frittered away; there I was
always in action, or, at least, in motion; and, except during
night, always on or in the sea, and on horseback. I am sadly
sick of my present sluggishness, and I hate civilization."[59]
This nostalgia for the East and for a life of action, this yearning
to escape from the constrictions and futilities of English Society
was one of the main impulses behind the verse tales, as Byron
himself confesses in the opening lines of *The Siege of Corinth*.

In these lines, as in *Childe Harold's Pilgrimage*, he tried to
convey the nature and value of his actual experiences, but in
the tales themselves he plunges boldly into fiction and invents
melodramatic plots to replace the feeble narrative interest of
his tour; so that the heroes are given much more striking and
important parts to play—indeed the main appeal of these tales,
both for the reading public and for Byron's own imagination,
lay in the character and actions of these central figures. In
portraying them he was following up the success of Harold,
whose melancholy, isolation and misanthropy had caught the
public's fancy, and the new protagonists retain these qualities,
though they have little of his *ennui*, which is replaced by fiery
courage and tumultuous passion. Yet even if Byron was
deliberately repeating a successful formula in each of these
tales, he was also satisfying some need of his own psyche: this
"Byronic" type of hero fascinated him, since it derived not only
from his reading, but from aspects of his own experience and
personality, and he had moods when he liked to think of himself
as just this kind of man. In his preface to *Werner* he tells us
that its original, *The German's Tale*, might be said to contain

---

[58] *L.J.*, III. 274 (cp. 266). *Parisina* is an exception in this respect, as in some
others. *Lara* is not set in the East, but it belongs to the same world as the Turkish
Tales, and Byron sanctioned the idea that it was a sequel to *The Corsair*.

[59] *Corr.*, I. 226 (cp. 161). Cp. also Moore, *Life*, p. 186.

the germs of much that he has written,[60] and this suggests how from an early age he was moved and attracted by some themes and characters in the sub-literature of the day: the idea of a prince or nobleman concealing guilt for a past crime, or of a young lord secretly involved with bands of "black banditti," is obviously important for the verse tales. Then the influence of Scott is unmistakable: the dark proud hero-villain Marmion, and Roderick Dhu, the bitter outlaw-rebel, have struck Byron's imagination, and he seems to have forgotten his own former condemnation of such figures (in *English Bards*); while many similar characters from fiction—Mrs Radcliffe's Schedoni, for example, Godwin's Bethlem Gabor, and Schiller's Charles de Moor—affected his portrayal of the Giaour and his successors. Factors in Byron's own life also contributed. As a boy he loved to think of his forebears and their glory, but he was fascinated too by the crimes and isolation of "the wicked Lord," his own immediate predecessor, whom he liked to imitate in some respects.[61] There was also his sense of guilt, or at least his interest in remorse and guilt, the origin of which is obscure— it may be the result of his Calvinist upbringing in Aberdeen, it may be related to the early sexual experience to which he had been subjected by his nurse, or it may derive from experiments in homosexuality or incest; but whatever its source, it certainly affects the picture he draws of these heroes. Then his former loneliness, his sense of having been without a circle of acquaintance proper to his rank, his awareness of having been an "outsider" when he came to London—these things made him think admiringly of haughty isolated men, exiles or outcasts, who spurned and despised society. This was easily related to his moods of discontent with civilised life—his yearnings for the East, for passion, violence, and adventure; and his admiration for the chiefs and warriors he had met in the Levant—his friendship, for example with the notorious Ali Pasha—helped to reinforce his interest in this hero-type. A wide range of allusion, therefore, literary, biographical, and psychological, would be needed to explain the genesis of Conrad, Lara, and the rest, and their attraction for the poet.

The literary value of these heroes, on the other hand, can

[60] *P.W.*, v. 338.   [61] Moore, *Life, pp.* 13-14.

be discussed without much reference to their origins.   And
first of all one has to note a great advance on the superficial
attitudinising of Childe Harold—when one passes from him
to the Giaour one finds an increase in vitality, a more detailed
and convincing picture of the hero, a more powerful and
dramatic presentation of his feelings:

> "The cold in clime are cold in blood,
> Their love can scarce deserve the name ;
> But mine was like the lava flood
>   That boils in Ætna's breast of flame.
> I cannot prate in puling strain
> Of Ladye-love, and Beauty's chain :
> If changing cheek, and scorching vein,
> Lips taught to writhe, but not complain,
> If bursting heart, and maddening brain,
> And daring deed, and vengeful steel,
> And all that I have felt, and feel,
> Betoken love—that love was mine,
> And shown by many a bitter sign.
> 'Tis true, I could not whine nor sigh,
> I knew but to obtain or die.
> I die—but first I have possessed,
> And come what may, I *have been* blessed.
> Shall I the doom I sought upbraid ?
> No—reft of all, yet undismayed
> But for the thought of Leila slain,
> Give me the pleasure and the pain,
> So would I live and love again." [62]

No doubt there are flaws in this passage—these scorching veins
and writhing lips are unfortunate touches which verge on the
ludicrous, and the whole speech has a stagy ring—but the
lines are alive, not dead on the page like most of Harold's
outbursts, and the hero's passion, pride, remorse and isolation
are brought before us as we read; while the same is true,
though to a lesser extent, in all the other tales.

Yet having acknowledged this one must insist on the
limitations of Byron's achievement here.   The intensity in his
portrayal of these heroes is the intensity not of tragic poetry,

[62] *P.W.*, III. 136.

but of adolescent day-dreams, and the over-writing and exaggerations are peculiarly revealing:

> See—by the half-illumined wall
> His hood fly back, his dark hair fall,
> That pale brow wildly wreathing round,
> As if the Gorgon there had bound
> The sablest of the serpent-braid
> That o'er her fearful forehead strayed. . . .[63]

> His bristling locks of sable, brow of gloom,
> And the wide waving of his shaken plume,
> Glanced like a spectre's attributes—and gave
> His aspect all that terror gives the grave.[64]

Byron's whole presentation of these characters confirms the suspicions roused by such stylistic excesses. He keeps returning to the notion of a great soul warped by suffering and injustice, changed from a beneficent force to an evil and destructive power. The Giaour's "crimes" had their origin in the violence of his own passions, and though we get one glimpse of an early friendship, we know nothing of the factors prior to the illicit love-affair which have made him the man we see; but all the others were potentially good and noble: their misanthropy and ruthless violence are the result of wrongs inflicted on them in their youth. Byron's treatment of this theme, however, is extremely superficial, as one can see by comparing the verse tales with *Wuthering Heights*, where this type of hero is raised for the first time to the level of great literature. Emily Brontë makes the reader feel and experience the wretchedness of Heathcliff's childhood, the cruelty and degradation to which he was subjected, and the thwarting of his love: all these are fully created for us, so that we can understand, even while detesting, his demonic thirst for vengeance. Byron shows no comparable depth of psychological insight, or powers of concrete presentation. These, it may be said, are qualities more easily developed in the novel than the verse tale, but his deficiency in this respect can be brought out just as well by a comparison with *The Ancient Mariner*. Byron and Coleridge

[63] *P.W.*, III. 127.   [64] *P.W.*, III. 331.

are both portraying men who have suffered greatly, who have "known the worst"—they share the characteristically romantic interest in abnormal mental states, and in the possibility of alienation from one's fellow-men. But Coleridge is fully as much concerned with the means of recovery, repentance, reconciliation; and he also recreates with nightmare vividness the experiences his hero has gone through, so that we participate emotionally and imaginatively in the process which has made him what he is. Byron, on the other hand, gives a mere rapid sketch or outline of *his* heroes' pasts, the only function of which is to suggest their innate superiority to other men, and to sanction their "interesting" display of pride, defiance, and rebellion:

> Yet was not Conrad thus by Nature sent
> To lead the guilty—Guilt's worst instrument—
> His soul was changed, before his deeds had driven
> Him forth to war with Man and forfeit Heaven.
> Warped by the world in Disappointment's school,
> In words too wise—in conduct *there* a fool ;
> Too firm to yield, and far too proud to stoop,
> Doomed by his very virtues for a dupe,
> He cursed those virtues as the cause of ill,
> And not the traitors who betrayed him still ; . . .
>
> Feared—shunned—belied—ere Youth had lost her force,
> He hated Man too much to feel remorse,
> And thought the voice of Wrath a sacred call,
> To pay the injuries of some on all.[65]

These heroes are all bent on vengeance, whether on individuals or social groups, nations or all mankind. This is not linked with any cause except their own hates and desires: the Romantic Outlaw was often the champion of the weak and the oppressed, or a fighter for his nation's independence, but Byron's characters are dissociated from all such activities. Except for Conrad's chivalry towards the inmates of Seyd's harem, they do not do generous or altruistic deeds. Lara has some compassion for the poor, but though he raises and leads a revolution, his motives are entirely selfish—he wants to

[65] *P.W.*, III. 236-7.

protect himself from punishment by the aristocracy for the murder of Ezzelin. Conrad is not presented as the enemy of Islam or of Turkish tyranny: he is a misanthropic pirate, warring on mankind, and he attacks Seyd only because the latter was preparing to attack him. Alp is fighting for no cause except his own revenge on Venice and his hope of winning his love, while the Giaour was pursuing a private feud when he killed Hassan. Selim has some revolutionary Greek patriots in his band, but he contemptuously dismisses their ideals in favour of his own:

> The last of Lambro's patriots there
>   Anticipated freedom share ;
> And oft around the cavern fire
> On visionary schemes debate,
> To snatch the Rayahs from their fate.
> So let them ease their hearts with prate
> Of equal rights, which man ne'er knew ;
> I have a love for freedom too.
> Aye ! let me like the ocean-Patriarch roam,
> Or only know on land the Tartar's home !
> My tent on shore, my galley on the sea,
> Are more than cities and Serais to me :
> Borne by my steed, or wafted by my sail,
> Across the desert, or before the gale,
> Bound where thou wilt, my barb ! or glide, my prow ! . . .
>
> Once free, 'tis mine our horde again to guide ;
> Friends to each other, foes to aught beside. . . .
>
> I like the rest must use my skill or strength,
> But ask no land beyond my sabre's length. . . .[66]

The heroes of these tales would all subscribe to this ideal of liberty, anarchic and individualistic. In them one sees a glorification of the outlaw, the rebel, the renegade, the Ishmaelite, the bold bad man.

Unlike Emily Brontë (or Milton in his portrayal of Satan), Byron preserves no detachment from his heroes. He abandons the moral realism of *English Bards*, and revels in their pride,

[66] *P.W.*, III. 194-5, 197, 198.

their sin, their hatred, and their violence. There is nothing to compare with the presentation of Heathcliff's mad obsession with revenge as it appears to sane observers, or with his final realisation that revenge has lost its meaning for him. Nor is there any attempt at viewing the heroes critically: we are invited to identify ourselves with them, and the voice of the narrator brings in no effective standards by which they are to be judged. There are lines in *The Giaour* which express views in sharp contrast with the values of the tale itself,[67] the passage in which they appear consists of additions to the original version, and it is virtually another poem (on the state of Greece), quite unconnected with the story—it does not modify one's attitude to the events which follow, because the two parts never seem related to each other. In the tales themselves there are some condemnations of the central characters, but these serve, like the earlier comments on Childe Harold's immorality, to emphasise the attractive qualities of evil. The monk's description of the *Giaour* highlights his passion and Satanic pride; at the beginning of *The Bride of Abydos* the reader's appetite is whetted by the exclamations on man's violence; the references to Conrad's crimes give us an agreeable thrill; and the account of Lara's death brings out, without really condemning, his daring and impiety. Indeed the deaths of these heroes are not in any way a judgment on their lives— there is no sense of a natural order being re-established after an unnatural rebellion, and except for Hugo they all die defiant and intransigent:

> Ere his very thought could pray,
> Unaneled he passed away,
> Without a hope from Mercy's aid,—
> To the last a Renegade.[68]

This is a typical ending for a Byronic hero, and it is clearly meant to be impressive, even admirable. In these verse tales Byron has abandoned any pretence of a didactic purpose: moral principles are invoked only for the greater glory of the men who defy them, and these men are never exposed to the most elementary critique, or subjected to the acid scrutiny of

---

[67] *P.W.*, III. 88.   [68] *P.W.*, III. 488.

common sense. There is often a parade of analysis and
judgment, but the effect is usually to attribute still more
greatness to the hero, to call for sympathy and admiration
which he hardly seems to merit, to suggest that he is worse
than other men only because he is basically so much finer and
more sensitive than they are:

> There was in him a vital scorn of all :
> As if the worst had fallen which could befall,
> He stood a stranger in this breathing world,
> An erring Spirit from another hurled ; . . .
>
> With more capacity for love than Earth
> Bestows on most of mortal mould and birth.
> His early dreams of good outstripped the truth,
> And troubled Manhood followed baffled Youth ;
> With thought of years in phantom chase misspent,
> And wasted powers for better purpose lent ;
> And fiery passions that had poured their wrath
> In hurried desolation o'er his path,
> And left the better feelings all at strife
> In wild reflection o'er his stormy life ; . . .
>
> So much he soared beyond, or sunk beneath,
> The men with whom he felt condemned to breathe,
> And longed by good or ill to separate
> Himself from all who shared his mortal state ;
> His mind abhorring this had fixed her throne
> Far from the world, in regions of her own . . .[69]

In Byron's portrayal of these figures there is a strong
element of silly self-dramatisation. In the prefatory letter to
The Corsair he deprecates the tendency of readers to identify
the poet with his creations, but even in this passage his deliberate ambiguity encourages the practice he professes to
condemn;[70] and an entry in his journal shows that he pre-
tended, even to himself, that he had had experiences like those
of Conrad:

> He told me an odd report,—that *I* am the actual Conrad, the
> veritable Corsair, and that part of my travels are supposed to

---

have passed in privacy. Um !—people sometimes hit near the truth ; but never the whole truth. H. don't know what I was about the year after he left the Levant ; nor does any one— nor—nor—nor—however, it is a lie—but, 'I doubt the equi- vocation of the fiend that lies like truth.'[71]

This impulse to present himself as a Byronic hero of the new type had appeared as early as October 1811, in a poem about his early love for Mary Chaworth. After describing his own grief, his suffering and his despair, Byron hints darkly (but with relish) at the possibility of his being driven by them to a life of crime, ruthless ambition, and anarchic savagery:

> . . . if, in some succeeding year,
> When Britain's 'May is in the sere,'
> Thou hear'st of one, whose deepening crimes
> Suit with the sablest of the times,
> Of one, whom love nor pity sways,
> Nor hope of fame, nor good men's praise ;
> One, who in stern Ambition's pride,
> Perchance not blood shall turn aside ;
> One ranked in some recording page
> With the worst anarchs of the age,
> Him wilt thou *know*—and *knowing* pause,
> Nor with the *effect* forget the cause.[72]

Francis Hodgson, to whom the poem was addressed, insisted that "the poor dear Lord *meant* nothing of this,"[73] but Moore's comment is more adequate: "It seemed as if, with the power of painting fierce and gloomy personages, he had also the ambition to be, himself, the dark 'sublime he drew', and that, in his fondness for the delineation of heroic crime, he endeavoured to fancy, where he could not find, in his own character, fit subjects for his pencil."[74] This mood never lasted long, but it was none the less recurrent, and it shows a funda- mental immaturity in Byron at this time. His heroes were projections of a private quasi-adolescent fantasy, and while one can enjoy them with the same indulgence that one brings to the works of P. C. Wren or Peter Cheyney, it is impossible to take them seriously, either as symbolic figures or as representations

[71] *L.J.*, ii. 399. [72] *P.W.*, iii. 30.
[73] Marchand, *Byron*, i. 297, n.4. [74] Moore, *Life*, p. 140.

of human nature. It is worth remembering, of course, that Byron himself in these years did not take his poetry very seriously. He was writing entertainments for the reader: for himself they were partly a source of further fame, and partly a means of escape from his own immediate problems and surroundings—he says that he wrote them as a relief to the fever of his mind,[75] to distract himself from his emotional difficulties,[76] "to wring [his] thoughts from reality, and take refuge in 'imaginings,' however 'horrible' "[77]—though actually these "horrible imaginings" were peculiarly attractive to him in such moods, so that he never applied to them within the poems the ironical intelligence he so often showed in normal life.

In the next phase of his career his "normal life" had virtually ceased to exist: after the separation scandal, the public outcry, and Society's rejection of him, Byron's attitudes and emotions tended to approximate to those he had merely played with in the verse tales, and he now presented himself openly as a Byronic hero. In doing so, however, he considerably modified this archetype, so that instead of its being a simple element in daydreams of escape and fantasy, it became a *persona* he could use to express his feelings and ideas about life in the present and his own predicament. Yet in spite of this development, and the greater pressure of experience that one senses in his poetry of this period, much even of his best work continues to be marred as the verse tales had been by his fatal distaste for self-criticism, and by his persistent insulation of his poetry from his realism and common sense.

[75] *Corr.*, I. 238.   [76] *L.J.*, II. 278 (cp. 314, 351).
[77] *L.J.*, II. 293 (cp. 361-2).

III

Childe Harold's Pilgrimage, Canto III

BY THE SPRING of 1816 Byron felt that he had written himself out.[1] *The Siege of Corinth* was the last of his Eastern tales, for he knew he had exhausted that particular vein; and for the time being he was not inclined to start on any other. The drama of the separation and his exile, therefore, can be seen as having come most opportunely, since they provided him with both material and stimuli for a new phase of creativity.

Considered from this point of view the rights and wrongs of the affair are unimportant. If Byron was the victim of misunderstanding or deceit, he had a real and major grievance, but even if (as seems most probable) he was to blame, he was quite capable of persuading himself that *he* was the injured party;[2] and this sense of intolerable wrong is what mattered for his poetry. The events of these months came as a great shock to him. "If he had left his wife and cut society," Trelawny says in an unkind but perceptive comment, ". . . he would have been content: that his wife and society should have cast him off, was a mortification his pride could never forgive nor forget."[3] Faced with this situation—forced both to come to terms with it in his own mind, and to decide what his public reaction should be, Byron found a model, or at least suggestions, in the character of his own heroes. He had always been attracted by their melancholy, isolation, and rebellious pride, but now he seemed to be living through their actual experiences—he was meeting in reality with emotions and events like those he had loved to imagine; and it was natural that, feeling himself ostracised, wronged like his heroes by

[1] *L.J.*, III. 274.

[2] Cp. Lady Byron's letter of June 15th, 1816 : "Habits of misrepresentation necessarily entail a degree of self-delusion—we say things to persuade others till we persuade ourselves—and I have always found this so true of Lord Byron, that I am inclined to think he *now* really *believes* himself the injured person. When the whole force of such an *imagination* is turned to deceive the conscience it is too easy to find 'a flattering unction'—and it is perhaps one of the most melancholy & fatal misapplications of human powers." (Milbanke, *Astarte*, p. 216).

[3] Trelawny, *Recollections*, p. 44.

both individuals and social groups, he should tend to adopt
their attitudes. He seems indeed to have felt a compulsive
desire to enact his former fantasies in real life—by going into
exile he increased the similarity between his lot and Conrad's,
or Alp's, or the Giaour's, and the approximation was remarked
on even by his friends: "Lord Byron," Scott wrote in May 1816,
". . . has Child Harolded himself and Outlawd himself into
too great a resemblance with the pictures of his imagination."[4]
This fusion of the poet with the hero-type he had created is
the central feature of *Childe Harold*, Canto III, which was
written to give utterance to his deep obsessive mood that summer. He was not, of course, continuously wretched, and the
poem is not a full account of his experiences: here again there
is no mention of his travelling companions, or of, say, his jokes
at the expense of Polidori; but it *is* true to his dominating and
recurrent thoughts and feelings of this period.

An immediate result of his new state of mind was the
obliteration of his earlier distinction between hero and narrator.
Byron begins by speaking unmistakably in his own person, and
then breaks off to introduce Childe Harold and insist on the
latter's fictional status:

> In my youth's summer I did sing of One,
> > The wandering outlaw of his own dark mind ;
> > Again I seize the theme, then but begun,
> > And bear it with me. . . .[5]

But his account of his poetic motives makes it clear that his
relation to this character is unique and intimate:

> 'T is to create, and in creating live
> > A being more intense that we endow
> > With form our fancy, gaining as we give
> > The life we image, even as I do now—
> > What am I ? Nothing : but not so art thou,
> > Soul of my thought ! with whom I traverse earth,
> > Invisible but gazing, as I glow
> > Mixed with thy spirit, blended with thy birth,
> And feeling still with thee in my crushed feelings' dearth.[6]

---

[4] *The Letters of Sir Walter Scott*, ed. H. J. C. Grierson, D. Cook, W. M. Parker
and others, London 1932-7, IV. 234.

[5] *P.W.*, II. 217.   [6] *P.W.*, II. 219-20.

D

Some such mixing and blending takes place almost at once, for even in the summary of Harold's recent fortunes we become aware that it is really Byron who is being described. By adopting this transparent fiction he gains first of all a means of avoiding direct treatment of his own domestic circumstances—this seemed promised by the opening stanzas with their explicit references to his wife and child, and to his wounded feelings, but with the transition to Childe Harold he can leave the quarrel and the separation wrapped in mystery: he can appeal for sympathy, in fact, without disclosing or discussing the real causes of his suffering. And secondly, he can be much more laudatory about Harold than he could about himself, without antagonising readers at the very outset of his poem. Having achieved these aims, however, Byron allows the distinction between Harold and himself to lapse. He may choose to present his idealised self-portrait in the first or the third person, but the portrait remains virtually the same: in passing from autobiographical statement to professed fiction, one finds only a change of grammatical number, with no corresponding change in personality, for there is no difference in mood, temperament or opinion between the new Childe Harold and the "I" of the narrator. In this canto, as Jeffrey wrote in reviewing it,

> . . . it is really impracticable to distinguish them.—Not only do the author and his hero travel and reflect together—but, in truth, we scarcely ever have any notice to which of them the sentiments so energetically expressed are to be ascribed ; and in those which are unequivocally given as those of the Noble author himself, there is the same tone of misanthropy, sadness and scorn, which we were formerly willing to regard as a part of the assumed costume of the Childe.[7]

The new protagonist, who thus combines the functions of both hero and narrator, shows a marked advance on all his predecessors. The main characters in the verse tales had been melancholy, misanthropic, lonely, proud, and passionate, but their lives were set in distant countries, often in past or

---

[7] *Edinburgh Review*, xxvii (Dec. 1816), 293.

unspecified periods; and although they embodied some of Byron's day-dreams and desires, they were remote from most of his immediate interests. The earlier Childe Harold had been a contemporary figure, in spite of his pseudo-medieval trappings, but his *ennui* and self-sufficiency had shut him off from the life around him, and he remained a detached spectator, little moved by what he saw. The new Harold retains most of the qualities which had appealed to Byron in these earlier heroes, but he has nothing of his namesake's *ennui*. Like the original narrator he responds readily to natural beauty, and is interested in modern life and politics—passionately aware of the state of Europe, and feeling intensely his own grief and grievances, he emerges as "the orator of the world's woes and his own."[8] The figure of the melancholy Wanderer is modified by Byron's own experiences, thoughts and feelings, and also by his reading of *Alastor*, so that it becomes a picture, no longer of the Sinner or the Outlaw, but of the Poet—the wronged and suffering Romantic Genius.

All objects and events are seen through the eyes of this narrator-hero, and the reflexions they give rise to are as alive and personal as the passages of introspection: as Scott notes in his review of Canto IV, "His descriptions of present and existing scenes however striking and beautiful, his recurrence to past actions however important and however powerfully described, become interesting chiefly from the tincture which they receive from the mind of the author."[9] It is this assimilation of facts to the poet-hero's personality and interests that gives Canto III its unity, and prevents it from degenerating into a mere travelogue. Battlefields, monuments, history, characters, and scenery are all viewed in relation to one or another of Childe Harold's main preoccupations—his own wrongs and sorrows, the fate of genius, the liberty of peoples, the value and significance of Nature; and these four major themes are not presented separately, but linked and interwoven so that they figure as related aspects of the hero's mind and character, imposing a coherence on his multitude of observations and reflexions.

[8] H. J. C. Grierson, *The Background of English Literature*, London 1925, p. 88.
[9] *Quarterly Review*, xix. (April, 1818), 228.

This new *persona* brings with it a distinctive mode of utterance. When we read this canto after Cantos I and II we get a general impression of much greater power and competence: there is none of the former uncertainty, the fumbling experiments with humour or archaic diction, or the awkward changes of tone. Byron seems to have much more definite ideas of what he wants to do and how to do it: he is aiming now not at variety and inclusiveness—ideals which he had abandoned in the verse tales—but at a stylistic elevation corresponding to his own intensity of feeling; and he does often achieve this. Yet while one can readily agree with those readers who thought Canto III his best work up to now, it is far from being wholly successful. The Spenserian stanza is too elaborate and difficult a verse form to lend itself to Byron's slapdash way of writing—he may seem to use it easily and fluently, but the ease and fluency often depend on carelessness in composition: in spite of the revisions which appear in his first draft, he seems to be improvising, catching at words and phrases which will carry on the stanza, without always thinking of their precise significance. This may result only in minor faults of craftsmanship, like the misrelated participle in

> Awaking with a start,
> The waters heave around me . . .[10]

but it can sometimes have more serious effects. Thus Byron often writes a striking opening for a stanza, and then lets it tail off in a succession of weak lines or phrases loosely strung together: this collapse of the rhetorical pitch which he began by setting himself is due partly to artistic carelessness or incompetence, partly also to a tendency to over-state even his strong feelings, and thus aim at a more elevated tone than he could easily sustain. The attempt at a high style is unfortunate in other ways as well. It can lead, for example, to a rather unscrupulous manipulation of the reader's responses—the comparison of Harold wrapped in his thoughts to a corpse wrapped in its shroud seems designed merely to evoke a vague sense of the terrible and the mysterious;[11] and although this is an exceptionally blatant case, there is very often an imprecision in the

---

[10] *P.W.*, II. 216.   [11] See below, p. 64 : cp. Chapter Two, p. 41.

diction and the imagery which makes Byron's style appear inflated rather than impressive. Occasionally too the tone of public utterance seems inappropriate—it is quite suitable for his thoughts on Waterloo, but not for his apostrophes to his infant daughter, and there is indeed a certain vulgarity in his orating on his own parental love.

Although such blemishes do not appear in every stanza, they soon force us to modify our first favourable impression of Canto III, since we are increasingly aware of faults, in taste as well as craftsmanship, which point to weaknesses in Byron-Harold's character and sensibility. From the very opening of the poem, indeed, one finds some causes for dissatisfaction with the central figure, through whose consciousness we apprehend the meaning. In addition to the faults already noted, there is Byron's irritating love of "mystifying" the reader—hinting at his sins and sorrows without ever stating clearly what they were, and thus achieving cheap effects of pathos or of horror:

Yet must I think less wildly :—I *have* thought
    Too long and darkly, till my brain became,
    In its own eddy boiling and o'erwrought,
    A whirling gulf of phantasy and flame :
    And thus, untaught in youth my heart to tame,
    My springs of life were poisoned. 'Tis too late ! . . .

    Long absent HAROLD re-appears at last ;
    He of the breast which fain no more would feel,
    Wrung with the wounds which kill not, but ne'er heal ; . . .

    Still round him clung invisibly a chain
    Which galled for ever, fettering though unseen,
    And heavy though it clanked not ; worn with pain,
    Which pined although it spoke not, and grew keen,
Entering with every step he took through many a scene. . . .[12]

A more fatal flaw appears in the account of Harold's distaste for his fellow-men. The alienation of the poet or genius from society is a common enough theme in romantic literature, but it can be treated on very different levels of moral seriousness

---

[12] *P.W.*, II. 220, 221.

and integrity. A good example, which will serve as a touch-stone, is provided by Wordsworth's description of his anguish, his conflicting loyalties, when England went to war with revolutionary France:

> . . . I felt
> The ravage of this most unnatural strife
> In my own heart ; there lay it like a weight
> At enmity with all the tenderest springs
> Of my enjoyments. I, who with the breeze
> Had play'd, a green leaf on the blessed tree
> Of my beloved country ; nor had wish'd
> For happier fortune than to wither there,
> Now from my pleasant station was cut off,
> And toss'd about in whirlwinds. I rejoiced,
> Yea, afterwards, truth most painful to record !
> Exulted in the triumph of my soul
> When Englishmen by thousands were o'erthrown,
> Left without glory on the Field, or driven,
> Brave hearts, to shameful flight. It was a grief,
> Grief call it not, 'twas anything but that,
> A conflict of sensations without name,
> Of which he only who may love the sight
> Of a Village Steeple as I do can judge
> When in the Congregation, bending all
> To their great Father, prayers were offer'd up,
> Or praises for our Country's Victories,
> And 'mid the simple worshippers, perchance,
> I only, like an uninvited Guest
> Whom no one own'd sate silent, shall I add,
> Fed on the day of vengeance yet to come ?[13]

Here Wordsworth succeeds in conveying both the intensity and the complexity of his feelings, and in the circumstances both these qualities command respect. His isolation was reluctant and unhappy, for although his deepest beliefs about human nature and society forced him out of sympathy with England, his basic love for her was still strong. Indeed his very feelings about France owed something to his upbringing: the "green leaf" metaphor, as well as emphasising his close

[13] *The Prelude*, ed. E. de Selincourt, 2nd edn, rev. Helen Darbishire, Oxford 1959, p. 382.

natural attachment to his country, also reminds us that it was
English Nature which had helped to form his moral being;
while the Village Steeple and Congregation suggest not only
the simple pieties now perhaps being misapplied, but the whole
context of rustic life which had done so much to develop his
love and respect for human nature. The passage deals then
with the clash between his major loyalties at that time, and
it gains from being read as part of the poem in which these
loyalties are fully discussed, but even taken by itself it can be
seen to give an honest, sensitive and convincing record of an
agonising inner conflict. When we pass from this to Byron's
presentation of Childe Harold, we find thoughts and feelings
of a very different order:

> But soon he knew himself the most unfit
> Of men to herd with Man, with whom he held
> Little in common ; untaught to submit
> His thoughts to others, though his soul was quelled
> In youth by his own thoughts ; still uncompelled,
> He would not yield dominion of his mind
> To Spirits against whom his own rebelled,
> Proud though in desolation—which could find
> A life within itself, to breathe without mankind.[14]

In place of Wordsworth's scrupulous precise description of his
feelings, Byron offers us flashy paradox and large rhetorical
gestures expressing a shoddy kind of self-approval. He complacently accepts isolation as the natural lot of genius—indeed
as something rather creditable; no conflict is involved because
"mankind" is lumped together as a homogeneous mass of
dullness and stupidity, to be easily rejected by the great or
sensitive soul; and this rejection is based simply on a firm
conviction of his own spiritual superiority. One sees here the
baneful influence of Shelley's notions of the difference between
poets and other men—notions which were all too easily
reconciled with certain favourite attitudes of Byron's own;
and the combination had an irresistible attraction for him at
that time. The long account of Harold is thus as much of an

[14] *P.W.*, II. 223.

indulgence, a dream fantasy, as anything in the verse tales; and it culminates in a passage of almost ludicrous exaggeration, which shows how completely Byron's critical intelligence is in abeyance:

> Self-exiled Harold wanders forth again,
> > With nought of Hope left—but with less of gloom ;
> > The very knowledge that he lived in vain,
> > That all was over on this side the tomb,
> > Had made Despair a smilingness assume,
> > Which, though 'twere wild,—as on the plundered wreck
> > When mariners would madly meet their doom
> > With draughts intemperate on the sinking deck,—
> Did yet inspire a cheer, which he forbore to check.[15]

Canto III, however, is not all like this. It is a remarkable blend of public and private interests, and we pass from thinly veiled autobiography to a meditation on the results of Britain's final victory over Napoleon:

> Fit retribution ! Gaul may champ the bit
> > And foam in fetters ;—but is Earth more free ?
> > Did nations combat to make *One* submit ?
> > Or league to teach all Kings true Sovereignty ?
> > What ! shall reviving Thraldom again be
> > The patched-up Idol of enlightened days ?
> > Shall we, who struck the Lion down, shall we
> > Pay the Wolf homage ? proffering lowly gaze
> And servile knees to Thrones ? No ! *prove* before ye praise !

> If not, o'er one fallen Despot boast no more !
> > In vain fair cheeks were furrowed with hot tears
> > For Europe's flowers long rooted up before
> > The trampler of her vineyards ; in vain, years
> > Of death, depopulation, bondage, fears,
> > Have all been borne, and broken by the accord
> > Of roused-up millions : all that most endears
> > Glory, is when the myrtle wreathes a Sword,
> Such as Harmodius drew on Athens' tyrant Lord.[16]

In stanzas such as these one finds fully developed some of the

---

[15] *P.W.*, ii. 225.   [16] *P.W.*, ii. 227-8.

ideas on war and politics which Byron held for the remainder
of his life. He hated despotisms of every kind, and sympathised
with peoples who were subject to domestic or to foreign
tyrants. He believed in liberty, for other men as well as for
himself, and his views on the French Revolution were like those
later expressed by Shelley in the preface to *The Revolt of Islam*:
in this canto he deplores the worst excesses of the revolutionaries, but argues that men warped by oppression could not be
expected to behave with perfect justice, and far from being
appalled by their mistakes, he looks forward eagerly to another
more decisive revolution. His views on war were closely
related to these few basic ideas: he detested wars of conquest
or aggression, or mere clashes between rival powers, stressing
their futility and the human misery which they involve—thus
in his thoughts on Waterloo he emphasises the sterility of
Britain's victory, the waste of life, and the sorrow which it
brought to thousands. But, like Godwin, he approved of
battles fought for liberty: young Marceau, as a general of the
French Republic, is commemorated as a champion of Freedom;
and the field of Morat, where the Swiss defeated the Burgun-
dians, is viewed with reverence instead of horror:

> While Waterloo with Cannae's carnage vies,
>> Morat and Marathon twin names shall stand ;
>> They were true Glory's stainless victories,
>> Won by the unambitious heart and hand
>> Of a proud, brotherly, and civic band,
>> All unbought champions in no princely cause
>> Of vice-entailed Corruption ; they no land
>> Doomed to bewail the blasphemy of laws
> Making Kings' rights divine, by some Draconic clause.[17]

All these beliefs were not newly conceived in 1816—they had
appeared in some of Byron's poems and letters before now;
but his sudden severance from English life, and his resentful
hostility to public opinion, made him voice his views more
openly and more intransigently than he had ever done before.
There is therefore an emotional connexion between his private

[17] *P.W.*, II. 255-6.

grievances and Harold's politics,[18] but in spite of this the quality of feeling differs greatly in his presentation of these subjects. The political stanzas can be prejudiced and unfair; they can also degenerate from eloquence into stilted rhetoric or frigid cliché; but they are never contaminated by the arrogance and self-pity which so often vitiate the speaker's treatment of his personal affairs.

Byron resists, too, the temptation to depict the lives of men like Rousseau and Napoleon as mere types or analogues of his own case. He is aware of similarities between his lot and theirs, and this awareness helps to give the poem its unity and strength of feeling; but he avoids crudely identifying them with himself. He sees Napoleon, for example, as another great man dragged down and humiliated by inferior beings, but he does not over-simplify and sentimentalise his story: ever since his schooldays Byron had felt an inclination to idealise the Emperor, but the inescapable facts of his hero's career forced him to recognise the complexity of his character; and though he still admires Napoleon, he does not attempt to minimise his weaknesses:

> Oh, more or less than man—in high or low—
>   Battling with nations, flying from the field ;
>   Now making monarch's necks thy footstool, now
>   More than thy meanest soldier taught to yield ;
>   An Empire thou couldst crush, command, rebuild,
>   But govern not thy pettiest passion, nor,
>   However deeply in men's spirits skilled,
>   Look through thine own, nor curb the lust of War,
> Nor learn that tempted Fate will leave the loftiest Star.[19]

Some parts of this analysis remind one of his antithetical descriptions of the verse-tale heroes—

>   In him inexplicably mixed appeared
>   Much to be loved and hated, sought and feared—[20]

but there is an important difference: Byron has to acknowledge

---

[18] This is particularly clear in letters of the period 1816-17, where he looks on revolution as a means of getting his revenge on the Society which had cast him out. See below, Chapter Eleven, pp. 183-4.

[19] *P.W.*, II, 240.

[20] *P.W.*, III. 334.

in Napoleon some traits—notably cowardice—which cannot
be glossed over or romanticised. He is faced with the complexity of life itself, which restricts the characteristic workings
of his imagination and forbids him to reduce real people to a
stereotyped formula. With this greater respect for truth there
sometimes comes increased maturity of judgment: in Rousseau
Byron finds another romantic genius who felt that those around
him were his enemies, but instead of treating him with the
uncritical indulgence shown to Harold, he proceeds to comment
on his errors and delusions:

> His life was one long war with self-sought foes,
>> Or friends by him self-banished ; for his mind
>> Had grown Suspicion's sanctuary, and chose,
>> For its own cruel sacrifice, the kind,
>> 'Gainst whom he raged with fury strange and blind.
>> But he was phrensied,—wherefore, who may know ?
>> Since cause might be which Skill could never find ;
>> But he was phrensied by disease or woe,
> To that worst pitch of all, which wears a reasoning show. . . .[21]

Through these more objective (although sympathetic) analyses
of real individuals, who resembled him in one way or another,
Byron achieves momentarily a sounder understanding of himself
and of the problems of "greatness" than he arrived at by direct
consideration of his own predicament. Thus when he comes to
relate Napoleon's character and situation to his own, he writes
about the restless romantic temperament with far more
penetration than he showed in his account of Harold:

> But Quiet to quick bosoms is a Hell,
>> And *there* hath been thy bane ; there is a fire
>> And motion of the Soul which will not dwell
>> In its own narrow being, but aspire
>> Beyond the fitting medium of desire ;
>> And, but once kindled, quenchless evermore,
>> Preys upon high adventure, nor can tire
>> Of aught but rest ; a fever at the core,
> Fatal to him who bears, to all who ever bore.

---

[21] *P.W.*, II. 266.

> This makes the madmen who have made men mad
>   By their contagion ; Conquerors and Kings,
>   Founders of sects and systems, to whom add
>   Sophists, Bards, Statesmen, all unquiet things
>   Which stir too strongly the soul's secret springs,
>   And are themselves the fools to those they fool ;
>   Envied, yet how unenviable ! what stings
>   Are theirs ! One breast laid open were a school
> Which would unteach Mankind the lust to shine or rule :
>
> Their breath is agitation, and their life
>   A storm whereon they ride, to sink at last,
>   And yet so nursed and bigoted to strife,
>   That should their days, surviving perils past,
>   Melt to calm twilight, they feel overcast
>   With sorrow and supineness, and so die ;
>   Even as a flame unfed, which runs to waste
>   With its own flickering, or a sword laid by,
> Which eats into itself, and rusts ingloriously.[22]

This is admirable, but Byron cannot stay long at this level—
in the very next stanza we are conscious of a falling-off, for
when he turns from the exceptional psychology of these men
to their relations with ordinary mortals, his reflexions are more
limited and personal, with a hint of self-pity; and his pretentious metaphor suggests perhaps an over-facile opposition
between genius and mediocrity:

> He who ascends to mountain-tops shall find
>   The loftiest peaks most wrapt in clouds and snow ;
>   He who surpasses or subdues mankind,
>   Must look down on the hate of those below.
>   Though high *above* the Sun of Glory glow,
>   And far *beneath* the Earth and Ocean spread,
>   *Round* him are icy rocks, and loudly blow
>   Contending tempests on his naked head,
> And thus reward the toils which to those summits led.[23]

The imagery of this stanza points to the important part
that Nature plays in Canto III. It is no longer described for
its own sake, as it had been in the earlier *Childe Harold*, but it

---

[22] *P.W.*, II. 242-3.   [23] *P.W.*, II. 243.

figures largely in the presentation of the poet-hero's emotional and spiritual states. Conscious of his wrongs and sorrows, and his own innate superiority, he flies to solitude among the mountains, where he sometimes looks on his surroundings simply as a refuge from the crowd and the turmoil of life:

> Is it not better, then, to be alone,
> And love Earth only for its earthly sake ?
> By the blue rushing of the arrowy Rhone,
> Or the pure bosom of its nursing Lake,
> Which feeds it as a mother who doth make
> A fair but froward infant her own care,
> Kissing its cries away as these awake ;—
> Is it not better thus our lives to wear,
> Than join the crushing crowd, doomed to inflict or bear ?[24]

Here one sees in the opening lines Byron's ability to give new and vigorous expression to quite commonplace ideas, but the effect is spoiled by the long simile, which may have originated in his feelings about Ada and her mother, but which is developed with so little reference to the actual relation of lake to river that it seems a crude sentimentalising of physical Nature. In the next stanza Byron passes without any explanation from his loving Earth only for her earthly sake to a kind of Nature mysticism which is not strictly that of Shelley or of Wordsworth, but which obviously owes a good deal to these authors. This peculiarly abrupt transition may lend substance to the view that he was not writing from his own experience, but exploiting various ideas that had already received literary treatment, and a curious imprecision in his phrasing sometimes gives the same impression.[25] Probably, however, he is speaking of things

---

[24] *P.W.*, II. 260-1.

[25] Wordsworth himself thought that Byron's enthusiasm for Nature was assumed or borrowed. Moore tells (*Memoirs*, III. 161) of a visit which the older poet paid to him in October 1820 : "[Wordsworth] spoke of Byron's plagiarisms from him ; the whole third canto of 'Childe Harold' founded on his style and sentiments. The feeling of natural objects which is there expressed, not caught by B. from nature herself, but from him (Wordsworth), and spoiled in the transmission. 'Tintern Abbey' the source of it all ; from which same poem too the celebrated passage about Solitude, in the first canto of 'Childe Harold', is (he said) taken, with this difference, that what is naturally expressed by him, has been worked by Byron into a laboured and antithetical sort of declamation." And Wordsworth expressed the same views in his letters.

he had really felt or thought he felt when under the influence of Shelley's talk and Wordsworth's poetry, and any vagueness in his account of the experience is due, not to its being a deliberate fake, but to its never having been much more than a vague yearning emotion:

> I live not in myself, but I become
>   Portion of that around me ; and to me
>   High mountains are a feeling, but the hum
>   Of human cities torture : I can see
>   Nothing to loathe in Nature, save to be
>   A link reluctant in a fleshly chain,
>   Classed among creatures, when the soul can flee,
>   And with the sky—the peak—the heaving plain
> Of Ocean, or the stars, mingle—and not in vain. . . .
>
> And when, at length, the mind shall be all free
>   From what it hates in this degraded form,
>   Reft of its carnal life, save what shall be
>   Existent happier in the fly and worm,—
>   When Elements to Elements conform,
>   And dust is as it should be, shall I not
>   Feel all I see less dazzling but more warm ?
>   The bodiless thought ? the Spirit of each spot ?
> Of which, even now, I share at times the immortal lot ?
>
> Are not the mountains, waves, and skies, a part
>   Of me and of my Soul, as I of them ?
>   Is not the love of these deep in my heart
>   With a pure passion ? should I not contemn
>   All objects, if compared with these ? and stem
>   A tide of suffering, rather than forego
>   Such feelings for the hard and worldly phlegm
>   Of those whose eyes are only turned below,
> Gazing upon the ground, with thoughts which dare not glow.[26]

These last few lines suggest (what one suspected all along) that the primary function of such fine "poetic" sentiments may simply be to differentiate Childe Harold from the herd, and demonstrate his great superiority of soul. The build-up of his character seems more important than the actual "religion"

[26] *P.W.*, II. 261-4.

he asserts here, and throughout the poem Nature provides him not so much with a system of beliefs as with a symbolism by means of which he can present more fully his own personality and feelings. In the scenes which he surveys he can find emblems, as it were, of his present situation:[27] the castles of the Rhine suggest the lofty mind's relation to the crowd; the river itself makes him wish that it were Lethe, though it would flow in vain over *his* memory; and a storm over Lake Léman seems to parallel his own emotional turmoil:

> Sky—Mountains—River—Winds—Lake—Lightnings ! ye !
>> With night, and clouds, and thunder—and a Soul
>> To make these felt and feeling, well may be
>> Things that have made me watchful ; the far roll
>> Of your departing voices, is the knoll
>> Of what in me is sleepless,—if I rest.
>> But where of ye, O Tempests ! is the goal ?
>> Are ye like those within the human breast ?
> Or do ye find, at length, like eagles, some high nest ?

> Could I embody and unbosom now
>> That which is most within me,—could I wreak
>> My thoughts upon expression, and thus throw
>> Soul—heart—mind—passions—feelings—strong or weak—
>> All that I would have sought, and all I seek,
>> Bear, know, feel—and yet breathe—into *one* word,
>> And that one word were Lightning, I would speak ;
>> But as it is, I live and die unheard,
> With a most voiceless thought, sheathing it as a sword.[28]

While, therefore, there are several foci of interest in this canto, the central interest always is the poet-hero himself. Byron has chosen to present his criticism of life, his meditations on his own experience, through this character, and our final judgment on the poem will depend, presumably, on what we think of "Harold" in his new role. I myself find him unsatisfactory: he is too histrionic and self-pitying a figure, and the

---

[27] The same habit of thought is to be found in *Manfred*, and in Byron's journal for September 1816 : "Passed *whole woods of withered pines, all withered* ; trunks stripped and barkless, branches lifeless ; done by a single winter,—their appearance reminded me of me and my family." (*L.J.*, III. 360).

[28] *P.W.*, II. 275-6.

admiration Byron obviously feels for him (as for the verse-tale heroes) seems excessive and unjustified. Harold lays claim to exceptional nobility of soul, but neither the greatness of his nature nor the fineness of his sensibility is sufficiently established by the poem itself; and while his thoughts are often interesting, they hardly warrant his conviction of their elevation above those of ordinary men. This self-flattering, self-dramatising self-deception is his greatest weakness, which appears again and again, producing some of the most famous, but most questionable, purple passages in Canto III:

> I have not loved the World, nor the World me ;
> I have not flattered its rank breath, nor bowed
> To its idolatries a patient knee,
> Nor coined my cheek to smiles,—nor cried aloud
> In worship of an echo : in the crowd
> They could not deem me one of such—I stood
> Among them, but not of them—in a shroud
> Of thoughts which were not their thoughts, and still could,
> Had I not filed my mind, which thus itself subdued.

> I have not loved the World, nor the World me,—
> But let us part fair foes ; I do believe,
> Though I have found them not, that there may be
> Words which are things,—hopes which will not deceive,
> And Virtues which are merciful, nor weave
> Snares for the failing ; I would also deem
> O'er others' griefs that some sincerely grieve—
> That two, or one, are almost what they seem,—
> That Goodness is no name—and Happiness no dream.[29]

Here we have the Byronic Byron at his best and worst. There is a natural temptation to adduce biographical evidence to prove that he is lying at this point—that he *had* loved "the World" and courted its approval with remarkable success; but confining ourselves to more reputable critical procedures, we may point not only to some loosenesses of thought and of expression, but also to the presentation of humanity as a crowd of base, hypocritical, rank-breathed idolators, forming a single monolithic entity ("the World") which is contrasted with the

[29] *P.W.*, II. 286-7.

one great individual—himself. The vanity and petulance of this are obvious and deplorable; and yet the stanzas cannot be rejected out of hand: one has to admit that these feelings are successfully created for us by the verse, in spite of—or rather by means of—its stylistic defects; so that it would probably be fairest to describe this passage (and the many others like it) as extremely good bad poetry, highly competent though vicious. Then again, as I have tried to show, this aspect of Childe Harold is not always in the foreground, for when Byron's interest was sufficiently engaged in other characters or other subjects he could escape almost completely from his worst faults and write poetry of a higher order, even though the balance he attains is a precarious one, and he is constantly in danger of lapsing into the cheap attitudes he nearly always strikes when considering his recent history or his relation to his fellow-men.

There is, moreover, some confusion in the actual conception of Childe Harold's character: his total detachment from mankind, his retreat to solitude and Nature, and his arrogant contempt for ordinary humanity, are difficult to reconcile with his professed enthusiasm for Revolution and Freedom for the People. Byron was trying for the first time to combine romantic liberalism with the "Byronic" attributes of pride, misanthropy, and isolation, and the result is not convincing psychologically. The conflict is never fully recognised, and it is far from being resolved by the glib formula "To fly from, need not be to hate, mankind"[30]; so that we see reflected here a contradiction in the author's own beliefs and feelings.

Clearly, then, in spite of the increased creative power that Byron shows in Canto III, he had not yet solved the two closely related problems of his style and his poetic personality.

[30] *P.W.*, ii. 259.

E

IV

The Prisoner of Chillon

The Prisoner of Chillon is the best of Byron's verse tales, and indeed the best of all his non-satiric works. One reads it with surprised delight, for it is strange to find, sandwiched between *Childe Harold*, Canto III, and *Manfred*, a dramatic monologue so different from them both, so free from their characteristic faults, and possessing such distinctive merits of its own.

Byron visited Chillon towards the end of June 1816, and the poem was written while his impressions were still fresh and vivid, but its quality cannot be attributed to this alone: he must have had a sudden, an immediate perception of how best to treat the subject, for he shows throughout an unexpectedly mature and fine artistic sense. The construction of the poem could hardly be bettered, and his return to narrative in a more flexible and less demanding verse form seems to have freed him instantly from the stylistic vices he had been developing. It was not that he became aware of them as vices, but that a happy instinct led him to avoid them, although some were to reappear almost immediately in other works. When he wrote his *Sonnet on Chillon*, for example, Byron seems to have felt that though his subject was the same the form required a more elevated "literary" style, and this was the result:

> Eternal Spirit of the chainless Mind !
> > Brightest in dungeons, Liberty ! thou art :
> > For there thy habitation is the heart—
> The heart which love of thee alone can bind ;
> And when thy sons to fetters are consigned—
> > To fetters, and the damp vault's dayless gloom,
> > Their country conquers with their martyrdom,
> And Freedom's fame finds wings in every wind.
> Chillon ! thy prison is a holy place,
> > And thy sad floor an altar—for 'twas trod,

> Until his very steps have left a trace
>   Worn, as if thy cold pavement were a sod,
> By Bonnivard !—May none those marks efface !
>   For they appeal from tyranny to God.[1]

In the octave here his noble sentiments fall flat because of the stilted dignity and lifeless metaphors, and also because the play of sentences against the pattern of the verse is not well-managed: the turn in the second half of each quatrain gives an effect of facile optimism—we feel that dungeons, fetters, and the damp vault's dayless gloom are being brushed aside too easily, and the view that only love of liberty can bind the heart seems sheer poetic cant when one contrasts it with the verse tale's realism. The sestet, however, is much better, in its own exclamatory way, partly because it is planned as a single rhetorical unit, and partly because Byron concentrates on the one specific character and situation. Even in this sonnet one can see that his genius was for the actual, the detailed, the particular, not for the general and abstract; and *The Prisoner of Chillon* gains incalculably both from his writing in a less pretentious style, and from his presenting the story of a single victim rather than orating on the ideas of Imprisonment and Freedom.

Some of Byron's greatest satire was to spring from his full realisation of what certain situations and experiences—in love, war, shipwreck, social life—are really like for people taking part in them; and in this poem he shows a similar ability and insight. Starting from his first-hand knowledge of the castle and its dungeons, and from the story he had heard told about Bonivard, he proceeded to make this vivid imaginative reconstruction of what long imprisonment might have been like for one man. This main character is not strictly historical, but when Byron modified the facts of history (in so far as he knew them) it was not in order to present another portrait of his favourite hero-type, but to make the poem more philosophical in Aristotle's sense: he designs his fable to bring out as fully and as powerfully as possible the implications and the horror of the fate he is describing. In *The Prisoner of Chillon*, therefore, Byron has a clearly conceived artistic-moral purpose,

---

[1] *P.W.*, IV. 7.

and it is carried out with an economy and force new in his writings.

The first section of the poem introduces the protagonist by emphasising the most obvious results of his imprisonment—the visible effect it has had on his physique. There is a rapid sketch of his family's history, which is kept deliberately slight, giving a background of religious persecution without distracting our attention from the central theme: the sentence on the brothers was unjust and arbitrary, and the poem implies a criticism of despotism and intolerance, but it does this by revealing the true nature and essential wrongness of imprisonment as such.

The narrator-hero goes on to describe the dungeon in an impressionistic "composition of place," stressing its unnatural corrupting quality—even sunlight, if it penetrates there, is perverted from its normal health and lightness; and he tells how his own years in the cell have affected him for life, in ways which are less immediately apparent. One notes here—it is obvious enough—that the references to fetters, chains, and wounds that never heal, which seemed exaggerated when used metaphorically in *Childe Harold*, are completely justified and meaningful in this new context:

> . . . in each pillar there is a ring,
>   And in each ring there is a chain ;
> That iron is a cankering thing,
>   For in these limbs its teeth remain,
> With marks that will not wear away,
> Till I have done with this new day,
> Which now is painful to these eyes,
> Which have not seen the sun so rise
> For years—I cannot count them o'er,
> I lost their long and heavy score
> When my last brother drooped and died,
> And I lay living by his side.[2]

Having revealed his brothers' fate, thus modifying our responses to the whole narration still to come, he returns to the early days

[2] *P.W.*, IV. 15.

of their imprisonment and the first deadening influence of
their surroundings:

> 'Twas still some solace in the dearth
> Of the pure elements of earth,
> To hearken to each other's speech,
> And each turn comforter to each
> With some new hope, or legend old,
> Or song heroically bold ;
> But even these at length grew cold.
> Our voices took a dreary tone,
> An echo of the dungeon stone,
> > A grating sound, not full and free,
> > As they of yore were wont to be :
> > It might be fancy—but to me
> They never sounded like our own.[3]

That phrase "it might be fancy" marks a difference between
this work and the early verse tales, or *Childe Harold's Pilgrimage*:
it suggests that the speaker is aware that his own emotions and
experiences may lead him to distort the truth, to overstate
things, to imagine rather than report; and it thus implies a
controlling judgment and a scrupulosity of statement which in
fact are to be found throughout the poem. We can put more
faith in this man's utterances than in those of Byron's other
romantic heroes or narrators; and later when his mental
balance is disturbed, we are made to realise this—not invited
to accept or admire his delusions.

The poem's fundamental contrast between Freedom and
Imprisonment is presented as a contrast between Life and
Death; and the description of the other brothers is meant to
emphasise the terrible negation of vitality in Chillon's dungeon:
one is young, pure, gay, and tender-hearted, with life all
before him, and the other more mature and manly, fit for
action, and accustomed to the freedom of a hunter. For both
Chillon is a living grave, and their existence there a living
death. The cruel paradox of their situation is made clear to
us by a fuller account of the chateau and its setting: Nature
and the elements, which are normally associated with liberty,

[3] *P.W.*, IV. 16.

combine here with the works of man to form a double prison,
and it is only in the violence of storms that the narrator
could conceive of an escape from misery—through death:

> Below the surface of the lake
> The dark vault lies wherein we lay :
> We heard it ripple night and day ;
>   Sounding o'er our heads it knocked ;
> And I have felt the winter's spray
> Wash through the bars when winds were high
> And wanton in the happy sky ;
>   And then the very rock hath rocked,
>   And I have felt it shake, unshocked,
> Because I could have smiled to see
> The death that would have set me free.[4]

This dramatic use of Nature in the story, and the controlled
force of the speaker's feelings, are far more effective than the
obtrusive symbolism and gusty yearnings of *Childe Harold*—

> . . . where of ye, O Tempests ! is the goal?
> Are ye like those within the human breast?

And this section has another function in the structure of the
poem—by interrupting the narrative it suggests the passage
of time, so that the hero can now go on to tell what happened
to his two companions:

> I said my nearer brother pined,
> I said his mighty heart declined,
> He loathed and put away his food ;
> It was not that 'twas coarse and rude,
> For we were used to hunter's fare,
> And for the like had little care. . . .
>
> My brother's soul was of that mould
> Which in a palace had grown cold,
> Had his free breathing been denied
> The range of the steep mountain's side ;
> But why delay the truth ?—he died.
> I saw, and could not hold his head,

---

[4] *P.W.*, iv. 18-19.

Nor reach his dying hand—nor dead,—
Though hard I strove, but strove in vain,
To rend and gnash my bonds in twain.
He died—and they unlocked his chain,
And scooped for him a shallow grave
Even from the cold earth of our cave.
I begged them, as a boon, to lay
His corse in dust whereon the day
Might shine—it was a foolish thought,
But then within my brain it wrought,
That even in death his freeborn breast ·
In such a dungeon could not rest.
I might have spared my idle prayer—
They coldly laughed—and laid him there :
The flat and turfless earth above
The being we so much did love ;
His empty chain above it leant,
Such Murder's fitting monument ![5]

Then comes the crushing blow of the younger brother's death, and after that the narrator's mental breakdown, which is presented with originality and complete success as another form of death in life:

What next befell me then and there
    I know not well—I never knew—
First came the loss of light and air,
    And then of darkness too :
I had no thought, no feeling—none—
Among the stones I stood a stone,
And was, scarce conscious what I wist,
As shrubless crags within the mist ;
For all was blank, and bleak, and grey ;
It was not night—it was not day ;
It was not even the dungeon-light,
So hateful to my heavy sight,
But vacancy absorbing space,
And fixedness—without a place ;
There were no stars—no earth—no time—
No check—no change—no good—no crime—

---

[5] *P.W.*, IV. 19-20.

> But silence and a stirless breath
> Which neither was of life nor death ;
> A sea of stagnant idleness,
> Blind, boundless, mute and motionless ![6]

This trance is broken by a bird's song, which recalls the prisoner to life, and his immediate reactions are described with genuine insight—first the impulse of joy, then a fresh realisation of his wretchedness, and then delight on seeing the bird itself. The delight soon shades into delusion, when he says that this might be his brother's soul come down to visit him, but though his thoughts here are absurd, they are not meant to be taken seriously: they are the fancies of a man beginning to recover from complete mental collapse, and as such they are perfectly acceptable; and similarly, his self-pity when the bird flies away is in keeping with his barely convalescent state of mind: it is shown as a natural weakness, not a virtue, and so does not alienate the reader's sympathy.

After his recovery we realise that the prisoner is not the same man as before: there is the possibility of a relapse, as we see from his physical-emotional distress over his brothers' graves; and still more important is the fact that he has now adapted himself so thoroughly to prison life. There is perhaps an ironic ambiguity in the lines where he says he was free to walk about:

> And it was liberty to stride
> Along my cell from side to side . . .[7]

This certainly was liberty, compared with being chained to a pillar, but it may also be the only liberty of which he could now conceive: his thoughts and life were narrowed to the dungeon's scope, and he had no idea of escape, for after his experiences there the whole earth would only be a wider prison to him. And yet he feels an impulse to look once again on the landscape which he used to know:

> . . . to ascend
> To my barred windows, and to bend

---

[6] *P.W.*, IV. 23.   [7] *P.W.*, IV. 25.

> Once more, upon the mountains high,
> The quiet of a loving eye.
> I saw them—and they were the same,
> They were not changed like me in frame ;
> I saw their thousand years of snow
> On high—their wide long lake below,
> And the blue Rhone in fullest flow ;
> I heard the torrents leap and gush
> O'er channelled rock and broken bush ;
> I saw the white-walled distant town,
> And whiter sails go skimming down . . .[8]

In this whole passage Byron makes good use of Wordsworth and his own knowledge of Lake Léman to produce not pseudo-mysticism but a simple picture of the scene, and a sense of the beauty, vitality and joy of Nature—of the trees, winds, water, flowers, fish, birds—and of men—everything which participates in the life which has been going on while the hero was in prison, the life which he has learned to do without. The sudden extension of our vision makes us realise with a shock that we, like the prisoner, have become accustomed to the dungeon, and it is difficult to readjust immediately to the outside world —this is why his own reactions are confused:

> And then new tears came in my eye,
> And I felt troubled—and would fain
> I had not left my recent chain ;
> And when I did descend again,
> The darkness of my dim abode
> Fell on me as a heavy load ;
> It was as is a new-dug grave,
> Closing o'er one we sought to save,—
> And yet my glance, too much opprest,
> Had almost need of such a rest.[9]

His mixed feelings here prepare us for the last section of the poem, where he is released as arbitrarily as he had been im-prisoned, only to find that he has become so used to dungeon life that he has almost lost the taste for freedom: his mind and spirit, just as much as his body, have suffered from the long

[8] *P.W.*, IV. 26.   [9] *P.W.*, IV. 27.

ordeal, and this is the poem's final horror—that a man can be broken by prison so that even Liberty loses its savour:

> At last men came to set me free ;
>   I asked not why, and recked not where ;
> It was at length the same to me,
> Fettered or fetterless to be,
>   I learned to love despair.
> And thus when they appeared at last,
> And all my bonds aside were cast,
> These heavy walls to me had grown
> A hermitage—and all my own !
> And half I felt as they were come
> To tear me from a second home :
> With spiders I had friendship made,
> And watched them in their sullen trade
> Had seen the mice by moonlight play,
> And why should I feel less than they ?
> We were all inmates of one place,
> And I, the monarch of each race,
> Had power to kill—yet, strange to tell !
> In quiet we had learned to dwell ;[10]
> My very chains and I grew friends,
> So much a long communion tends
> To make us what we are :—even I
> Regained my freedom with a sigh.[11]

The Prisoner of Chillon is a more finished, satisfying work of art than any of Byron's poems up to this date. Its superiority is not simply a matter of improved technique, though certainly the planning and the writing are much better than before—indeed the praise which T. S. Eliot gives to his handling of plot and metre in *The Giaour*[12] might have been given with more justice to this later poem. But *The Prisoner of Chillon* also shows a deeper understanding of human nature, a sounder sense of values, and a greater integrity of feeling than we are accustomed to in his "romantic" works. The new narrator-hero is different from his predecessors, for he is more credible

---

[10] These lines suggest a contrast with the intolerance and cruelty of real rulers, and man's inhumanity to man as we have seen it in the poem.

[11] *P.W.*, IV. 28.

[12] T. S. Eliot, *On Poetry and Poets*, London 1957, pp. 196-8.

and consistent as a character, he has more maturity and dignity, and above all he is free from the now familiar faults of "Byronism." In *Childe Harold*, Canto III, the passages on Liberty were least affected by the speaker's own peculiarities, by Byron's prevailing mood, and in *The Prisoner of Chillon*, where his subject is the loss of liberty, he achieves a similar impersonality of treatment. Here, however, there are new exciting qualities, as well as the merely negative virtue of avoiding such faults: Byron shows a hitherto unsuspected power of dramatic imagination—an ability to create and sustain a different type of character, to "imitate" convincingly emotions and psychological states that he himself had not experienced; and his whole presentation of the story is controlled by a new sense of purpose: the verse tale has now become a serious art form, which he uses to express his real beliefs, not just to entertain the reader or amuse himself.

The Prisoner of Chillon stands alone, however, amid Byron's poetry of this period. In spite of its excellence, it does not mark a turning-point in his career as writer, for the escape from his usual weaknesses was only temporary, and he soon returned to them with gusto. In *The Dream*, for example, which was published in the same collection, he portrays himself as a thoroughly Byronic figure, modelled on his former heroes. He then went on, almost immediately, to a still more ambitious presentation of this hero-type in *Manfred*. And one feels a weariness of spirit as one finds him ringing the changes on the same old formula, showing no awareness of its limitations, dangers, and occasional absurdity.

V

Manfred

FORMALLY, *Manfred* is a new departure for Byron—an experiment in semi-lyrical romantic drama, which derives from Goethe's *Faust*;[1] but its content is familiar to a reader of *Childe Harold* and the verse tales. *Manfred* expresses, through a new set of conventions, Byron's own familiar notions, his own *Weltanschauung*, and Goethe was one of the first to acknowledge that the work was of completely different import from *his* masterpiece.[2] It was only the failure of some readers to perceive this difference, and their talk of plagiarism, that made Byron once deny indignantly that he had used the German or the English Faustus.[3] Normally he would admit quite readily that he had known the former, though he claimed it was of limited importance in the composition of his own poem:

> [Goethe's] *Faust* I never read [he told John Murray], for I don't know German ; but Matthew Monk Lewis . . . at Coligny, translated most of it to me *vivâ voce*, and I was naturally much struck with it ; but it was the *Staubach* and the *Jungfrau* and something else, much more than Faustus, that made me write *Manfred*. The first Scene, however, and that of Faustus are very similar.[4]

---

[1] *Faust* certainly gave Byron the idea of writing *Manfred*, and suggested this dramatic form ; but in his handling of plot and character he drew on a wide field of other reading. There are obvious reminiscences of Hamlet, Milton's Satan, and Prometheus, as well as of popular romantic works. Professor S. C. Chew sees both *Faust* and Chateaubriand's *René* as important sources and he traces parallels or minor debts in Walpole's *Castle of Otranto* and *The Mysterious Mother*, Shelley's *St. Irvyne or The Rosicrucian* and perhaps some of his poems, Beckford's *Vathek*, Lewis's *Monk*, Coleridge's *Remorse*, and Maturin's *Bertram*. (*The Dramas of Lord Byron*, Göttingen 1915). Bertrand Evans stresses the extent to which Byron was drawing on a common stock of "Gothic" incidents and properties ; and he makes out a convincing case for the influence of characters and conventions well established in the Gothic dramas of the period. ("Manfred's Remorse and Dramatic Tradition," in *P.M.L.A.*, LXII. (1947), pp. 752 ff.

[2] *L.J.*, v. 506 : cp. E. M. Butler, *Byron and Goethe*, London 1956, p. 33.

[3] *L.J.*, IV. 177.

[4] *L.J.*, v. 37 (cp. IV. 97, 173-4).

His repeated emphasis on the part played by Alpine scenery is borne out by the work, for many passages of natural description echo phrases from his Journal to Augusta; yet this hardly provides an adequate account of the poem's genesis, far less its meaning. Byron's interest, after all, lies primarily in the hero, not the landscapes: they provide an appropriate setting for the action, but remain subordinate to the play's main purpose of displaying Manfred's character and problems. It was therefore disingenuous on Byron's part to say that he wrote it "for the sake of introducing the Alpine scenery in description,"[5] or that the "Journal . . . of my journey in the Alps . . . contains all the germs of *Manfred*"[6]; yet this last remark comes nearer to the truth, since his journal was a record of his states of mind as well as of his travels and surroundings :

> In the weather for this tour (of 13 days), I have been very fortunate—fortunate in a companion (Mr. He.)—fortunate in our prospects, and exempt from even the little petty accidents and delays which often render journeys in a less wild country disappointing. I was disposed to be pleased. I am a lover of Nature and an admirer of Beauty. I can bear fatigue and welcome privation, and have seen some of the noblest views in the world. But in all this—the recollections of bitterness, and more especially of recent and more home desolation, which must accompany me through life, have preyed upon me here ; and neither the music of the Shepherd, the crashing of the Avalanche, nor the torrent, the mountain, the Glacier, the Forest, nor the Cloud, have for one moment lightened the weight upon my heart, nor enabled me to lose my own wretched identity in the majesty, and the power, and the Glory, around, above, and beneath me.[7]

In its rather histrionic insistence on the intensity of his sufferings, and on the inefficacy of Nature as a cure, this passage is clearly related to the mood of *Manfred*. As one might expect, Byron's own feelings are the ultimate source for the poem—the "something else" which made him write it was presumably his recent history—not his domestic circumstances this time, but

[5] *L.J.*, iv. 80.   [6] *L.J.*, v. 342.   [7] *L.J.*, iii. 364.

his relations, real or imagined, with Augusta, and their psychological aftermath. Incestuous guilt, or at least the idea of such guilt, seems to have been the mainspring of his inspiration, and if there are parallels with *René* and *The Mysterious Mother* it is probably because their themes chimed with his own preoccupations; and its basis in his own life was perhaps the reason for his trying to divert attention to more incidental "sources" like the Alpine scenery.

Manfred is not, however, autobiographical, nor does it stand in the fairly close relation that *Childe Harold* does to Byron's own experience. He draws on his life (and reading) only to create a work of more general significance, a fantastic drama of the supernatural which will embody his ideal of human greatness. Here more than in any other poem we see him as a maker of myths, and the play is in an important sense the culmination of his whole romantic phase, since it is his supreme attempt to claim significance and value for the character of the Byronic hero.

Yet in spite of this uncompromising affirmation, Byron's attitude to *Manfred* varied even while he was at work on it. The play was begun in Switzerland in the autumn of 1816, and he wrote the first two acts while his enthusiasm for romantic literature was at its height, and while his bitterness and melancholy were still most acute. The third act was added in Venice, when his mental state was very different, and not only does a note of farce appear among the Gothic horrors,[8] but his first account of the completed poem shows an ironic detachment from the mood in which it had been written:

> I forgot to mention to you that a kind of Poem in dialogue (in blank verse) or drama, . . .begun last summer in Switzerland, is finished ; it is in three acts ; but of a very wild, metaphysical, and inexplicable kind. Almost all the persons—but two or three—are spirits of the earth and air, or the waters ; the scene is in the Alps ; the hero a kind of magician, who is tormented

---

[8] See *P.W.*, IV. 122-3, n. :
>   "ASHTAROTH *disappears with the* ABBOT, *singing as follows* :—
>   A prodigal son, and a maid undone,
>   And a widow re-wedded within the year ;
>   And a worldly monk, and a pregnant nun,
>   Are things which every day appear."

by a species of remorse, the cause of which is left half unexplained. He wanders about invoking these spirits, which appear to him, and are of no use ; he at last goes to the very abode of the Evil principle . . . to evocate a ghost, which appears, and gives him an ambiguous and disagreeable answer ; and in the 3ᵈ act he is found by his attendants dying in a tower where he studied his art. You may perceive by this outline that I have no great opinion of this piece of phantasy. . . .

I have not even copied it off . . . ; but when I have, I will send it to you, and you may either throw it into the fire or not.[9]

As Byron gradually returned to normal after the emotional crises of 1816, he realised that *Manfred* might seem silly rather than sublime, and he also felt some diffidence at entering what was for him an untried literary field, so that we find him telling Murray that he has no idea whether the play is good or bad—if bad it must on no account be risked in publication.[10] At his own request it was shown to his old advisor, Gifford, who praised Act I as "wonderfully poetical," but disapproved of Act III. Byron himself had already realised that this part was inferior to the rest, and accepting Gifford's criticism without resentment or demur he went back to work on it, and soon produced a greatly improved version which was forwarded from Rome early in May, so that the play had now assumed its final shape.

Although Byron himself described it as "inexplicable," his general intention is quite clear: as E. H. Coleridge observes, "the *motif* of *Manfred* is remorse—eternal suffering for inexpiable crime,"[11] and the play consists of a progressive revelation of the hero's character and history, and of the stages in his search for an escape from guilt.

In the opening scene Manfred appears at midnight in a Gothic gallery, to soliloquise about his mental torment, and to invoke the Spirits of Earth, Ocean, Air, Night, Mountains, Winds, and his own Star. They come in answer to his final summons, which expresses his sense of fatality—of being under

[9] *L.J.*, IV. 54-5 (February 15th, 1817).
[10] *L.J.*, IV. 68, 86.
[11] *P.W.*, IV. 82.

a curse, and this idea is developed by the Seventh Spirit's first speech:

> The Star which rules thy destiny
> Was ruled, ere earth began, by me :
> It was a World as fresh and fair
> As e'er revolved round Sun in air ;
> Its course was free and regular,
> Space bosomed not a lovelier star.
> The Hour arrived—and it became
> A wandering mass of shapeless flame,
> A pathless Comet, and a curse,
> The menace of the Universe ;
> Still rolling on with innate force,
> Without a sphere, without a course,
> A bright deformity on high,
> The monster of the upper sky !
> And Thou ! beneath its influence born—
> Thou worm ! whom I obey and scorn—
> Forced by a Power (which is not thine,
> And lent thee but to make thee mine)
> For this brief moment to descend
> Where these weak Spirits round thee bend
> And parley with a thing like thee—
> What would'st thou, Child of Clay ! with me ?[12]

These lines are much better than the jingles sung or spoken by the other Spirits. Byron is writing about something which he really felt and imagined vividly—he has returned with new power to the conception of a noble nature doomed by some fate, blasted, and perverted from Promethean potentialities to almost Satanic evil. It is difficult, however, to say precisely what this passage means in terms of the play's action. If this Spirit rules the star under which Manfred was born, has he controlled or influenced the hero's life? Was it he, or some external Fate, who was responsible for the dire change in the star, and was this change the cause of Manfred's sin? Or was "the Hour" not predetermined by any agency, supernatural or astrological? Was it simply the hour of sin, committed of the hero's own accord, and is the change in the star a mere

[12] *P.W.*, IV. 89.

symbolical description of the change in Manfred's soul? These questions are unanswered and unanswerable, so that there is a serious confusion or obscurity in the play's metaphysics, and these are still further complicated by the Spirit's later comments which suggest a devil trying to win the hero's soul. Byron is using some ideas that fascinated him, and expressing them well enough to give us an agreeable *frisson* of horror, but he does not seem to have defined them clearly even to himself, or to have worked them into a coherent system, even in this one poem. There is, indeed, an almost wilful confusion on the question of Free Will *versus* Predestination, and this enables him to have it both ways: Manfred has all the glamour which in Byron's eyes attached itself to a doomed hero, "fatal and fated in [his] sufferings";[13] but he is also shown as a kind of superman, choosing his own course in defiance of all supernatural powers, and the contradiction is never examined or resolved.

There is a less important ambiguity about the status of the other Spirits. Byron may be writing allegorically, in which case they represent aspects of physical Nature, or he may be suggesting, through this new mythology, some spiritual life behind natural phenomena; but the basic interpretation of the scene would be the same in either case. Manfred asks these Spirits for "forgetfulness," though the cause of his unrest is still a secret. They reply that they can give him mastery of the elements which are under their control, but that they have no power to grant oblivion; and as they are immortal, they cannot tell him whether death will bring what he desires. Here Byron seems to be rejecting the Wordsworthian and Shelleyan notions of *Childe Harold*, Canto III: he is denying the power of Nature (physical or spiritual) to minister to a mind diseased, or to provide a haven for the disembodied soul.

Towards the end of the scene the Seventh Spirit rather maliciously assumes the form of "a beautiful female figure," and from Manfred's frenzied outburst we deduce that it was that of his lost love (Astarte). The Incantation which follows, spoken presumably by this spirit or the lady, adds to our sense

[13] *P.W.*, IV. 103.

F

of mystification, but fills out our picture of the hero as a man accursed and sinful, isolated from his fellows by his agony and guilt:

> By thy cold breast and serpent smile,
> By thy unfathomed gulfs of guile,
> By that most seeming virtuous eye,
> By thy shut soul's hypocrisy ;
> By the perfection of thine art
> Which passed for human thine own heart ;
> By thy delight in others' pain,
> And by thy brotherhood of Cain,
> I call upon thee ! and compel
> Thyself to be thy proper Hell ! [14]

Many of the faults, however, which are thus attributed to Manfred, are not shown in his soliloquies or actions in the play, and this would seem to be another case of Byron "having it both ways." All his heroes in the early verse tales had been paradoxical mixtures of good and evil, vice and virtue, but their more unpleasant crimes were never fully presented in the poems, so that the reader—like the author—could enjoy the romantic villainy without ever facing its real implications. Something of the same kind happens now in *Manfred*, for the hero's sinful past is emphasised to make him seem more interesting and awe-inspiring, but the more objectionable qualities (like hypocrisy or delight in others' pain) are excluded from the actual portrayal of his character, by an artistic sleight of hand amounting to dishonesty.

In Scene Two Manfred appears alone on the Jungfrau, meditating on his condition. Spirits, spells, and superhuman aid have failed to obliterate the past, and though all around him he sees the beauty of Nature, it provides no cure—unless the opportunity for suicide: as he contemplates his life, and the prospect that lies before him, he grows desperate and finally decides to plunge into the abyss. Saved by the Chamois Hunter, he goes with him to his cottage, and the Second Act begins with a long dialogue between the Byronic superman and

[14] *P.W.*, IV. 93 ; S. C. Chew, *The Dramas of Lord Byron*, p. 59, n.1.

this representative of ordinary humanity. This establishes the fact that Manfred is an aristocrat—

> One of the many chiefs, whose castled crags
> Look o'er the lower valleys [15]

—and suggests that his great sin was that of incest. A hint of murder is soon discredited, for it was his *love* that had proved fatal—an idea that had appealed to Byron ever since *The Giaour*; and another favourite notion reappears when Manfred says he has lived so intensely that he has packed long years into his relatively short life, and his desolation is beyond the comprehension of more normal men. He contrasts the Chamois Hunter's simple life and virtues with his own blighted and tormented soul, but—very significantly—he rejects the other's attempt at consolation, since he despises Christian piety and Christian ethics:

CHAMOIS HUNTER

> Man of strange words, and some half-maddening sin,
> Which makes thee people vacancy, whate'er
> Thy dread and sufferance be, there's comfort yet—
> The aid of holy men, and heavenly patience—

MANFRED

> Patience—and patience ! Hence—that word was made
> For brutes of burthen, not for birds of prey !
> Preach it to mortals of a dust like thine,—
> I am not of thine order.[16]

And his spiritual pride and self-sufficiency are further emphasised by his reception of the Hunter's final words:

CHAMOIS HUNTER

> Heaven give thee rest !
> And Penitence restore thee to thyself ;
> My prayers shall be for thee.

MANFRED

> I need them not,
> But can endure thy pity. I depart. . . .[17]

In the next scene Manfred turns again to magic, and calls up the Witch of the Alps, giving her a long account of himself

[15] *P.W.*, IV. 99.   [16] *P.W.*, IV. 100.   [17] *P.W.*, IV. 102.

in a speech where once again we see a blend of the Byronic
and the Shelleyan rejections of humanity:

> From my youth upwards
> My Spirit walked not with the souls of men,
> Nor looked upon the earth with human eyes ;
> The thirst of their ambition was not mine,
> The aim of their existence was not mine ;
> My joys—my griefs—my passions—and my powers,
> Made me a stranger ; though I wore the form,
> I had no sympathy with breathing flesh,
> Nor midst the Creatures of Clay that girded me
> Was there but One who—but of her anon.
> I said with men, and with the thoughts of men,
> I held but slight communion ; but instead,
> My joy was in the wilderness,—to breathe
> The difficult air of the iced mountain's top,
> Where the birds dare not build—nor insect's wing
> Flit o'er the herbless granite ; or to plunge
> Into the torrent, and to roll along
> On the swift whirl of the new-breaking wave
> Of river-stream, or Ocean, in their flow.
> In these my early strength exulted ; or
> To follow through the night the moving moon,
> The stars and their development ; or catch
> The dazzled lightnings till my eyes grew dim ;
> Or to look, list'ning, on the scattered leaves,
> While Autumn winds were at their evening song.
> These were my pastimes, and to be alone ;
> For if the beings, of whom I was one,—
> Hating to be so,—crossed me in my path,
> I felt myself degraded back to them,
> And was all clay again. . . .[18]

He goes on to describe his love for Astarte, her death, and his
consequent search for oblivion. The witch, having heard his
story, offers to assist him on condition that he swears obedience
to her, but he refuses scornfully, preferring to endure his agony
rather than submit to such a degradation:

> I will not swear—Obey ! and whom ? the Spirits
> Whose presence I command, and be the slave
> Of those who served me—Never ![19]

---

[18] *P.W.*, IV. 104-5.   [19] *P.W.*, IV. 107.

This parallels his rejection of Christianity, but the exact meaning of the episode is far from clear. The Witch of the Alps would seem to be a higher kind of Spirit than those who had first appeared, since she can help Manfred where they could not; but if she represents Nature, or Natural Beauty, or a spirit behind Nature—and something of this sort seems to be implied—Byron is surely contradicting himself, since these powers have already been considered, and found wanting.[20] I suspect that she has no real allegorical or symbolic function, and that the scene is fundamentally "inexplicable": Byron is inventing actions and situations which show Manfred's pride and independence, but which have no further meaning, no relation to life as we know it, and no correspondence to an intellectual concept.

This is again apparent in the next scene, when the hero seeks help from the devil Arimanes and his servants, who control the affairs of this world—they include the Destinies, who are responsible for the disasters which afflict mankind, Nemesis who (oddly enough) assists reactionary monarchs to crush demands for Freedom, and various unnamed Spirits. Manfred interrupts their ceremonies, but refuses to kneel to Arimanes, in another episode designed only to show his greatness, pride, and strength of will:

ALL THE SPIRITS
Prostrate thyself, and thy condemnéd clay,
Child of the Earth ! or dread the worst.

MANFRED
I know it ;
And yet ye see I kneel not. . . .

FIFTH SPIRIT
Dost thou dare
Refuse to Arimanes on his throne
What the whole Earth accords, beholding not
The terror of his Glory ?—Crouch ! I say.

---

[20] See the opening scene, and the soliloquy on the Jungfrau.

MANFRED

Bid *him* bow down to that which is above him,
The overruling Infinite—the Maker
Who made him not for worship—let him kneel,
And we will kneel together.

THE SPIRITS

Crush the worm !
Tear him in pieces !—

FIRST DESTINY

Hence ! Avaunt !—he's mine.
Prince of the Powers invisible ! This man
Is of no common order, as his port
And presence here denote : his sufferings
Have been of an immortal nature—like
Our own ; his knowledge, and his powers and will,
As far as is compatible with clay,
Which clogs the ethereal essence, have been such
As clay hath seldom borne ; his aspirations
Have been beyond the dwellers of the earth. . . .[21]

The First Destiny's claim on Manfred is, to say the least, obscure; and we are never told why he goes to the Devil for aid instead of to the God whom he acknowledges to be superior —presumably it is because he thinks he can meet Arimanes on equal terms, whereas the other would require some form of worship or submission. Arimanes for his part seems to look on him with favour, and the Phantom of Astarte is now summoned. Manfred pleads with her to speak to him, to say that she forgives him, to assure him she is not being punished for their sin, but she replies only by informing him of his approaching death, and then she disappears. This gives his audience another opportunity to admire his fortitude:

A SPIRIT

He is convulsed—This is to be a mortal,
And seek the things beyond mortality.

---

[21] *P.W.*, IV. 114.

ANOTHER SPIRIT

> Yet, see, he mastereth himself, and makes
> His torture tributary to his will.
> Had he been one of us, he would have made
> An awful Spirit.[22]

The weakness of the original third act lay in its lack of significant action. The Abbot was a caricature of religious intolerance, his threatening message was an insult to the hero's spiritual torment, Manfred's treatment of him was a piece of trivial farce, and even his own death came as something of an anticlimax. In the revised version Byron changes all this: he omits the "pranks fantastical," and makes two important alterations in the story. In the first place, "the Abbot is become a good man,"[23] expressing a truly Christian doctrine of repentance and forgiveness—he asserts with greater force and authority the advice of the Chamois Hunter, but in vain. Manfred refuses to admit an intermediary between himself and Heaven, and declares that religion has no power to cure *his* anguish:

> Old man ! there is no power in holy men,
> Nor charm in prayer, nor purifying form
> Of penitence, nor outward look, nor fast,
> Nor agony—nor, greater than all these,
> The innate tortures of that deep Despair,
> Which is Remorse without the fear of Hell,
> But all in all sufficient to itself
> Would make a hell of Heaven—can exorcise
> From out the unbounded spirit the quick sense
> Of its own sins—wrongs—sufferance—and revenge
> Upon itself ; there is no future pang
> Can deal that justice on the self-condemned
> He deals on his own soul.[24]

The same idea lies behind the second major change in Act III —a band of devils is brought in at the end to carry off Manfred's soul, but he drives them away (although the Abbot was unable to repulse them): his power, he says, was not derived from them, but from his own genius and industry, and so he will not let himself be dragged to Hell. (But why, one wants to ask,

---

[22] *P.W.*, IV. 118.   [23] *L.J.*, IV. 115.   [24] *P.W.*, IV. 123.

did the Seventh Spirit and the Witch of the Alps say that his power did come from other Powers,[25] and why did he not contradict them at the time?) Manfred admits that he has committed crimes, and he regards his own remorse as the inevitable punishment; but he refuses to allow devils to increase his torments, just as he denies the ability of the Church to mitigate them. This is a corollary of the spiritual pride which had led him to reject the Christian discipline of repentance, and to refuse to kneel to Arimanes or serve the Witch of the Alps. Byron is asserting the autonomy and isolation of the human soul—or rather of the *great* human soul: not its freedom from moral laws, but its independence of any system of rewards or punishments administered by an external power, and the impossibility of its escaping from the mental consequences of its sins, which must simply be accepted and endured.

This is very far from being ignoble or absurd—there are touches of real spiritual dignity in *Manfred*. And yet no one who has read it critically could agree with S. C. Chew when he says that Byron "points to an ideal truer and nobler than Goethe's," and that the play's "chief message is one of encouragement and hope;"[26] or with Professor Butler when she maintains that "the ethical content is the triumph of the unconquerable spirit of man."[27] Such claims ignore the extent to which the courage, endurance, and integrity which Byron celebrated in his poem *Prometheus* are here vitiated by their involvement with the more disreputable qualities and attitudes of the Byronic hero.

Manfred, after all, is not in any sense a representative or champion of Mankind. Byron was undoubtedly attracted by the notion of a hero who, though greater than his fellows in both rank and genius, none the less devotes himself to their cause, and Prometheus provided him with a prototype which was often in his mind that summer.[28] Yet this conception does not affect Manfred—he shows pity and consideration for the human beings whom he despises, but he is not interested

---

[25] See p. 80 ; *P.W.*, IV. 103.
[26] *The Dramas of Lord Byron*, pp. 83, 84.
[27] E. M. Butler, *Byron and Goethe*, p. 33.
[28] See *L.J.*, IV. 174-5.

in bettering their lot. In his youth he had had "noble aspirations" of this kind:

> To make my own the mind of other men,
> The enlightener of nations . . .[29]

but in reality he shrank from all contact with men, even as their leader and benefactor:

> I could not tame my nature down ; for he
> Must serve who fain would sway ; and soothe, and sue,
> And watch all time, and pry into all place,
> And be a living Lie, who would become
> A mighty thing amongst the mean—and such
> The mass are ; I disdained to mingle with
> A herd, though to be leader—and of wolves.
> The lion is alone, and so am I.[30]

It is tempting to contrast this with the unfailing common sense and patience with which Byron managed the dishonest, quarrelsome, unreliable Greeks at Missolonghi—he himself, in that last chapter of his life, provides us with a standard by which Manfred's bombast can be judged and found contemptible—by which Manfred himself is seen to be sadly defective as an ideal. But quite apart from this question of the value and propriety of the hero's attitudes, it is clear that he is no Prometheus but a Prometheus *manqué*, and that although he defies supernatural powers this does not affect the material or spiritual condition of mankind. His is an entirely private martyrdom, and he cannot be said to represent humanity or the mind of man—he is an exceptional, unique phenomenon, his problems are peculiar to himself, and their solution (if there is one) has no bearing on the situation of *nous autres*.

This difference between Men and Manfred is insisted on throughout the poem, yet one is never quite persuaded of its truth. Here, as in almost all of his "romantic" works, Byron seems to demand more sympathy and admiration for the hero than he shows him to deserve. We are always hearing about Manfred's greatness, for not only do we have his own descriptions of himself, but almost every character acts as a foil or as a chorus voicing some kind of awed respect and praise. Yet his superiority is a matter of repeated assertion rather than

[29] *P.W.*, IV. 124.   [30] *P.W.*, IV. 125.

convincing demonstration. All the posturings of pride and defiance, all the nursing of his melancholy and misanthropy, all the clamouring about his love and agony, do not make him an impressive or a tragic figure: there is little or no advance on the morality and characterisation of *The Giaour*, for Byron is absorbed with the same vision of a noble and passionate lover blasted by sins, racked by remorse and grief, but defying everyone and everything. The only difference is that Manfred is portrayed more fully, and an attempt is made to read deeper significance into his favourite attitudes and feelings, but the effect of this is to make us realise more clearly than ever before the faults and limitations of this hero-type, and its inadequacy for the role imposed upon it here. The treatment of the central problem of guilt, to take one crucial aspect of the work, consists of triviality masquerading as grandeur: just as in *The Giaour*, Byron distinguishes between repentance and remorse only so that the hero can reject the former, which he sees as an indignity, to wallow in the latter. This new spiritual superman, in fact, has an emotional and intellectual immaturity of a kind usually associated with adolescence, and while this would not have mattered so much in a verse-tale entertainment, it is fatally disabling in a moral-metaphysical play like *Manfred*. The more seriously we are asked to take the hero, the more serious must be our criticism of his defects; and the more we study him and his career, the more we see the truth of Eliot's comment that "It is . . . impossible to make out of [Byron's] diabolism anything coherent or rational."[31]

The failure of *Manfred*, then, is largely due to the deficiencies of the hero, and to Byron's inability to "place" these, or alternatively to convince us that they are virtues, but it is also due in part to the hopeless confusion of the supernatural machinery. This has sometimes been defended—W. J. Calvert, for example, argues that the incongruity of the *dramatis personae* is not to be considered as a fault, since "the work can be interpreted only as 'an attempt to give objective expression to intensely subjective emotion.' "[32]   The problem cannot, however, be

[31] *On Poetry and Poets*, p. 195.

[32] W. J. Calvert, *Byron : Romantic Paradox*, Chapel Hill (North Carolina) 1935, pp. 140-1. The phrase is quoted from S. C. Chew, *op. cit.*, p. 36.

disposed of quite as easily as this, for Byron's intention obviously goes beyond mere self-expression to the assertion of beliefs and values, and these are obscured by the sheer incoherence of the play's mythology. Cosmic rebellion, whether Promethean or Satanic, can be judged only with reference to the God or Universal Order which is being defied, but this is what we never fully understand in *Manfred*. Byron's supernatural characters do not all exist on the same level of reality. Some are more or less allegorical in nature, others mythological, while others again purport to be members of an actual divine or diabolic hierarchy: "The over-ruling Infinite—the Maker" (is he the Christians' God?) is "real," presumably, in a sense that the Witch of the Alps is not; Arimanes, the devils and the Spirits occupy a rather doubtful position between the two, while Nemesis and the Destinies present still further difficulties. Byron was, of course, following the example of *Faust*, but Goethe had a firm grasp of his poem's complex meaning, and his symbols, though of varied types, are part of a meaningful and consistent statement—they create significance, not vagueness and confusion. Lacking this intellectual substructure, *Manfred* soon becomes repetitive, obscure and muddled; and the moral-philosophic value of the hero's pride and defiance is never adequately defined, because it is not formulated in terms of the author's own theological beliefs, or in an imaginative equivalent of these. Yet even if it had been so presented, it might still have failed to be impressive: in *Cain*, Byron's next "metaphysical drama," he draws on Old Testament events and eighteenth-century philosophy, but the effect of this explicit treatment of such issues is to bring us face-to-face with his poverty of religious ideas. He had no talent for this kind of thinking—his opinions were confused and contradictory, and his conversations with Dr Kennedy show how far he was from having worked out any real critique of Christianity. He was incapable of ever becoming a philosopher or theologian, and his attempts to write poetry which he himself described as "metaphysical"[33] reveal an ignorance of his own limitations, and a misconception of his true poetic powers.

It is only in *ottava rima* satire that he finds how to

[33] E.g., *L.J.*, IV. 54-5 ; v. 361.

philosophise without being dull, pretentious or banal. Or if even in *Don Juan* he falls into such faults, it is only for short passages, and the poem's quick pace prevents us from lingering over them and becoming too aware of them as blemishes, while usually Byron will himself break off, refusing to go intellectually out of his depth, and making fun of his own portentousness. Yet in this very humility and self-ridicule there is often an ironic scrutiny of beliefs and motives for belief, which culminates in *The Vision of Judgment*—and which constitutes an attack on Orthodoxy infinitely more effective than the blundering frontal assaults of *Cain* and *Manfred*.

VI

Childe Harold's Pilgrimage, Canto IV

CANTO III of *Childe Harold* and *Manfred* show the limitations of the Byronic hero as *persona* or protagonist, and it seems unnecessary to examine Canto IV in the same detail. Yet this poem contains new elements as well as familiar weaknesses, for there are some changes and developments which constitute a real departure from Byron's mood of 1816, and look forward to the coming revolution in his whole poetic manner and technique. It should be seen, then, as essentially transitional in nature, using themes and attitudes which had appeared before, but sometimes modifying them in important ways, especially by coming closer to his normal everyday feelings and idiom.

For the most part he adopts the same conventions as he had evolved for Canto III: his journey from Venice to Rome provides the basic structure of the work, just as his route through Belgium, Germany and Switzerland gave him the framework for the former poem; and he now abandons even the pretence of a distinction between poet and hero:

> With regard to the conduct of the last canto [he writes], there will be found less of the pilgrim than in any of the preceding, and that little slightly, if at all, separated from the author speaking in his own person. The fact is, that I had become weary of drawing a line which every one seemed determined not to perceive : like the Chinese in Goldsmith's *Citizen of the World*, whom nobody would believe to be a Chinese, it was in vain that I asserted, and imagined that I had drawn, a distinction between the author and the pilgrim ; and the very anxiety to preserve this difference, and disappointment at finding it unavailing, so far crushed my efforts in the composition, that I determined to abandon it altogether—and have done so.[1]

In the poem itself then he speaks openly in his own person

[1] *P.W.*, II. 323.

mentioning the Pilgrim only as a once-convenient fiction, or a fancy of the past.[2]

This does not mean, however, that he has abandoned the whole complex of ideas and feelings associated with Harold. Byron's mood had changed during his months in Italy, but he had not altogether lost his melancholy and resentment, or his desire to voice them to the world, and in some new stanzas his tone is indistinguishable from that of the most violent, emotional, and self-regarding passages of Canto III:

> . . . There are some feelings Time can not benumb,
> Nor Torture shake, or mine would now be cold and dumb.

> But from their nature will the Tannen grow
>   Loftiest on loftiest and least sheltered rocks,
>   Rooted in barrenness, where nought below
>   Of soil supports them 'gainst the Alpine shocks
>   Of eddying storms ; yet springs the trunk, and mocks
>   The howling tempest, till its height and frame
>   Are worthy of the mountains from whose blocks
>   Of bleak, gray granite into life it came,
> And grew a giant tree ;—the Mind may grow the same.

> Existence may be borne, and the deep root
>   Of life and sufferance makes its firm abode
>   In bare and desolated bosoms : mute
>   The camel labours with the heaviest load,
>   And the wolf dies in silence—not bestowed
>   In vain should such example be ; if they,
>   Things of ignoble or of savage mood,
>   Endure and shrink not, we of nobler clay
> May temper it to bear,—it is but for a day.[3]

One cannot help noticing that Byron's own endurance, on which he so prides himself, is far from being as silent as this might suggest. He breaks out, just as in the former canto, in wild indignation and self-pity; and even when he speaks about Forgiveness, our impression is not one of genuine emotional or

---

[2] *P.W.*, II. 448-9, 462-3.
[3] *P.W.*, II. 343-5. The Alpine imagery suggests the close relationship of such a passage to Byron's feelings and experiences of the previous year.

spiritual change, but rather of his continued self-approval—of his admiration for his own superior deportment in adversity:

> And if my voice break forth, 'tis not that now
>   I shrink from what is suffered : let him speak
> Who hath beheld decline upon my brow,
> Or seen my mind's convulsion leave it weak ;
> But in this page a record will I seek.
> Not in the air shall these my words disperse,
> Though I be ashes ; a far hour shall wreak
> The deep prophetic fulness of this verse,
> And pile on human heads the mountain of my curse !
>
> That curse shall be Forgiveness.—Have I not—
>   Hear me, my mother Earth ! behold it, Heaven !—
> Have I not had to wrestle with my lot ?
> Have I not suffered things to be forgiven ?
> Have I not had my brain seared, my heart riven,
> Hopes sapped, name blighted, Life's life lied away ?
> And only not to desperation driven,
> Because not altogether of such clay
> As rots into the souls of those whom I survey.[4]

"Why do you indulge this despondency?" asked Shelley, after reading *Manfred*,[5] and his choice of verb shows critical and psychological perception, for there is a kind of relish and self-satisfaction in the gloom with which Byron surveys his fate; and the same is true of some of his more general reflexions about human life:

> We wither from our youth, we gasp away—
>   Sick—sick ; unfound the boon—unslaked the thirst,
> Though to the last, in verge of our decay,
> Some phantom lures, such as we sought at first—
> But all too late,—so are we doubly curst.
> Love, Fame, Ambition, Avarice—'tis the same,
> Each idle—and all ill—and none the worst—
> For all are meteors with a different name,
> And Death the sable smoke where vanishes the flame. . . .

---

[4] *P.W.*, II. 428-9.
[5] *Corr.*, II. 58.

> Our life is a false nature—'tis not in
>   The harmony of things,—this hard decree,
>   This uneradicable taint of Sin,
>   This boundless Upas, this all-blasting tree,
>   Whose root is Earth—whose leaves and branches be
>   The skies which rain their plagues on men like dew—
>   Disease, death, bondage—all the woes we see,
>   And worse, the woes we see not—which throb through
> The immedicable soul, with heart-aches ever new.[6]

This ranting pessimism, which provoked Peacock's amusing satire in *Nightmare Abbey*, is one of the characteristic notes of Canto IV, yet it does not pervade the whole poem. And while Byron's treatment of his wrongs and sorrows often resembles that of Canto III, his poetic personality has changed in other ways. This can be seen, for example, in his attitude to Nature. His passing from Switzerland to Italy made in itself for a change of emphasis—the new poem, he told Murray, "necessarily treats more of works of art than of Nature":[7] but his own approach is different too. Once freed from the immediate influence of Shelley, Byron threw off his vague mysticism, and except for two stanzas added at a very late stage, we hear nothing in this canto about mingling with the Universe,[8] and very little about flying from Men to Solitude. When he turns to scenery he is not searching for a refuge or religion—he is interested in Nature simply for its beauty, or its associations, literary and historical. He has returned in fact to the viewpoint of an ideal tourist, even if he departs from it at times to reappear as a Romantic Genius. Byron's mood—in spite of all the "darkness and dismay"—has ceased to be obsessive, and though he can still work up his grief and indignation to a high pitch, they are no longer fused in a single intense emotional state, governing the selection and use of material throughout the poem. We find as a consequence that the narrator's personality does not always blend and unify his observations as it did in Canto III, for some things, like the Falls of Terni, are described in detail only because Byron saw them and thought they were

[6] *P.W.*, II. 421, 422.
[7] *L.J.*, IV. 153.
[8] "There are no metaphysics in it ; at least I think not," he told Murray (*L.J.*, IV. 155).

beautiful and interesting—not because they have any bearing on his main emotional or intellectual preoccupations. And the same centrifugal tendency appears in his handling of other topics such as War and Liberty.

Of course one must not try to force this canto into the mould of its predecessor: here we have a new mood and new theme—the elegiac—which could hardly be avoided in Italy, and which is more important than the subjects carried forward from 1816. All around him Byron saw the ruins or the relics or achievements of past civilisations, and he began to see his own fall in relation to that of great cities and great geniuses of former ages. Indeed Canto IV is best regarded as a long meditation on Time's works, defeats, and victories, culminating in the address to Ocean, which for Byron is a symbol of Eternity. This meditation is not simply a long melancholy musing on the impermanence of earthly glory: for all Byron's pessimism he can see that true nobility and greatness triumph over mutability and death—poets, for example, who had been disgraced, exiled or imprisoned by their countrymen or rulers are now reverenced, while their enemies (despots or populace) are remembered only with contempt.[9] Here was another aspect of "the fate of genius"—one that brought some consolation to his wounded pride, while the long perspectives which Italian history provided helped him to adjust emotionally to his own changed circumstances.

Even when we do full justice to this new and central theme, however, we must acknowledge Canto IV to be the most loosely organised as well as the longest section of *Childe Harold's Pilgrimage*. This is partly a consequence of his additions to the poem: his second thoughts are often admirable in themselves, but they detract occasionally from the work's coherence. Stanzas 51 and 52 add little to what Byron has already said,

---

[9] He had already treated this idea in *The Lament of Tasso*, written earlier in 1817. Tasso, of course, could almost be regarded as the arch-example of a persecuted poet, and it is not surprising that Shelley found some passages "most wonderfully impressive" : ". . . those lines," he wrote to Byron, "in which you describe the youthful feelings of Tasso ; that indistinct consciousness of its own greatness, which a heart of genius cherishes in solitude, amid neglect and contempt, have a profound and thrilling pathos which I will confess to you, whenever I turn to them, make my head wild with tears." (*Corr.*, ii. 59).

G

but interrupt the argument which runs naturally on from st. 50 to st. 53; sts. 27-9, which he wrote after seeing a wonderful sunset on his evening ride, form an isolated piece of natural description; and there are other examples of unskilful dovetailing of new with old. But most of the sixty stanzas added to the original one hundred and twenty-six are worked in very well, and the looseness of construction is due less to the stages in which Canto IV was written than to some confusion in the poet's own feelings, and in the aims he sets himself. In Canto III he had created a particular narrator-hero, and presented his account of his surroundings through this character: here his purpose is ostensibly the same, but he finds it much more difficult to maintain the personality he had assumed, while his interest in the scenes around him tends to get out of control. There were so many things to see and to describe in Italy— Byron himself says that "the text, within the limits I proposed, I soon found hardly sufficient for the labyrinth of external objects, and the consequent reflections"[10]—and he comes nearer here than he had ever done before to the methods of a guide-book, trying to include everything of interest to the tourist.[11] And this eagerness to comment and describe, together with a certain instability in his own feelings, leads him to neglect the characterisation of the narrator-hero.

When the poem opens the speaker is as much an object of attention as the scene which he surveys—he is an important figure in the foreground of his own composition, which would hardly be complete without him there as an observer and participant:

> I stood in Venice, on the "Bridge of Sighs ;"
>> A Palace and a prison on each hand :
>> I saw from out the wave her structures rise
>> As from the stroke of the Enchanter's wand :
>> A thousand Years their cloudy wings expand
>> Around me, and a dying Glory smiles

---

[10] *P.W.*, II. 323.

[11] Hobhouse supplemented this endeavour with his voluminous notes appended to the poem, and with his volume of *Historical Illustrations of the Fourth Canto of Childe Harold*.

O'er the far times, when many a subject land
Looked to the wingéd Lion's marble piles,
Where Venice sate in state, throned on her hundred isles ![12]

We remain aware of this narrator's personality, but it seems to
vary as the poem progresses—sometimes he is less a meditative
tourist than a sufferer and victim, for whom sad surroundings
are an appropriate and congenial setting:

But my Soul wanders ; I demand it back
To meditate amongst decay, and stand
A ruin amidst ruins. . . .[13]

In discussing his own ruin, too, he can lapse (as we have seen)
into anger and self-pity, and an exaggerated pessimism couched
in violent and turgid rhetoric. At other times, however, as he
gazes on the real ruins around him, his own sorrows are
dwarfed and his mood becomes much calmer, though still
melancholy:

Upon such a shrine
What are our petty griefs ?—let me not number mine.

Cypress and ivy, weed and wallflower grown
Matted and massed together—hillocks heaped
On what were chambers—arch crushed, column strown
In fragments—choked up vaults, and frescoes steeped
In subterranean damps, where the owl peeped,
Deeming it midnight :—Temples—Baths—or Halls ?
Pronounce who can : for all that Learning reaped
From her research hath been, that these are walls—
Behold the Imperial Mount ! 'tis thus the Mighty falls. . . .

---

[12] *P.W.*, ii. 327-8. Rogers has a comment on this stanza which is particularly
interesting in view of Byron's admiration for him as "the last of the *best* school" :
"There is a great deal of incorrect and hasty writing in Byron's works ; but it is
overlooked in this age of hasty readers. For instance,
'I stood in Venice, on the Bridge of Sighs,
A palace and a prison *on each hand*.'
He meant to say, that on one hand was a palace, on the other a prison.—And
what think you of:—
'And dashest him again to earth:—there let him *lay*' ?"
(Rogers, *Table-Talk*, p. 244).

[13] *P.W.*, ii. 347.

Tully was not so eloquent as thou,
    Thou nameless column with the buried base !
    What are the laurels of the Caesar's brow ?
    Crown me with ivy from his dwelling-place.
    Whose arch or pillar meets me in the face,
    Titus or Trajan's ? No—'tis that of time :
    Triumph, arch, pillar, all he doth displace
    Scoffing ; and apostolic statues climb
To crush the imperial urn, whose ashes slept sublime,

Buried in air, the deep blue sky of Rome,
    And looking to the stars : they had contained
    A Spirit which with these would find a home,
    The last of those who o'er the whole earth reigned,
    The Roman Globe—for, after, none sustained,
    But yielded back his conquests :—he was more
    Than a mere Alexander, and, unstained
    With household blood and wine, serenely wore
His sovereign virtues—still we Trajan's name adore.[14]

Here, even as he celebrates Time's triumph, Byron shows how virtue triumphs over time, and there are many other passages like this, propounding views of life quite different from the vision of futility and gloom which Harold sometimes gives us; and the style, significantly, is much less pretentious and extravagant than in his wilder outbursts—it can become stilted and awkward, but at best he has a dignified descriptive-meditative manner admirably suited to his elegiac theme. Then there are stanzas where the emotional temperature is lower still— where Byron seems not frenzied, grief-stricken, or even mildly melancholy, but normal and contented as he enjoys the scene before him, though too often in such moods he tries to work up his ideas and observations into "poetry," giving them a factitious and unnecessary elevation.[15] Sometimes, on the other hand, he seems to be feeling his way towards a more familiar style of easy discourse (as in his very unconventional remarks on Horace[16]), and this can approximate for brief moments to the colloquial pungency of satire:

[14] *P.W.*, II. 406-7, 410, 411.   [15] *P.W.*, II. 364-5.
[16] *P.W.*, II. 386-8.

Was she as those who love their lords, or they
  Who love the lords of others ? such have been
  Even in the olden time, Rome's annals say. . . .[17]

I leave to learnéd fingers, and wise hands,
  The Artist and his Ape, to teach and tell
  How well his Connoisseurship understands
  The graceful bend, and the voluptuous swell :
  Let these describe the undescribable. . . .[18]

While occasionally one feels that Byron is trying to achieve in this not very suitable verse-form some effects of contrast and deflation like those of his own later satires:

" While stands the Coliseum, Rome shall stand :
  When falls the Coliseum, Rome shall fall ;
  And when Rome falls—the World." From our own land
  Thus spake the pilgrims o'er this mighty wall
  In Saxon times, which we are wont to call
  Ancient ; and these three mortal things are still
  On their foundations, and unaltered all—
  Rome and her Ruin past Redemption's skill—
The World—the same wide den—of thieves, or what ye will.[19]

The failure represented by the trailing weak conclusion was due mainly to the structure of the Spenserian stanza; and it was soon to be transformed into success when he discovered the potentialities of *ottava rima*, with its crisp epigrammatic final couplet to replace the needless Alexandrines of *Childe Harold*.

There is, then, no one style in Canto IV. The tone is governed neither by a firmly-held conception of the narrator's character, nor by singleness of feeling in the author. Byron could pass at this time from gloom and despondency to a delighted interest in the world around him, and these contradictory emotions are reflected in the poem, which thus by its

---

[17] *P.W.*, II. 404. [18] *P.W.*, II, 368.

[19] *P.W.*, II. 434-5. This stanza contains another example of the "incorrect and hasty writing" characteristic of Byron's *Childe Harold* manner : he does not really mean that the three things he mentions are unaltered, but that two are greatly altered, while the third—in spite of the pilgrims' prophecy—remains the same as ever.

very inconsistencies and contrasts helps to bridge the amazing gulf between *Manfred* and *Beppo*. The inclusion of these varied moods, moreover, with their appropriate levels of style, shows that Byron was working round again to the problem he had been faced with in *Childe Harold*, Cantos I and II—that of finding a form and a convention which would enable him to express adequately his own complex nature. For years he had been evading this artistic problem, writing from a limited area of his experience and feelings, mainly in a fruitless exploration of the possibilities of the Byronic hero, but he now seems to be searching once again for a more personal, a more authentic, a more vital idiom than he had yet discovered; and this time the solution was at hand, for his long apprenticeship was nearly over, and with *Beppo* we pass from the realm of largely vain experiment, of repeated trial and error, into that of positive achievement and great poetry.

VII

Beppo

THE new line Byron's poetry took in 1817 was heralded and accompanied by changes in his critical ideas. The literary conservatism of *English Bards* had been modified in his "years of fame": he still admired Pope and the Augustans, but his own works were more deeply influenced by writers (such as Moore and Scott) whom he had once condemned, but whom he now came to respect and to enjoy; and his enthusiasm for romantic poetry reached its highest point in the summer and autumn of 1816. By September of the next year his opinions had been drastically altered. He continued to think highly of *Childe Harold*, but his sympathies were now more with the central eighteenth-century tradition, and he felt that he himself and the other "moderns" were on the wrong lines altogether.

With regard to poetry in general [he wrote to Murray], I am convinced, the more I think of it, that [Moore] and *all* of us—Scott, Southey, Wordsworth, Moore, Campbell, I,—are all in the wrong, one as much as another ; that we are upon a wrong revolutionary poetical system, or systems, not worth a damn in itself, and from which none but Rogers and Crabbe are free ; and that the present and next generations will finally be of this opinion. I am the more convinced in this by having lately gone over some of our classics, particularly *Pope*, whom I tried in this way,—I took Moore's poems and my own and some others, and went over them side by side with Pope's, and I was really astonished (I ought not to have been so) and mortified at the ineffable distance in point of sense, harmony, effect, and even *Imagination*, passion, and *Invention*, between the little Queen Anne's man, and us of the Lower Empire. Depend upon it, it is all Horace then, and Claudian now, among us ; and if I had to begin again, I would model myself accordingly. Crabbe's the man, but he has got a coarse and impracticable subject, and Rogers, the Grandfather of living

Poetry, is retired upon half-pay . . . and has done enough, unless he were to do as he did formerly.[1]

He was not wholly steadfast in this new position—when Moore challenged him about the letter Byron gave rather a different account of it, attributing more value to the present generation of Romantics:

> I called Crabbe and Sam the fathers of present Poesy [he wrote in February 1818] ; and said, that I thought—except them—*all* of '*us youth*' were on a wrong tack. But I never said that we did not sail well. Our fame will be hurt by *admiration* and *imitation*. When I say *our*, I mean *all* (Lakers included), except the postscript of the Augustans. The next generation (from the quantity and facility of imitation) will tumble and break their necks off our Pegasus, who runs away with us ; but we keep the *saddle*, because we broke the rascal and can ride. But though easy to mount, he is the devil to guide ; and the next fellows must go back to the riding-school and the manège, and learn to ride the 'great horse.'[2]

In his reply to the *Blackwood's* review of *Don Juan*, however, Byron elaborated his original statement (though he now grouped Campbell with Crabbe and Rogers), and his letters from 1817 onwards show an antagonism to many contemporary poets, and a lowered estimate of their achievement. Moore and Scott he still liked and admired, though he sometimes qualified his praises of their works, but towards the Lake Poets and the Cockneys he developed an implacable hostility. His distaste for the first of these groups had appeared as early as July 1817,[3] and it was soon intensified by a variety of grievances. He was annoyed by the ingratitude which he thought Coleridge showed in attacking the Drury Lane Committee, and he was furious to hear rumours of Southey's "League of Incest" slander, and of Coleridge's having helped to spread it. Then as Byron identified himself more and more with the cause of liberty, he came to despise the Lake Poets for their political apostasy, and from now on this was one of his main charges against them. In June 1818, for example, he was infuriated

[1] *L.J.*, IV. 169-70 : cp. *Corr.*, II. 139.   [2] *L.J.*, IV. 196-7.
[3] *L.J.*, IV. 151.

by Hunt's claim that Wordsworth was the greatest poet of the day: "Let them take Scott," he wrote to Moore, "Campbell, Crabbe, or you, or me, or any of the living, and throne him;— but not this new Jacob Behmen, this x x x whose pride might have kept him true, even had his principles turned as perverted as his *soi-disant* poetry."[4] Hunt himself could not be accused of any such apostasy, and Byron was grateful for his public support at the time of the separation; but he was now acutely aware of the other's personal and social defects—of the vulgarity and limited experience which Byron saw as characteristic of the whole Cockney group. A further reason for his frequent attacks on all these writers was that they were rebels, both in theory and practice, from the school of Pope: they denigrated the great master; they subscribed to critical heresies; and their own works were full of faults and weaknesses. These faults and weaknesses were often technical—defects in diction, for example, or in versification—obscurity, affected simplicity, over-ornateness, metrical looseness or irregularity—but Byron's most fundamental criticisms of modern poetry referred to its subject matter ("bad materials") and content. This was the period when he wanted to see poetry reconciled with truth and wisdom, asserting values and expressing attitudes to life acceptable to a civilised and cultured gentleman of his own day. And he now condemned, with the aggressive common sense that he had shown in *English Bards*, the lowness and triviality of some of Wordsworth's anecdotes in verse, the "unintelligible" mysticism and metaphysics of Wordsworth and Shelley, the improbable verse tales of adventure produced by Scott (and himself), the mawkishness and immaturity of Keats, and other types of romantic sentiment which he dismissed as foolishness. All these he saw as opposed to the urbane wit and mature good sense of Pope, "the moral poet of all civilisation,"[5] and he felt it his duty as a critic and a satirist to attack such aberrations. This duty was the more compelling since he knew that he himself was one of the worst offenders—he had fallen into, and encouraged, the bad taste of the times: "no one," he admitted, "has done more through negligence to corrupt the

---

[4] *L.J.*, IV. 238 : cp. VI. 381 and *P.W.*, VI. 174-7.
[5] *L.J.*, V. 560 (cp. 590, 554).

language"[6]—". . . no man has contributed more than me in my earlier compositions to produce that exaggerated and false taste."[7] In his later period he tried to atone for this by embarking on a one-man crusade in defence of what he now saw as true poetic standards. In April 1818, for example, he announced his intention of defending Pope publicly against "the unjustifiable attempts at depreciation begun by Warton and carried on to and at this day by the new School of Critics and Scribblers, who think themselves poets because they do *not* write like Pope. I have no patience," he went on, "with such cursed humbug and bad taste; your whole generation are not worth a canto of the *Rape of the Lock*, or the *Essay on Man*, or the *Dunciad*, or 'anything that is his'."[8]

Along with this change in Byron's critical opinions came a change in his emotional condition, for his mood of 1816, with its melancholy, anguish, and defiant pride, did not last very long. In Italy he moved in a society quite unperturbed by his domestic scandal; his genius was fully acknowledged; he enjoyed his love-affairs without reproach; and he was "partial to the people, the language and the habits of life" in Venice, finding it a city "very agreeable for Gentlemen of desultory habits. . . ."[9] In this new milieu he soon ceased to think and feel habitually as he had done in Switzerland. There seems to have been a compulsive element in his debauchery, which suggests that he had not fully regained mental balance, and he could easily relapse into fits of gloom or angry brooding on the separation, but his letters show that his usual state of mind was now quite different from that of the preceding summer. As early as January 1817 he was able to look back with some amusement on his melancholy and despair,[10] while in March he repudiated Jeffrey's identification of the author with Childe Harold as he had appeared in Canto III: "I wish

---

[6] *L.J.*, v. 82. [7] *L.J.*, vi. 67.
[8] *L.J.*, iv. 224-5 (cp. 278). [9] *L.J.*, iv. 233.
[10] "I am glad you like it," he wrote to Moore about *Childe Harold*, Canto III : "it is a fine indistinct piece of poetical desolation, and my favourite. I was half mad during the time of its composition, between metaphysics, mountains, lakes, love unextinguishable, thoughts unutterable, and the nightmare of my own delinquencies. I should, many a good day, have blown my brains out, but for the recollection that it would have given pleasure to my mother-in-law ; . . ." (*L.J.*, iv. 49).

you would also add," he wrote to Moore, "what you know, that
I was not, and, indeed, am not even *now*, the misanthropical and
gloomy gentleman he takes me for, but a facetious companion,
well to do with those with whom I am intimate, and as
loquacious and laughing as if I were a much cleverer
fellow."[11]

It is as such a facetious companion that he appears in most
of his letters from Venice. His accounts of Italian society—
and of his *amorosa*—were so very entertaining that John Murray
asked him for some poetry in the same vein: "Give me a
poem," he wrote in January 1817, "—a good Venetian tale
describing manners formerly from the story itself, and
now from your own observations, and call it 'Marianna'."[12]
Nothing came of this request, however, because Byron was still
working from the creative impulses of 1816, even though he
had some doubts about their value. Thus he finished *Manfred*,
but at first thought little of "this piece of phantasy": "It is
too much in my old style;" he declared, ". . . I certainly am
a devil of a mannerist, and must leave off. . . ."[13] Yet after
writing *The Lament of Tasso* he returned to *Manfred*, and revised
the third act; and he then went on to the fourth canto of
Childe Harold, which he thought extremely good, although (as
we have seen) he came to think that it was written in the wrong
tradition. The inconsistencies in this last work, moreover, and
the difficulty that Byron obviously found in maintaining the
romantic character he had assumed, point to the conflict
between his normal and his poetic modes of thought and feeling,
and the resulting tensions made him modify the Byronic hero's
mode of utterance at times—but he could not escape from it
entirely since he had as yet no satisfactory alternative, no other
way of writing poetry. Certainly (as his letters show) he had
developed in his prose a richly comic vision and a witty colloquial style which were soon to appear in *Beppo*, but at this
stage they were still excluded from his serious compositions,
and a catalyst was needed to precipitate them into poetry.

---

[11] *L.J.*, IV. 72-4.
[12] Samuel Smiles, *A Publisher and his Friends*, London 1891, I. 372. The reference
is, of course, to Byron's mistress, Marianna Segati.
[13] *L.J.*, IV. 71-2.

This was provided in September 1817 by his reading of Frere's *Whistlecraft*,[14] which arrived, by a freak of good fortune, just when in his changed mood and new-found dissatisfaction with romantic poetry, he was ready to profit by its example. From the very first he made no secret of the influence this work had had on him: "I have . . . written a poem," he told John Murray on October 12th, "(of 84 octave stanzas), humourous, in or after the excellent manner of Mr. Whistlecraft (whom I take to be Frere), on a Venetian anecdote which amused me. . . .";[15] and on October 23rd he reaffirmed this debt.[16] Its importance can hardly be overestimated, for this was the great turning-point in Byron's own career as poet. Shortly before this he had written some amusing doggerel which showed the inclination of his mind,[17] but now he had a model which suggested an entirely new style, and inspired him to a sustained satiric effort on lines different from anything that he had done before.

Frere's *jeu d'esprit*, in fact, transformed Byron's satirical technique, which up to this time had been based on false assumptions about his own talents and his affinity with the best poets of the eighteenth century. In *English Bards*, *Hints from Horace*, *The Curse of Minerva* and *The Waltz*, he had modelled himself on Pope and his followers, but the results were disappointing, showing a failure—not surprising in a young poet—to perceive his own unfitness for this kind of writing; and another misconception of his true satiric *métier* is to be found in a letter of 1814:

> . . . truth to say, my satires are not very playful. . . . As to mirth and ridicule, that is out of my way ; but I have a tolerable fund of sternness and contempt, and, with Juvenal before me, I shall perhaps read [the Prince Regent] a lecture he has not lately heard in the Cabinet.[18]

Now, in September 1817, he was re-asserting his high estimate

---

[14] *Prospectus and Specimen of an Intended National Work, By William and Robert Whistlecraft . . .*, London 1817.
[15] *L.J.*, IV. 172-3.
[16] *L.J.*, IV. 176.
[17] *L.J.*, IV. 29, 30-1, 79, 87-8 ; *Self-Portrait*, II. 415-17.
[18] *L.J.*, III. 58.

of Pope, and saying that if he had to begin again he would model himself accordingly, but if he had done this it would have been disastrous. It is one thing to admire a writer—quite another to succeed in imitating his style; and though Byron had a deep and genuine regard for Pope, he lacked even now the moral poise, the subtlety of wit and feeling, and the artistic economy, which made possible the best of Pope's work. Byron's *Sketch* of 1816, *Hints from Horace*, which he tried to resurrect in 1820, and *The Age of Bronze*, written in 1822-3, provide ample evidence of his continued incapacity for this satiric mode. Frere's *Whistlecraft* was therefore doubly valuable, since it not only helped to turn Byron away from romantic poems of doubtful value, but it also kept him (for the time being) from further vain attempts at realising his ideal of Augustan satire; and it did this by directing him to a completely different *genre*, peculiarly suited to his character and talents.

Whistlecraft was written in the style and manner of Italian "burlesque" poetry in *ottava rima*, Byron's acquaintance with which was limited at this time. Pulci he seems to have known only through Merivale's *Orlando in Roncesvalles*,[19] and perhaps through the latter's articles in the *Monthly Magazine*; but these do not convey the real qualities of Pulci's style, for in his contributions to the periodical Merivale selected only serious passages for translation, while in the *Orlando* he aimed at "an epic and heroic atmosphere, an elevated and earnest tone."[20] Byron's first reference to Berni occurs in a letter dated March 25th, 1818—some five months after the completion of *Beppo*; and here, even while asserting that "the style is not English, it is Italian," and that "Berni is the father of that kind of writing," he admits that "Whistlecraft was *my* immediate *model!*"[21] There is indeed no evidence to suggest that he had any first-hand knowledge of the poetry of Berni or of Pulci in September 1817, and though he had read Ariosto and Boiardo, they are rather different in effect and tone. He had, on the other hand, enjoyed the works of Casti, but neither these nor any of his other readings in Italian had so far affected his

---

[19] Mentioned *L.J.*, III. 5.
[20] *The Monks and the Giants*, ed. R. D. Waller, Manchester 1926, p. 27.
[21] *L.J.*, IV. 217.

poetic practice.[22] *Whistlecraft* revolutionised it, by showing him how the form and manner of these poets could be adapted to the English language, and by suggesting a technique by which he could express himself in verse with the same freedom, wit, urbanity and ease as he did in his letters and conversation.

Byron believed that he had profited, both as a man and as a writer, by his knowledge of Society. Thus in September 1821, when criticising Milman and Barry Cornwall, he maintained that their work suffered from the limitations of the circles in which they moved:

> The pity of these men is, that they never lived either in *high life*, nor in *solitude* : there is no medium for the knowledge of the *busy* or the *still* world. If admitted into high life for a season, it is merely as *spectators*—they form no part of the Mechanism thereof. Now Moore and I, the one by circumstances, and the other by birth, happened to be free of the corporation, and to have entered into its pulses and passions, *quarum partes fuimus*. Both of us have learnt by this much which nothing else could have taught us.[23]

And in his second letter on the Bowles controversy Byron seems to be feeling his way towards a social analysis of tone:

> The grand distinction of the under forms of the new school of poets is their *vulgarity*. By this I do not mean that they are *coarse*, but 'shabby-genteel,' as it is termed. A man may be *coarse* and yet not *vulgar*, and the reverse. Burns is often coarse, but never *vulgar*. Chatterton is never vulgar, nor Wordsworth, nor the higher of the Lake school, though they treat of low life in all its branches. It is in their *finery* that the new under school are *most* vulgar, and they may be known by this at once ; as what we called at Harrow 'a Sunday blood' might be easily distinguished from a gentleman, although his cloathes might be the better cut, and his boots the best blackened, of the two :

---

[22] In 1816 he had used *ottava rima* in an *Epistle to Augusta* (*P.W.*, IV. 57-62), but in spite of some touches of humour, this poem shows no awareness of the stanza's great potentialities.

[23] *L.J.*, v. 362-3 : cp. III. 119 : "I think very highly of [Hogg], as a poet ; but he, and half of these Scotch and Lake troubadours are spoilt by living in little circles and petty societies. London and the world is the only place to take the conceit out of a man—in the milling phrase."

—probably because he made the one, or cleaned the other, with his own hands. . . . Far be it from me to presume that there ever was, or can be, such a thing as an *aristocracy* of *poets* ; but there *is* a nobility of thought and of style, open to all stations, and derived partly from talent, and partly from education,— which is to be found in Shakespeare, and Pope, and Burns, no less than in Dante and Alfieri, but which is nowhere to be perceived in the mock birds and bards of Mr. Hunt's little chorus. If I were asked to define what this gentlemanliness is, I should say that it is only to be defined by *examples*—of those who have it, and those who have it not. In *life*, I should say that most *military* men have it, and few *naval* ;—that several men of rank have it, and few lawyers ; . . . It is the *salt* of society, and the seasoning of composition. *Vulgarity* is far worse than downright *blackguardism* ; for the latter compre- hends wit, humour, and strong sense at times ; while the former is a sad abortive attempt at all things, 'signifying nothing.' It does not depend upon low themes, or even low language, for Fielding revels in both ;—but is he ever *vulgar* ? No. You see the man of education, the gentleman, and the scholar, sporting with his subject,—its master, not its slave.[24]

Similar ideas may have been responsible for the distaste with which he regarded Wordsworth's theories of diction and Hunt's advocacy of the spoken language as a literary medium. This distaste seems curious when one thinks of Byron's own *ottava rima* poetry, but he may have felt (for one thing) that this kind of style was inappropriate except in satire, and still more important was the social prejudice that underlay his critical opinions: Wordsworth's colloquialism was avowedly based on the language of rustics or "the middle and lower classes of society," while that of Hunt and Keats reflected the cheap tone of their suburban circle, whereas he himself drew on the speech of wits and gentlemen.

Up to 1817, however, Byron's poetry had not benefited by his *milieu*—by his familiarity with the best English society. His various styles were based not on social but on literary models and ideals, and were therefore quite distinct from his characteristic modes of expression in real life, and sometimes

[24] *L.J.*, v. 591-2.

(as a consequence of this) he was ashamed of the personality he had built up in his works. The importance of *Whistlecraft* lay in its showing him a way of writing verse in the colloquial but gentlemanly idiom which he habitually used, and of establishing in poetry a tone and attitude which he need not repudiate in his capacity of man of fashion. His manner now, instead of being portentous and emotional, is casual, amusing, conversational, for *Beppo* is almost completely free from pseudo-elevation—he presents it as an entertaining trifle he has scribbled off, not anything "inspired," "romantic," or designed (as his own early works had been) to meet the public's vulgar taste for the exotic and sensational:

> Oh ! that I had the art of easy writing
>   What should be easy reading ! could I scale
> Parnassus, where the Muses sit inditing
>   Those pretty poems never known to fail,
> How quickly would I print (the world delighting)
>   A Grecian, Syrian, or *Ass*yrian tale ;
> And sell you, mixed with western Sentimentalism,
> Some samples of the *finest Orientalism*.

> But I am but a nameless sort of person,
>   (A broken Dandy lately on my travels)
> And take for rhyme, to hook my rambling verse on,
>   The first that Walker's Lexicon unravels,
> And when I can't find that, I put a worse on,
>   Not caring as I ought for critics' cavils ;
> I've half a mind to tumble down to prose,
> But verse is more in fashion—so here goes ![25]

This deprecating, quizzical, informal treatment of his own works is characteristic of Byron's social personality, which now appears in poetry for the first time, governing his choice of tone and sentiments, and bringing with it some ideas and feelings hitherto found only in his letters or his talk. He continues, for example, to despise professional writers, but he can now voice his contempt *in verse*, in the very accents of the bored aristocrat:

[25] *P.W.*, IV. 175-6.

One hates an author that's *all author*—fellows
    In foolscap uniforms turned up with ink,
So very anxious, clever, fine, and jealous,
    One don't know what to say to them, or think,
Unless to puff them with a pair of bellows ;
    Of Coxcombry's worst coxcombs e'en the pink
Are preferable to these shreds of paper,
These unquenched snuffings of the midnight taper.

Of these same we see several, and of others,
    Men of the world, who know the World like Men,
Scott, Rogers, Moore, and all the better brothers,
    Who think of something else besides the pen ;
But for the children of the 'Mighty Mother's,'
    The would-be wits, and can't-be gentlemen,
I leave them to their daily 'tea is ready,'
Smug coterie, and literary lady.[26]

Here then one finds a new integration of the dandy and the poet in Byron, and the transformation of his style which made this possible was effected primarily by his reading *Whistlecraft*.

Another work, however, probably contributed in a different way to his conception of the satire. When he was in Brussels in 1816 he had been given a copy of Casti's *Novelle Galanti*, which he thoroughly enjoyed:

> I cannot tell you [he wrote to the donor] what a treat your gift of Casti has been to me ; I have almost got him by heart. I had read his *Animali Parlanti*, but I think these *Novelle* much better. I long to go to Venice to see the manners so admirably described.[27]

These tales provided him with examples of witty, satirical, and licentious stories in *ottava rima*, in place of the Arthurian knights and adventures of *Whistlecraft*; and in his choice of subject Byron may have been influenced by this, as well as by Murray's request for a tale of Venetian manners, for in *Beppo* he breaks with the comic-heroic tradition represented by Frere, and

---

[26] *P.W.*, IV. 183-4.   [27] *L.J.*, IV. 217, n.2.

H

bases his poem on an anecdote which had amused him—a scandalous story of life in modern Venice.[28]

This was much more in accordance with his own tastes, for chivalric legend meant so little to Byron that he was not even interested in guying it; and his poetry now becomes a poetry not of humorous fantasy like Frere's, but of reality, of truth: he uses his new poetic idiom, derived from his real every-day manner of speech, to present his own real every-day ideas and interests. The constituents of his "reality" are very different, of course, from those of Wordsworth's, for while both poets deal with the commonplace, Byron finds his material in a decadent urban Society of the kind which Wordsworth saw as utterly opposed to the integrity of rustic life. Byron himself is fully aware of the corruptness of Venetian Society, but instead of being disgusted by its vanity, frivolity, and immorality, he accepts them with amused delight; and he writes about the trivialities of daily life there with a zest and a vitality which had been lacking in his set-piece meditations on great subjects in *Childe Harold*. *Beppo's* excellence, indeed, lies partly in the infectious joy with which Byron observes the actual, however sordid or unedifying—especially the actual facts of human behaviour, like the absurdities he finds in an Italian Lent:

> This feast is named the Carnival, which being
> Interpreted, implies 'farewell to flesh :'
> So called, because the name and thing agreeing,
> Through Lent they live on fish, both salt and fresh.
> But why they usher Lent with so much glee in,
> Is more than I can tell, although I guess
> 'Tis as we take a glass with friends at parting,
> In the Stage-Coach or Packet, just at starting.

---

[28] This original anecdote, told by Segati (Marianna's husband) on the evening of August 29th, is recorded in Hobhouse's diary : "A Turk arrived at the Regina di Ungheria inn at Venice and lodged there—he asked to speak to the mistress of the inn a buxom lady of 40 in keeping with certain children & who had lost her husband many years before at sea—after some preliminaries my hostess went to the Turk who immediately shut the door & began questioning her about her family & her late husband—She told her loss—when the Turk asked if her husband had any particular mark about him she said—yes he had a scar on his shoulder. Something like this said the Turk pulling down his robe—I am your husband—I have been to Turkey—I have made a large fortune and I make you three offers—either to quit your amoroso and come with me—or to stay with your amoroso or to accept a pension and live alone." (Marchand, *Byron*, II. 708).

And thus they bid farewell to carnal dishes,
 And solid meats, and highly spiced ragouts,
To live for forty days on ill-dressed fishes,
 Because they have no sauces to their stews ;
A thing which causes many 'poohs' and 'pishes,'
 And several oaths (which would not suit the Muse),
From travellers accustomed from a boy
To eat their salmon, at the least, with soy ;

And therefore humbly I would recommend
 'The curious in fish-sauce,' before they cross
The sea, to bid their cook, or wife, or friend,
 Walk or ride to the Strand, and buy in gross
(Or if set out beforehand, these may send
 By any means least liable to loss),
Ketchup, Soy, Chili-vinegar, and Harvey,
Or, by the Lord ! a Lent will well nigh starve ye ;

That is to say, if your religion's Roman,
 And you at Rome would do as Romans do,
According to the proverb,—although no man,
 If foreign, is obliged to fast ; and you,
If Protestant, or sickly, or a woman,
 Would rather dine in sin on a ragout—
Dine and be d——d ! I don't mean to be coarse,
But that's the penalty, to say no worse.[29]

These stanzas also show how Byron's entertaining and seemingly random reflexions about trivialities help to establish his main satiric attitudes. He sees the Carnival as being a "farewell to flesh" in the sense of lust as well as of meat dishes, and he makes it clear that the Venetians have their fill of both before the fast begins—a fact which throws doubt on the value of the fast itself. This doubt is intensified by his account of the Italians' diet during Lent, for their fishes' being ill-dressed seems so perverse and unnecessary a mortification that it discredits the whole notion of asceticism, and the English travellers, creatures of appetite, appear more sensible. They too are in their way ridiculous—particularly in their irritation—for it is absurd that a man's comfort and happiness should depend on

[29] *P.W.*, IV. 161-2.

things like having Soy and Ketchup with his fish. Yet this
often is the truth—the ludicrous kind of truth that Byron now
delights in—and because it is the truth, it is quite reasonable
(he implies) for the traveller to arrange for his supplies of
sauces—or, better still, to disregard Lenten restrictions and
eat anything he wants. The Church which would condemn
this course of action is itself condemned by Byron's tone as
bigoted, illiberal, not to be taken seriously, and it has already
been discredited as venal,[30] so that there seems no good reason
for abstaining from the flesh-pots. And this preference of
indulgence to restraint, of appetite to the dictates of religion,
is characteristic of the poem's whole ethos.

Characteristic also is the way that Byron plays one nation's
standards off against another's, in order to establish his own
private, hedonistic scale of values. Living in Venice as an
exile, he viewed both English and Italian society with the eyes
at once of an *habitué* and an outsider; and while a combination
of knowledge and detachment is essential to the genesis of any
satire, it is its reference in this case to two different civilisations
—the author's experience of both but total commitment to
neither—that makes possible the satiric modes of *Beppo*. Byron
writes now as an expatriate, a critic of his country and a rebel
from her moral code, acknowledging this attitude by the
epigraph from *As You Like It*:

> "Farewell, Monsieur Traveller ; Look, you lisp, and wear
> strange suits : disable all the benefits of your own country ;
> be out of love with your Nativity, and almost chide God for
> making you that countenance you are ; or I will scarce think
> you have swam in a *Gondola*."

> That is, *been at Venice*, which was much visited by the young
> English gentlemen of those times, and was *then* what *Paris* is
> *now*—the seat of all dissoluteness.[31]

For the most part the narrator of the story enjoys Southern
ways of life, describing them with sympathetic tolerance and
vivid detail. Byron calls it "a poem . . . where I have said
all the good I know or do not know of [the Italians], and none
of the harm,"[32] and the object of this careful selection was to

---

[30] *P.W.*, IV. 160.   [31] *P.W.*, IV. 153.   [32] *L.J.*, IV. 205.

contrast Italy with England to the disadvantage of the latter. This opposition is implied throughout a great part of the poem, and it becomes explicit in some stanzas where the weather, language, and women of Albion are compared unfavourably with their Italian counterparts:

> With all its sinful doings, I must say,
>> That Italy's a pleasant place to me,
> Who love to see the Sun shine every day,
>> And vines (not nailed to walls) from tree to tree
> Festooned, much like the back scene of a play,
>> Or melodrame, which people flock to see,
> When the first act is ended by a dance
> In vineyards copied from the South of France.
>
> I like on Autumn evenings to ride out,
>> Without being forced to bid my groom be sure
> My cloak is round his middle strapped about,
>> Because the skies are not the most secure ;
> I know too that, if stopped upon my route,
>> Where the green alleys windingly allure,
> Reeling with *grapes* red wagons choke the way,—
> In England 'twould be dung, dust or a dray. . . .
>
> I love the language, that soft bastard Latin,
>> Which melts like kisses from a female mouth,
> And sounds as if it should be writ on satin,
>> With syllables which breathe of the sweet South,
> And gentle liquids gliding all so pat in,
>> That not a single accent seems uncouth,
> Like our harsh northern whistling, grunting guttural,
> Which we're obliged to hiss, and spit, and sputter all.
>
> I like the women too (forgive my folly !)
>> From the rich peasant cheek of ruddy bronze,
> And large black eyes that flash on you a volley
>> Of rays that say a thousand things at once,
> To the high Dama's brow, more melancholy,
>> But clear, and with a wild and liquid glance,
> Heart on her lips, and soul within her eyes,
> Soft as her clime, and sunny as her skies.[33]

---

[33] *P.W.*, IV. 172, 173.

Having thus established an extremely sympathetic attitude to Italy, and a critical one towards England, Byron proceeds to weight the scales still further by stressing her political and social defects, but in doing this he unobtrusively drops his comparative method, so that the question of Venice's political status is never allowed to arise. The logical fallacy is skilfully camouflaged by a short digression on Italian Beauty, and by the conversational manner which enables Byron to pass easily from one topic to another, and to change his standpoint without drawing attention to the shift of values that this implies. So that no thought of Italy's degradation is allowed to intrude on our enjoyment of Byron's ironical, half-flippant and half-serious attack on his own country:

> "England ! with all thy faults I love thee still,"
>   I said at Calais, and have not forgot it ;
> I like to speak and lucubrate my fill ;
>   I like the government (but that is not it) ;
> I like the freedom of the press and quill ;
>   I like the Habeas Corpus (when we've got it) ;
> I like a Parliamentary debate,
> Particularly when 'tis not too late ;
>
> I like the taxes, when they're not too many ;
>   I like a seacoal fire, when not too dear ;
> I like a beef-steak, too, as well as any ;
>   Have no objection to a pot of beer ;
> I like the weather,—when it is not rainy,
>   That is, I like two months of every year.
> And so God save the Regent, Church, and King !
> Which means that I like all and every thing.
>
> Our standing army, and disbanded seamen,
>   Poor's rate, Reform, my own, the nation's debt,
> Our little riots just to show we're free men,
>   Our trifling bankruptcies in the Gazette,
> Our cloudy climate, and our chilly women,
>   All these I can forgive, and those forget,
> And greatly venerate our recent glories,
> And wish they were not owing to the Tories.[34]

---

[34] *P.W.*, IV. 174-5.

The contrast between Italy and England is developed more subtly in the story of Beppo, Laura and the Count. The point of the anecdote lies in the deliberate frustration of the reader's expectations, which are based on a number of stock responses—on the idea of the sacredness of marriage, in particular, and the associations of Italians with pride, passion, and stilettos. The absence of violence at the *dénouement* reflects Byron's own experience of Venetian behaviour: "You need not be alarmed," he wrote to Moore, after describing how Segati had surprised him with his wife, "—jealousy is not the order of the day in Venice, and daggers are out of fashion; while duels, on love matters, are unknown,—at least, with the husbands."[35] The contrast is not only with the English view of marriage, but with the former attitude of the Venetians themselves, or at least with that of their most famous servant. In the opening stanzas, which establish the poem's moral atmosphere, the final anticlimax is foreshadowed by the comments on Othello, whose agony of jealousy appears not tragic but ridiculous in the eyes of this narrator:

> Shakespeare described the sex in Desdemona
> As very fair, but yet suspect in fame,
> And to this day from Venice to Verona
> Such matters may be probably the same,
> Except that since those times was never known a
> Husband whom mere suspicion could inflame
> To suffocate a wife no more than twenty,
> Because she had a "Cavalier Servente."
>
> Their jealousy (if they are ever jealous)
> Is of a fair complexion altogether,
> Not like that sooty devil of Othello's,
> Which smothers women in a bed of feather,
> But worthier of these much more jolly fellows,
> When weary of the matrimonial tether
> His head for such a wife no mortal bothers
> But takes at once another, or *another's*.[36]

---

[35] *L. J.*, IV. 51.

[36] *P. W.*, IV. 164-5. The name Laura too is probably intended to suggest a contrast between Byron's heroine and the virtuous married lady of whom Petrarch sang—and between the latter's pure love and the Count's more practical arrangements.

Throughout Byron's letters of this period we see his amusement at the general acceptance of adultery as a regular code of conduct:

> . . . a woman is virtuous (according to the code) who limits herself to her husband and one lover ; those who have two, three, or more, are a little *wild* ; but it is only those who are indiscriminately diffuse, and form a low connection . . . who are considered as overstepping the modesty of marriage.[37]

His gay acceptance in *Beppo* of this Venetian ethic implies a criticism of English morality, which in its outraged indignation at the separation scandal and such peccadilloes is seen to be absurd—as absurd as Othello's feelings about marital infidelity. The poem is based, in fact, on a moral relativism which suggests that there is no absolute set of values, that they vary from country to country, and that those of modern Italy are by far the most civilised and pleasant.

They too, on the other hand, are full of comedy for the observer, and while Byron praises Venice he preserves enough detachment to make fun of many aspects of the life there—the pretensions of Religion or Society, the cupidity of priests, or the motives and psychology of women, which he describes with a wealth of comic detail:

> Now Laura moves along the joyous crowd,
>   Smiles in her eyes, and simpers on her lips ;
> To some she whispers, others speaks aloud ;
>   To some she curtsies, and to some she dips,
> Complains of warmth, and this complaint avowed,
>   Her lover brings the lemonade, she sips ;
> She then surveys, condemns, but pities still
> Her dearest friends for being dressed so ill.
>
> One has false curls, another too much paint,
>   A third—where did she buy that frightful turban ?
> A fourth's so pale she fears she's going to faint,
>   A fifth's look's vulgar, dowdyish, and suburban,
> A sixth's white silk has got a yellow taint,
>   A seventh's thin muslin surely will be her bane,
> And lo ! an eighth appears,—"I'll see no more !"
> For fear, like Banquo's kings, they reach a score.

---

[37] *L.J.*, IV. 40 : cp. IV. 24, 26-8, 41, 51-2, 81, and *Corr.*, II. 27.

Meantime, while she was thus at others gazing,
    Others were levelling their looks at her ;
She heard the men's half-whispered mode of praising
    And, till 'twas done, determined not to stir ;
The women only thought it quite amazing
    That, at her time of life, so many were
Admirers still,—but "Men are so debased,
Those brazen Creatures always suit their taste.[38]

Such passages are often just as applicable to the women he had known and the *beau monde* he had observed in London, for these two societies, contrasted as they are in some respects, have many qualities in common; and it is part of his satiric method to display the sameness of human nature, with its vanities and weaknesses, in completely different environments.

We are not, however, asked to take a serious view of these vices or follies. *Beppo* is more than an amusing comic poem— it is a satire on manners and morals; but it is extremely tolerant and essentially light-hearted. Byron may use the flexibility of his medium to pass to a more venomous attack on "Botherby," the professional literary man, or to a few stanzas of sentiment, but these variations do not affect his larger unity of tone, for he excludes from *Beppo* all ideas or emotions which would conflict with or destroy its gaily cynical view of human life. He had put what he described as his "own sentiments on Venice"[39] into *Childe Harold*, Canto IV, where he stressed the city's melancholy fall from greatness to subjection, and he returned to this theme, elegiac and political, in the *Ode on Venice*, written not long after the publication of *Beppo*: but there is no trace of such sad thoughts in this poem. Its position between these two laments shows that the isolating of its mood was not an automatic product of Byron's changed emotional state, but the result of a process of selection, whether instinctive or deliberate, which shows considerable artistic sensitivity. His new style too, casual, amusing, and irreverent, is perfectly adapted to the spirit of the poem, so that Byron's success here is unquestionable and complete within the limits that he sets himself.

And yet if we judge *Beppo* by the highest standards, these

[38] *P.W.*, IV. 180-1.   [39] *L.J.*, IV. 189.

limits force themselves on our attention. Here we have the rare and paradoxical phenomenon of a great satire based not on morality but immorality—on a hedonism which asks us to disapprove only of bores (social, intellectual, or religious) who would spoil the fun; and the poem's success depends on the exclusion of the poet's profounder moral attitudes and deepest beliefs about mankind and society. Byron has at last succeeded in "shaking off his sables"[40] in his own imagination and the public's, but in his reaction from his former style and personality he swings here to the opposite extreme; and though he writes both well and wittily as a man of the world, he seems committed to the latter's cynicism and frivolity, "laughing at all things mundane."[41] This necessarily detracts from *Beppo's* value as a satire, forcing us to realise that Byron's new poetic manner, brilliant though it is, tends to impose some limitations on his vision—limitations which he was often to transcend in later works, but which in this poem he accepts without demur. Yet even here Byron's success is of a major order, for his cynicism, though potentially disabling, is in fact considerably modified by its sheer gaiety: he may choose to hymn adultery, to deny most moral values, to take sensual pleasure as the *summum bonum* for the civilised man, but he shows throughout such real zest and enjoyment that the effect is one of vitality, not of negation. He lacks many of the qualities of his greater contemporaries—he has nothing, for example, of Keats's appreciation of sensuous beauty, or Wordsworth's insight into the emotional and moral greatness of ordinary men and women; but more than any other poet—much more even than Burns— Byron conveys the *fun* of being alive and sinning, or of living a normal social life made up of commonplace activities like dining, drinking, talking, riding, making love, and so on. This, indeed, is one of his great positive and individual achievements as a poet, and *Beppo* is the first—but also one of the finest —of the works he wrote in this new and exciting vein.

[40] *L.J.*, IV. 74.   [41] See above, Chapter One, p. 13.

VIII

The Composition of *Don Juan*

I N *Beppo* Byron had written for the first time in a style completely suited to his genius—one that immediately transformed his work from mediocre competence to assured accomplishment and greatness of a kind—but he himself was slow to recognise the supreme importance of his new discovery. He seems to have thought of *Beppo* not as the unique achievement which it was, but as a gratifying proof of his versatility[1]— a mere experiment in this new satiric *genre* which he found interesting, but which he was not prepared to adopt immediately in place of his accustomed ways of writing. Indeed he showed a surprising readiness to leave *ottava rima* for other verse forms, other styles, and to abandon the urbane assurance of his new poetic manner for "romantic" attitudes and histrionic intensities of tone like those which had appeared in former works. Thus on completing *Beppo* he went back to the fourth canto of *Childe Harold*, and composed a number of new stanzas, two of which might have come from the most "metaphysical" parts of Canto III:

> Oh ! that the Desert were my dwelling-place,
>   With one fair Spirit for my minister,
>   That I might all forget the human race,
>   And, hating no one, love but only her !
>   Ye elements !—in whose ennobling stir
>   I feel myself exalted—Can ye not
>   Accord me such a Being ?   Do I err
>   In deeming such inhabit many a spot ?
> Though with them to converse can rarely be our lot.
>
> There is a pleasure in the pathless woods,
>   There is a rapture on the lonely shore,
>   There is society, where none intrudes,
>   By the deep Sea, and Music in its roar :
>   I love not Man the less, but Nature more,
>   From these our interviews, in which I steal

---

[1] *L.J.*, IV. 218.

> From all I may be, or have been before,
> To mingle with the Universe, and feel
> What I can ne'er express—yet can not all conceal.[2]

His next work was the *Ode on Venice*, which resembles parts of Canto IV in theme and mood, and in the occasional weaknesses of its declamatory style:

> Oh Venice ! Venice ! when thy marble walls
>   Are level with the waters, there shall be
> A cry of nations o'er thy sunken halls,
>   A loud lament along the sweeping sea !
> If I, a northern wanderer, weep for thee,
> What should thy sons do ?—anything but weep :
> And yet they only murmur in their sleep.
> In contrast with their fathers—as the slime,
>   The dull green ooze of the receding deep,
> Is with the dashing of the spring-tide foam,
>   That drives the sailor shipless to his home,
> Are they to those that were ; and thus they creep,
> Crouching and crab-like, through their sapping streets.
> Oh ! agony—that centuries should reap
> No mellower harvest ! . . .[3]

Here his moral-political beliefs are more positive than those of *Beppo*, but in order to express them Byron has had to revert to an earlier, less satisfactory poetic style. After the first few lines his rhetoric lapses into ineffectiveness, and he goes on to develop his sea-image without any controlling sense of relevance—he is thinking of the force and vigour of the earlier Venetians, and their violent destruction of their enemies, but there is confusion in the idea of a storm which wrecks ships but conveys the sailor safely home, and almost certainly this line reads as it does only because of the need to rhyme with "foam." Some time later Byron confessed (as a joke, admittedly) that when he aimed at an elevated style he was not concerned with precision of statement—

> I don't pretend that I quite understand
> My own meaning when I would be *very* fine [4]

---

[2] *P.W.*, II. 456-7.   [3] *P.W.*, IV. 193.
[4] *P.W.*, VI. 184 : cp. *Self-Portrait*, II. 516 : ". . . for my own part I don't understand a word of the whole four cantos [of *The Prophecy of Dante*], and was therefore lost in admiration of their sublimity."

—and the *Ode on Venice* is an example of this carelessness: he himself was soon to refer to it depreciatingly as "not very intelligible."[5]

Meantime Byron was still interested in his new satiric type of poetry. In March 1818 he read Rose's translation of the *Animali Parlanti*, and in May he received a verse epistle in the *Beppo* style from the same author. He seems also to have been investigating Frere's Italian models: on March 25th we find his first reference to Berni,[6] and Pulci is mentioned in November.[7] On the first of these occasions he told Murray that this kind of writing seemed well-suited to the English language, and that if *Beppo* proved successful he might send another volume in the same style on Italian life and manners. A month later, after dashing off some squibs and parodies which are indicative of his prevailing humour, he returned to this idea of a poem in *ottava rima*—"If *Beppo* pleases, you shall have more in a year or two in the same mood."[8] For his part Murray was delighted with this new aspect of Byron's genius—on June 16th (1818) he wrote to tell him (among other things) how well the poem was selling,[9] and on July 7th he asked him if he had not got "another lively tale like 'Beppo'."[10] But by this time Byron had already started on *Don Juan*.

On July 10th he wrote to say that the *Ode on Venice* was completed, and that he had in hand "two Stories, one serious and one ludicrous (*à la Beppo*), not yet finished, and in no hurry to be so."[11] These were *Mazeppa* and *Don Juan*, Canto I, works which he thought "not very important in themselves";[12] and since he had doubts about their quality, he waited for more news of his recent poems before going on with these experiments:

> If you would tell me exactly [he wrote to Murray], (for I know nothing, and have no correspondents except on business) the state of the reception of our late publications, and the feeling upon them, without consulting any delicacies (I am too seasoned to require them), I should know how and in what manner to proceed.[13]

---

[5] *Corr.*, II. 89.   [6] *L.J.*, IV. 217.
[7] *Corr.*, II. 89.   [8] *L.J.*, IV. 231.
[9] Samuel Smiles, *A Publisher and his Friends*, I. 394.
[10] *Op. cit.*, I. 396.   [11] *L.J.*, IV. 245.
[12] *L.J.*, IV. 245.   [13] *L.J.*, IV. 248.

This clearly implies a readiness to let public opinion determine the line of his development—he was attracted to *ottava rima* satire, but he hesitated to commit himself to his new project till he had heard of the relative success of *Beppo* and *Childe Harold*, Canto IV; and as late as August 26th he was writing that "the tales . . . are in an unfinished state, and I can fix no time for their completion: they are also *not* in the best manner."[14] In spite of these doubts and hesitations, however, the first draft of *Don Juan*, Canto I, was finished by September 19th, and both works were sent to Hobhouse by the middle of November.

The satire is of course our main concern, but *Mazeppa* deserves some attention, both for its intrinsic merit and for its interest as a transitional work—an attempt not to revive the verse-tale formula of Byron's London years, but to improve on it, by blending humour with romance in an entirely new way. This change is effected primarily by the more sophisticated narrative technique: the main story of Mazeppa's youthful passion, his sufferings, adventure, and revenge, is set within another narrative, so that he tells his tale in a particular situation of which we are kept aware, and which modifies our reactions to the central plot. The last lines of the poem, for example, form a trick ending, unexpected and deflatory, which forces a quick readjustment on the reader's mind; and throughout the work Mazeppa is fully and convincingly presented as a mature, experienced old soldier, who can look back on his early days with a detachment and a sense of humour foreign to Byron's thoroughly romantic heroes. He resembled them in some respects—in courage, and in reckless passion which even now he is not willing to repudiate:

> " I loved her then, I love her still ;
> And such as I am, love indeed
>   In fierce extremes—in good and ill.
> But still we love even in our rage,
> And haunted to our very age
> With the vain shadow of the past,—
> As is Mazeppa to the last."[15]

---

[14] *L.J.*, IV. 251.   [15] *P.W.*, IV. 214-15.

But however congenial these sentiments would have been to Conrad and the Giaour, one cannot imagine them describing *their* youth in a tone like this:

> "I think 'twas in my twentieth spring,—
> Aye 'twas,—when Casimir was king—
> John Casimir,—I was his page
> Six summers, in my earlier age !
> A learned monarch, faith ! was he,
> And most unlike your Majesty ;
> He made no wars, and did not gain
> New realms to lose them back again ;
> And (save debates in Warsaw's diet)
> He reigned in most unseemly quiet ;
> Not that he had no cares to vex ;
> He loved the Muses and the Sex ;
> And sometimes these so froward are,
> They made him wish himself at war ;
> But soon his wrath being o'er, he took
> Another mistress—or new book :
> And then he gave prodigious fêtes—
> All Warsaw gathered round his gates
> To gaze upon his splendid court,
> And dames, and chiefs, of princely port.
> He was the Polish Solomon,
> So sung his poets, all but one,
> Who, being unpensioned, made a satire,
> And boasted that he could not flatter.
> It was a court of jousts and mimes,
> Where every courtier tried at rhymes ;
> Even I for once produced some verses,
> And signed my odes 'Despairing Thyrsis.' "[16]

Mazeppa speaks like a man of this world, and his application of an older, wiser mind to the events of youth is one of the most interesting features of his narrative, for the changed vision of maturity appears in many of his comments—on the foolishness and triviality of the game he had played with the Countess, on the factors which disposed her to adultery, and on his own lack of self-control.[17]   Yet Mazeppa's reminiscences are far from

[16] *P.W.*, IV. 211-12.   [17] *P.W.*, IV. 215, 212-13, 216.

being merely deflatory, for he still believes in his early love as an unique, invaluable experience:

> " My days and nights were nothing—all
> Except that hour which doth recall,
> In the long lapse from youth to age,
>   No other like itself : I'd give
>   The Ukraine back again to live
> It o'er once more, and be a page,
> The happy page, who was the lord
> Of one soft heart, and his own sword. . . ".[18]

And he is completely serious in the central portion of his narrative—in the long account of his terrible ride on the wild horse—which perhaps it is not entirely fanciful to see as a symbolic presentation of the lot of the Byronic hero, carried away by an ungovernable passion. *Mazeppa* then, as a tale of love and adventure distanced to some extent and qualified, but not repudiated by the teller, is an extremely interesting and promising experiment, though it is overshadowed by the excellence of its companion-piece, *Don Juan*, Canto I.

On completing the latter work, however, Byron felt the lack of confidence he usually showed over new ventures:

> I have finished the first canto [he wrote on September 19th] (a long one, of about 180 octaves) of a poem in the style and manner of *Beppo*, encouraged by the good success of the same. It is called *Don Juan*, and is meant to be a little quietly facetious upon every thing. But I doubt whether it is not—at least, as far as it has yet gone—too free for these very modest days. However, I shall try the experiment, anonymously ; and if it don't take, it will be discontinued.[19]

He was particularly apprehensive about the public's reaction to his ribaldry—to his using "that freedom which Ariosto, Boiardo, and Voltaire—Pulci, Berni, all the best Italian and French—as well as Pope and Prior amongst the English— permitted themselves."[20] But although he expected disapproving comments, he soon came to feel that the poem was good, and when moralistic criticism did arrive from friends in England, he resented them as mere tributes to "the *Cant* of the day,

---

[18] *P.W.*, IV. 217.   [19] *L.J.*, IV. 260.   [20] *Corr.*, II. 90.

which still reads the *Bath Guide*, *Little's poems*, Prior and Chaucer, to say nothing of Fielding and Smollett."[21] "If you admit this prudery," he exclaimed, "you must omit half Ariosto, La Fontaine, Shakespeare, Beaumont, Fletcher, Massinger, Ford, all the Charles Second writers; in short, *something* of most who have written before Pope and are worth reading, and much of Pope himself."[22] And he refused to be trammelled by this uncritical and inconsistent moral censorship.

Yet while he rejected his friends' strictures, their effect was to discourage him a little. At one point he even agreed, under protest, that *Don Juan* should remain unpublished, asking only that fifty copies should be printed for private circulation;[23] and though Canto II had almost been completed when these criticisms reached him, he did not transcribe it until some six weeks had passed: "I have not yet begun to copy out the second Canto . . .," he wrote on February 1st, 1819, "from natural laziness, and the discouragement of the milk and water they have thrown upon the first."[24] It was eventually dispatched to Murray early in April, by which time Byron had decided that *Don Juan should* be published,[25] but he was doubtful about writing any more of it, in face of all the opposition: "You ask me," he exclaimed on June 29th, "if I mean to continue *D.J.*, etc. How should I know? what encouragement do you give me, all of you, with your nonsensical prudery? publish the two Cantos, and then you will see."[26] "If it don't take," he added on August 12th, "I will leave it off where it is, with all due respect to the Public; but if continued, it must be in my own way."[27]

It is clear, moreover, that though from the first he had thought of *Don Juan* as (potentially at any rate) a long poem, at this stage he had no clear conception of the finished work. In referring to twelve books[28] he was merely poking fun at epic theory; and his choice of hero did not necessarily commit him to following the existing legend of Don Juan, which he

---

[21] *L.J.*, IV. 276 : cp. *Corr.*, II. 97 and *L.J.*, IV. 366-7, 381-2.
[22] *L.J.*, IV. 277-8 : cp. IV. 295, 385, and *P.W.*, VI. 210.
[23] *L.J.*, IV. 277.
[24] *L.J.*, IV. 279.
[25] *L.J.*, IV. 280, 281-2 ; *Corr.*, II. 104-5.
[26] *L.J.*, IV. 321.   [27] *L.J.*, IV. 342.   [28] *P.W.*, VI. 73.

I

alters freely in these first two cantos. Almost certainly he visualised the poem as a series of amatory adventures, to take place in different countries, and to give scope for both sentiment and satire; and he probably had many incidents in mind, culled from his reading and his own experience; but he had not yet worked out a complete narrative framework. "You ask me for the plan of Donny Johnny," he wrote in this same letter of August 12th: "I *have* no plan—I *had* no plan; but I had or have materials. . . ."[29]

Cantos I and II were published on July 15th, 1819, but even before this Byron had begun some stanzas on the Duke of Wellington, which he meant to use in another canto; and even after hearing of the hostile reception which the first instalment met with, he embarked on a third canto in September. This, however, progressed slowly, for his feelings about the poem were now extremely mixed—his letters show that he had come to think highly of the early cantos, and to despise the outcry which they had evoked,[30] yet these hostile criticisms, together with the news that sales were poor, did damp his spirits: "The third Canto is in advance about 100 stanzas," he wrote to Hoppner on October 28th: "but the failure of the two first has weakened my *estro*, and it will neither be so good as the two former, nor completed unless I get a little more *riscaldato* [warmed up] in its behalf."[31] And he told Murray that "the reception of the two first [cantos] is no encouragement to you nor me to proceed."[32] Murray, however, wanted a continuation for the winter, and though Byron's composition was

---

[29] *L.J.*, IV. 342.

[30] See, for example, his letter to Kinnaird, October 26th, 1819 : "As to 'Don Juan', confess, confess—you dog and be candid—that it is the sublime of *that there* sort of writing—it may be bawdy but is it not good English ? It may be profligate but is it not *life*, is it not *the thing* ? Could any man have written it who has not lived in the world ?—and tooled in a post-chaise ?—in a hackney coach ?—in a gondola ?—against a wall ?—in a court carriage ?—in a vis à vis ?—on a table ? and under it ? I have written about a hundred stanzas of a third canto, but it is damned modest ; the outcry has frightened me. I had such projects for the Don, but Cant is so much stronger than Cxxx now-a-days, that the benefit of experience in a man who had well weighed the worth of both monosyllables, must be lost to despairing posterity. After all what stuff this outcry is—Lalla Rookh and Little are more dangerous than my burlesque poem can be." (Marchand, *Byron*, II. 823-4 ; *Self-Portrait*, II. 491).

[31] *L.J.*, IV. 366 : cp. Moore, *Life*, p. 421.   [32] *L.J.*, IV. 368.

interrupted by fever and a crisis in his relations with the Guicciolis, he completed the first draft of this canto by the end of November, and it was later subdivided to form Cantos III and IV. He felt himself that he had been inhibited by all the criticism, and that this section of the poem had suffered as a consequence: "I have finished a third canto of Don Juan," he wrote to Kinnaird, "very *decent,* but dull—damned dull";[33] and he told Murray that these new instalments "have not the Spirit of the first: the outcry has not frightened but it has *hurt* me, and I have not written *con amore* this time."[34] It was galling, however, to find that the Albemarle Street circle tended to agree with him, and his waning enthusiasm for *Don Juan* perished in this atmosphere of disapproval, so that by the spring of 1820 he did not even care very much whether these new cantos were suppressed or not.[35]

In February, however, he had finished another experiment in *ottava rima*—a translation of Pulci's *Morgante Maggiore,* Canto I—which he *was* anxious to have published. By this time Byron knew that Pulci was the founder of this kind of writing, and he hoped that by presenting his readers with part of the original example of Italian "burlesque" poetry, he could make them more aware of the conventions of the *genre,* and show them that he had good literary precedent for his manner— and irreverence—in *Don Juan.*[36] He took great pains with this translation, and was very proud of its fidelity to the original, insisting that the Italian text should be printed with his version so that readers could compare them; yet the work is very disappointing. He was hampered and restricted by the need to make his verses correspond to Pulci's, "servilely translating, stanza for stanza, and line for line, two octaves every night,"[37] and the poem is unexpectedly stilted, lacking the felicity, vitality, and ease of his own *ottava rima* satires. He himself

---

[33] *Corr.,* ii. 132 : cp. *L.J.,* iv. 383.

[34] *L.J.,* iv. 402 : cp. v. 16.

[35] *Corr.,* ii. 145-6. Another effect of the outcry was to make Byron reluctant to admit authorship of the poem, even to protect his copyright, in case he might be deprived of his parental authority over Ada, as Shelley had lost his children in 1817.

[36] *L.J.,* iv. 402, 407 ; *P.W.,* iv. 283-4.

[37] *L.J.,* iv. 405.

was strangely blind to its defects: in March 1820 he referred to it as "close and rugged,"[38] but with the perverseness of judgment that he often showed in these years, he soon came to rate it ludicrously highly: "You can steal the two Juans into the world quietly, tagged to the others," he told Murray in September. "The play as you will—the Dante too; but the *Pulci* I am proud of: it is superb; you have no such translation. It is the best thing I ever did in my life."[39] While in January 1821, with *Beppo* and five cantos of *Don Juan* behind him, he declared "I look upon the Pulci as my grand performance."[40]

To return, however, to the early months of 1820: in his disappointment with *Don Juan* Byron turned to other, non-satiric projects. *The Prophecy of Dante*, begun at the suggestion of Teresa Guiccioli, had been written in the summer and autumn of 1819, but he now sent it to Murray, saying that if it proved successful, he would continue it in further cantos; and he forwarded *Francesca of Rimini* by the next post. Then between April and July he wrote *Marino Faliero*, the first and probably the best of his experiments in tragedy. His turning to the drama at this stage in his career was largely the result of his belief that he had failed in his continuation of *Don Juan*—having, for the time being, an extremely low opinion of Cantos III and IV,[41] he was casting about for some new line to follow, though without great hopes of being successful: ". . . I begin to think I have mined my talent out," he noted ruefully, "and proceed in no great phantasy of finding a new vein."[42] He was also influenced at this time by his interest in Marino Faliero's story, and by his own critical theories—he had just been attacking modern poetry in his reply to *Blackwood's*, and he now thought of correcting public taste and demonstrating his own loyalty to eighteenth-century traditions by writing a regular tragedy in accordance with neoclassical precept and example.

[38] *Corr.*, II. 136.

[39] *L.J.*, v. 82-3 (cp. 64). The works referred to here are *Don Juan*, Cantos III and IV—"the others" are Cantos I and II—*Marino Faliero* and *The Prophecy of Dante*.

[40] *L.J.*, v. 225 (cp. 362).

[41] *L.J.*, v. 16, 42, 63, 66, 82, 96.   [42] *L.J.*, v. 25

Similar motives made him think of reviving *Hints From Horace*, and of publishing it with some omissions and alterations. It would form part of his new campaign against modern literary fashions, and at one time he meant to have it printed along with his defence of Pope in the reply to *Blackwood's*.[43] It would also be for him a return to the style he praised in the Augustans: he was now aware of the discrepancy between his critical opinions and most of his own works,[44] but he thought he could remedy this by writing his old type of satire (in heroic couplets), as well as by new experiments in neoclassical tragedy. In the autumn of 1820, therefore, he urged Murray to send out the text so that he could revise it; and although his enthusiasm for the project varied, it was very much in his mind for the next few months. In fact he never carried out the proposed revision (though he seems to have made a start on it), and the poem remained unpublished until 1831. Yet it is interesting to see how high an estimate he had of it: ". . . the fact is," he remarked in January 1821, "(as I perceive), that I wrote a great deal better in 1811, than I have ever done since";[45] and in March he declared "I look upon it and my Pulci as by far the best things of my doing."[46]

In October 1820 Byron had, however, felt another much more fruitful creative impulse, and by the end of November he had finished the first draft of *Don Juan*, Canto V, adding to it in the course of December. He now thought that although Canto III was "dull" the other four were better, and he wanted to see Cantos III, IV, and V in print.[47] He was also full of plans for a continuation of the poem, which he spoke of with his former zest, and in February 1821 he gave his first detailed account of his intentions, although even now the length of the poem was still undecided:

> The 5th is so far from being the last of *D.J.*, that it is hardly the beginning. I meant to take him the tour of Europe, with a proper mixture of siege, battle, and adventure, and to make him finish as *Anarcharsis Cloots* in the French Revolution. To how many cantos this may extend, I know not, nor whether

---

[43] *Self-Portrait*, II. 516 ; *L.J.*, V. 77.   [44] *L.J.*, IV. 486, 488 (cp. V. 559).
[45] *L.J.*, V. 222 (cp. 77).   [46] *L.J.*, V. 255.
[47] *L.J.*, V. 216, 224-5, 241-2.

(even if I live) I shall complete it ; but this was my notion :
I meant to have made him a *Cavalier Servente* in Italy, and a
cause for a divorce in England, and a Sentimental 'Werther-
faced man' in Germany, so as to show the different ridicules
of the society in each of those countries, and to have displayed
him gradually *gâté* and *blasé* as he grew older, as is natural.
But I had not quite fixed whether to make him end in Hell, or
in an unhappy marriage, not knowing which would be the
severest. The Spanish tradition says Hell : but it is probably
only an Allegory of the other state. You are now in possession
of my notions on the subject.[48]

Yet in spite of these plans Byron's interest at this time lay
mainly in other projects, and in the summer of 1821 Teresa
Guiccioli managed to persuade him not to go on with his great
satire: "At the particular request of the Contessa G.," he
announced to Murray in July, "I have promised *not* to continue
Don Juan. You will therefore look upon these 3 cantos as the
last of that poem. She had read the two first in the French
translation, and never ceased beseeching me to write no more
of it."[49]   The three cantos now in Murray's hands, however,
were published in August, and in spite of Byron's submission
to Teresa's importunities, he thought more highly of the work
now on re-reading it:

You have been careless of this poem [he wrote to Murray]
because some of your Synod don't approve of it ; but I tell
you, it will be long before you see any thing half so good as
poetry or writing. . . . I have read over the poem carefully,
and I tell you, *it is poetry*. Your little envious knot of parson-
poets may say what they please : time will show that I am not
in this instance mistaken.[50]

And again :

I read over the *Juans*, which are excellent. Your Synod was
quite wrong ; and so you will find by and bye. I regret that
I do not go on with it, for I had all the plan for several cantos,
and different countries and climes.[51]

---

[48] *L.J.*, v. 242-3.
[49] *L.J.*, v. 320-1 : cp. *Corr.*, II. 176 and Milbanke, *Astarte*, p. 308.
[50] *L.J.*, v. 351-2.
[51] *L.J.*, v. 359.

This new access of confidence in his *ottava rima* satire may have been responsible for his returning in September 1821 to *The Vision of Judgment*, which he had begun on May 7th but abandoned the same day—whereas now he wrote the whole poem in a single triumphant burst of creative energy.[52]

For the greater part of 1821, however, Byron was less interested in satire than in his experiments in drama. In January he had begun a second tragedy—on Sardanapalus—and was pondering the subjects of three more, on Cain, Tiberius, and Francesca of Rimini. After writing his letters on the Bowles controversy, he went on to finish *Sardanapalus* by May 27th; in June and July he wrote another drama, *The Two Foscari*; and immediately after this he began working on *Cain*, which he completed on September 9th. This play, with its deliberately provocative ideas, suggests that Byron was now more inclined to defy and outrage public opinion than to court its approval; and in fact he now made an effort to cut himself off from English influences: late in September he forbade Murray to send him any modern publications (except by a few specified authors), any periodical criticism, or anyone's opinions, "*good, bad,* or *indifferent,*" about his poetry; his reason being that he wanted to leave his genius free to take its natural direction.[53] At this time he was writing *The Vision of Judgment*, which might seem to justify his policy, yet he went on from this unquestionable masterpiece to three of his worst works, the plays *Heaven and Earth*, *Werner*, and *The Deformed Transformed*. Byron seems to have been reluctant to admit, even to himself, that he had not succeeded as a dramatist, and he kept experimenting doggedly in this field. To begin with, certainly, he had been doubtful of the merits of *Marino Faliero*,[54] and as recently as June of this year he told Murray that he would give up his attempts if this play was not well received:

> I am quite ignorant how far *the Doge* did or did not succeed. . . . It is proper that you should apprize me of this, because I am in the *third* act of a *third* drama [*The Two Foscari*] ; and if I have nothing to expect but coldness from the public and hesitation from yourself, it were better to break off in time. I had pro-

---

[52] *P.W.*, IV. 525, n.3.   [53] *L.J.*, V. 373-5 (cp. VI. 40-1).   [54] *L.J.*, V. 66.

posed to myself to go on, as far as my Mind would carry me, and I have thought of plenty of subjects. But *if* I am trying an impracticable experiment, it is better to say so at once.[55]

As time went on, however, and his plays did not meet with acclaim, he became obstinate, insisting that posterity would judge them good. By May 1822 he was convinced that the volume containing *Sardanapalus*, *The Two Foscari*, and *Cain* would come to be preferred to all his other writings,[56] and he regarded its lack of immediate success as further evidence of the uneducated and debased taste of his readers. "You see what it is to throw pearls to swine," he exclaimed in a letter to Shelley:

> As long as I write the exaggerated nonsense which has corrupted the public taste, they applauded to the very echo, and, now that I have really composed, within these three or four years, some things which sh^d 'not willingly be let die,' the whole herd snort and grumble and return to wallow in their mire. However, it is fit I sh^d pay the penalty of spoiling them. . . . It is a fit retribution that any really classical production sh^d be received as these plays have been treated.[57]

Here Byron seems to have attained a real artistic integrity, in however dubious a cause; but his parade of indifference to public opinion does not give us the whole truth. He had greatly enjoyed his phenomenal successes in former years, and although he now despised his own best-sellers, he alternated between a genuine defiance of the bad taste of the times, and a very natural longing for his works to be received enthusiastically, as they had been in the past. Hence he was still prepared (occasionally at any rate) to cater for the public taste, and his departure in *Werner* and *The Deformed Transformed* from his repeatedly asserted principles of drama can only be accounted for by a desire on his part to win interest and approval by writing plays of a more popular or more sensational variety.

This yearning for further successes (even for a *succès de scandale*) may also have helped to bring him back to his great

[55] *L.J.*, v. 313 (June 29th, 1821).
[56] *L.J.*, vi. 64 (cp. 75).
[57] *L.J.*, vi. 67 (May 20th, 1822) : cp. vi. 88-9.

satire—all his recent publications had been failures or near-
failures, but he knew that the second instalment of *Don Juan*
had sold very well indeed.[58] Other factors influenced him too,
of course: he had thought very highly of the poem when he
re-read it in August 1821, and he now realised more fully its
tremendous potentialities—its value as a weapon against everything he saw as evil; and all these considerations must have
weighed with him to make him appeal against Teresa's pro-
hibition, though the first we hear of his intention is the news
that her ban has actually been lifted:

> It is not impossible [he wrote on July 8th, 1822] that I may
> have three or four cantos of *D. Juan* ready by autumn, or a little
> later, as I obtained a permission from my Dictatress to continue
> it,—*provided always* it was to be more guarded and decorous
> and sentimental in the continuation than in the commence-
> ment. How far these Conditions have been fulfilled may be
> seen, perhaps, by and bye ; but the Embargo was only taken
> off upon these stipulations.[59]

In fact, Byron deliberately flouted the Contessa's stipulations,
making Canto VI outrageous in both plot and incidental
innuendo; and this defiance of her wishes was in effect a
declaration of independence—from now on his attitude to the
poem was not to be changed by anyone else's opinions. All his
former doubts and apprehensions, all his sensitivity to the
views of publisher and friends, have disappeared, and for ten
months or so he devotes himself almost entirely to *Don Juan*, in
the most sustained creative effort of his whole life. Cantos VI,
VII, and VIII were finished by August 8th,[60] and sent off with
Canto IX in the first fortnight of September. Cantos X and
XI were completed by October 17th, Canto XII by December
7th. There was then a pause of two months, during which he
worked on a few minor poems, but he soon came back to *Don
Juan*, and Cantos XIII, XIV, XV, and XVI were all written

[58] *Corr.*, II. 198. See also *Self-Portrait*, II. 662-3.
[59] *L.J.*, VI. 95 (cp. 109).
[60] *L.J.*, VI. 101. There is reason to suppose that Canto VI may have been
begun as early as April 14th, and that Cantos VI and VII may both have been
drafted *before* Byron got Teresa's permission to go on. See *Byron's 'Don Juan'*, ed.
T. G. Steffan and W. W. Pratt, Austin (Texas) 1957, (henceforth cited as Steffan
and Pratt), I. 384-5, n.

between February 12th and May 6th, 1823, while the opening stanzas of Canto XVII are dated May 8th. This astonishing creative period was then brought to an abrupt end by his decision to help the Greeks, for once he had resolved on going to the seat of war, he abandoned "scribbling" for the prospect of action, and in spite of Teresa's talk of further cantos written in Cephalonia and Missolonghi, Byron never touched *Don Juan* after putting it aside in May. But his work on the poem in 1822 and 1823 proves that he had at last come to full recognition of its greatness.

Even in this period, however, he did not abandon the idea of other literary projects, nor does he seem to have doubted the value of his heterogeneous experiments of 1821 and early 1822. Indeed he shows a rather undiscriminating eagerness to thrust all his recent works before the public. "*The Mystery* [i.e. *Heaven and Earth*] I look upon as good," he had told Murray in April 1822, "and *Werner* too, and I expect that you will publish them speedily";[61] in October he was still asking impatiently "With regard to *Werner* and *H[eaven] and E[arth]*, why are they not published?"[62] *Werner* was at last issued by Murray in November 1822—it was the last of Byron's works which he published in the poet's lifetime, for their relations had been strained for months now, and at last Byron transferred his whole allegiance to the radical John Hunt, who published all the later cantos of *Don Juan*. Hunt was also the publisher of the periodical *The Liberal*, which Byron made use of to print not only *The Vision of Judgment*, but *Heaven and Earth*, *The Blues* (" a mere buffoonery"),[63] and his translation of Pulci; and he also thought of having these pieces collected in a volume by themselves.[64] Moreover, he had still not given up all hope of writing new works in modes other than *ottava rima*: he paused in the composition of *Don Juan* to write *The Age of Bronze*, a topical political satire in heroic couplets, and *The Island*, a belated verse tale with a most unskilful mixture of romance and humour. Byron realised that these poems were not very good,[65] but for all that he had them published—they

[61] *L.J.*, VI. 49. [62] *L.J.*, VI. 121 (cp. 125, 129, 130).
[63] *L.J.*, V. 338. [64] *L.J.*, VI. 159.
[65] *L.J.*, VI. 160-1, 164-5.

were intended to appeal to the public taste, and he was ready to continue *The Age of Bronze* if it should prove successful.[66] Then he sent Mary Shelley some further scenes of "the drama before begun"[67]—presumably *The Deformed Transformed*, which John Hunt published a year later; he also thought of writing two more cantos of *Childe Harold* in the spring of 1823—an idea which was still in his mind when he sailed for Greece;[68] and in Cephalonia he began a poem on Aristomenes, although in Missolonghi his thoughts kept returning to his satire.

To sum up: *Don Juan* was composed over a period of five years (1818-23), but its progress was irregular and it was often subject to delays and interruptions. These were due partly to the influence of Byron's friends and his sensitivity to public opinion; for although he frequently asserted his indifference to such factors, it seems certain that he sometimes allowed them to divert him from his true course. Then his critical opinions were at times a harmful influence, for while they did provide (to some extent) a theoretical basis for his *ottava rima* satire, they also encouraged him in other less fortunate experiments— his return to *Hints From Horace* and his stubborn persistence with the drama were caused largely by misguided zeal for his own theories. Fundamentally, however, the main reason for Byron's erratic and uneven work in these years was the unreliability of his own critical judgment: he was capable of writing masterpieces, but not always of distinguishing between success and failure in his own work; and one of the most striking features of his later period is his failure to recognise how much better his *ottava rima* poetry was than any other kind he wrote. He was not prepared to defend *Beppo* when his friend Hodgson attacked it,[69] and although he often spoke

---

[66] *P.W.*, v. 578. Murray had suggested early in 1822 that Byron might write a poem in his old *Corsair* style to please the ladies, but Byron, influenced perhaps by Shelley, had rejected the idea with scorn : "As to 'a poem in the old way, to interest the women,' as you call it, I shall attempt of that kind nothing further. I follow the bias of my own mind, without considering whether women or men are or are not to be pleased . . ." (*L.J.*, VI. 40-1). Nevertheless, Murray's suggestion may have been partly responsible for Byron's writing *The Island*, for Christian is a throw-back to the old type of Byronic hero.

[67] *L.J.*, VI. 165.

[68] *L.J.*, VI. 157 ; Trelawny, *Recollections*, p. 122.

[69] *L.J.*, v. 282-3.

highly of *Don Juan* and *The Vision of Judgment*, he was ready to give equal praise to works of lower quality—to his Pulci translation, for example, or the plays. It was only in his final phase, beginning in the summer of 1822, that he attained to a clear, firm, and constant realisation of the greatness of his satire, and even then he was still interested in poems and projects of a very different order. So that while Byron fully intended to go on with *Don Juan* if he lived, he might easily have wasted time on a continuation of *Childe Harold*, or in the pursuit of some other *ignis fatuus* of popular taste or private critical theory.

It would be easy, by discreet manipulation of the evidence, to give a different picture—to suggest that Byron, after his early years of floundering experiments and slick successes, passed into a period of full artistic self-awareness and integrity, of consistent and assured achievement; but the facts of his development form a less simple pattern. And in critical discussion of *Don Juan* it is important to remember that though Byron gave more time to it than he did to any other single poem, it was only one of many projects, so that his work on it was intermittent, and sometimes hurried. Even as it is, of course, *Don Juan* is a masterpiece; but one of the great might-have-beens of literature is the poem that Byron *could* have written if he had clearly recognised his own real gifts and limitations, and concentrated on *ottava rima* satire for the whole five years after completing *Beppo*.

It is not simply that he could have given us more poetry of the same kind, but that he might have strengthened and improved the poem he actually wrote. We now know from the evidence of his manuscript revisions that he took considerable pains with *Don Juan*, and the sustained excellence of its style is his reward. But he did not give to the planning of his satire the same close attention that he gave to individual lines and stanzas, and the way in which it was composed undoubtedly made for weaknesses of structure. These were encouraged by the apparent formlessness of Byron's models, for the Italian romantic epic and the picaresque novel both seemed to sanction a carelessness—all too congenial to Byron—in architectonic; and in fact he never planned *Don Juan* as a whole. His ideas for its development and final length changed as he worked, so that it has no plot in the strictest sense of the term—no pre-conceived narrative complete in itself, informing the whole poem and embodying in concrete form the writer's "meaning." There are certainly traces of an attempt to pass beyond the primitive structural principle of linking incidents by showing the same protagonist in each: in 1819 Byron said that the individual episodes were to ridicule society in different countries, but that the larger narrative structure of the work was also to have significance—it was to portray the corruption of a normal youth by Society and Experience—to display him "gradually *gâté* and *blasé* as he grew older, as is natural"—to tell in fact the story of a representative human life. Yet even at best this plot would have been loose and episodic; and in any case the statement merely gives us Byron's plans for the satire at one stage in its composition—not an account of his intention at all times. He kept having ideas for new episodes and for great extensions of the poem; and since a work of this expanding scope could not be seen as a whole even by the author himself, he soon abandoned any attempt at moulding it into a single meaningful design. And so Byron's comic epic became something of a large, loose, baggy monster, full of life, but lacking the concentrated power which comes only with organic unity such as we admire in *Paradise Lost,* or *The Rape of the Lock,* or *Tom Jones,* or for that matter in *Beppo* and *The Vision of Judgment.*

Yet in its own peculiar way *Don Juan* is an order, not a chaos. Byron admittedly conceived it not as a whole but as instalments of varying length, but these instalments were designed to express and illustrate his own ideas and feelings about certain subjects, so that they do, *within themselves,* have significant action or "plot" in the fullest sense; and since the same ideas and preoccupations tend to recur, one can discern relationships, not formal but thematic, between the different episodes, which thus acquire a cumulative force.[70]   The

[70] Cp. Georges Gendarme de Bévotte : "A l'ancien drame Byron a substitué un poème divisé en un nombre indéterminé de chants.   Il prend le héros dès sa naissance, et le suit pas à pas à travers les mille incidents de son existence, chaque

general satiric intention, therefore, serves to unify the work; but more fundamental is the unity (if one can call it that), the consistency even in inconsistencies, that comes from its being unmistakably the product of a single although complex mind or consciousness: *Don Juan* is of its age in being a triumph of self-revelation. It is at once the author's criticism of life and the expression of his own personality, and at best these aspects are completely fused, the satiric excellence depending on Byron's being the kind of man he now reveals himself to be—although at other times the very fullness of his self-expression seems to detract from the poem's significance and force. Probably, therefore, the best way to approach this work (which cannot be discussed exhaustively because of its great length) is to examine Byron's treatment of some of his main satiric themes, considering at the same time their relation to his personality as it is presented to us by the poem.

---

aventure n'étant qu'un prétexte à peindre et à satiriser l'humanité, à faire connaître les idées de l'auteur sur toutes choses : morale, religion, politique, littérature . . . . L'œuvre est donc sans unité extérieure, mais elle a une unité intime qui réside dans l'intention satirique et morale dont elle est inspirée d'un bout à l'autre." (*La Légende de Don Juan*, Paris 1911, 1. 267, 270).

IX

Don Juan: Satire, Sentiment, and Cynicism

IN *Don Juan*, as in *Beppo*, Byron speaks for the most part as his normal aristocratic self. In his draft of a preface[1] he sketched a fictitious character for the narrator, but this was not so much a statement of his own intention as a parody of Wordsworth's elaborate note to "The Thorn," and in any case he never had the preface published. In the poem itself there is again a brief pretence of the narrator's being a Spaniard, or at least a resident in Seville, but this is not meant to be taken seriously—even in Canto I Byron's identity is an open secret, and his tone is that of gentlemanly English speech, while in Canto II he describes himself without prevarication as

> A wanderer from the British world of Fashion,
> Where I, like other 'dogs, have had my day.'[2]

This choice of *persona*, with the attitudes, ideas and feelings it involves, is of the first importance to *Don Juan*.

It means for one thing that the poem (like *Beppo*) is firmly rooted in reality as Byron knows it. His poetic manner implies an awareness of a whole context of social behaviour, so that he now writes knowingly, like a man of the world, about human nature, human weaknesses and human follies, though instead of issuing in dreary and repellent cynicism, this mode of perception leads with Byron to high comedy. To take only one example, when he notes the boredom of being married to a "perfect" wife, he strikes a completely individual, amusing note of witty and irreverent sophistication:

> Perfect she was, but as perfection is
>> Insipid in this naughty world of ours,
> Where our first parents never learned to kiss
>> Till they were exiled from their earlier bowers,
> Where all was peace, and innocence, and bliss,
>> (I wonder how they got through the twelve hours),
> Don José, like a lineal son of Eve,
> Went plucking various fruit without her leave.[3]

---

[1] *L.J.*, VI. 380-3.   [2] *P.W.*, VI. 128.   [3] *P.W.*, VI. 19.

Here Byron formulates in passing his own version of the Fortunate Fall—sin is more fun than innocence or virtue, and
Man's life may be less pure now than it was in Eden, but it is
also (as a consequence) far more enjoyable. Here, as in many
other passages, one finds the same gay cynicism as in *Beppo*,
sounding cheap enough in paraphrase, but paradoxically vital
in the poem itself.

This is, however, far from being the only effect achieved
by Byron in his new style, for it also suggests a quality of self-
control and humorous detachment, which is clearly a feature
of his social personality, and to some extent a consequence of
socially-imposed restraints. This acts as a check on self-
dramatisation, and prevents him from lapsing into the crude
emotionalism and attitudinising of his earlier works—he had
always tended to repudiate such lapses with one part of his
mind and personality, and it was that part which was now
finding expression in his *ottava rima* poetry. So that his style is,
as it were, a guarantee of the whole poem's integrity, its
freedom from emotional exaggeration. The value of this new
restraint appears immediately in his portrayal of Don Juan's
parents, for although they are based on himself and his wife[4]
he avoids the histrionics of his former treatments of the
separation. He succeeds in transmuting the events of 1815-16
into an extremely entertaining narrative, which has all the
piquancy of a "personal document," but which can and should
be read for its own sake; and his description of Donna Inez
(Lady Byron) is no mere vulgar lampoon, no piece of personal
abuse, but an accomplished satiric portrait:

> His mother was a learnéd lady, famed
>   For every branch of every science known—
> In every Christian language ever named,
>   With virtues equalled by her wit alone :
> She made the cleverest people quite ashamed,
>   And even the good with inward envy groan,
> Finding themselves so very much exceeded,
> In their own way, by all the things that she did. . . .

---

[4] This was emphasised by the poem's original motto, "Domestica Facta",
which is preserved in a MS copy of the Dedication, in the possession of Sir John
Murray.

> Her favourite science was the mathematical,
>   Her noblest virtue was her magnanimity,
> Her wit (she sometimes tried at wit) was Attic all,
>   Her serious sayings darkened to sublimity ;
> In short, in all things she was fairly what I call
>   A prodigy—her morning dress was dimity,
> Her evening silk, or, in the summer, muslin,
> And other stuffs, with which I won't stay puzzling.[5]

In this stanza the "praise" of Inez is developed with mock seriousness, although qualified by the rhymes "Attic all" and "what I call," but where one might expect a climax there is the devastating "turn" in line six, with its implications on the depth and nature of her learned interests, while the shock of "dimity" also causes a retrospective change in our responses to the rhyme-words "magnanimity," "sublimity."

This kind of effect, with its abrupt reversal of the feelings first excited, suggests still further potentialities in Byron's new style: it is peculiarly fitted for exposing the discrepancies between illusion and reality, appearance and essential truth; and this indeed would seem to have been his main aim in *Don Juan*. He did not make this clear in his early comments on the poem, for he said it was to be "ludicrous (*à la Beppo*)"[6] and "a little quietly facetious upon every thing,"[7] and he even went so far as to disclaim all serious intention: "You are too earnest and eager," he told Murray in August 1819, "about a work never intended to be serious. Do you suppose that I could have any intention but to giggle and make giggle?—a playful satire, with as little poetry as could be helped, was what I meant. . . ."[8] But he did not take this line consistently, and six months before he had gone to the opposite extreme in defending the morality of *Don Juan*: "I maintain," he wrote, "that it is the most moral of poems; but if people won't discover the moral, that is their fault, not mine."[9] His account of his intentions could thus vary according to his mood and the occasion, but the poem itself from the Dedication onwards does

---

[5] *P.W.*, VI. 16-17.   [6] *L.J.*, IV. 245.   [7] *L.J.*, IV. 260.

[8] *L.J.*, IV. 343. "Poetry" here presumably means "poetical" sentiments expressed in a "poetical" style.

[9] *L.J.*, IV. 279.

K

express some of his strongest feelings and beliefs. They are not presented with consistent seriousness and intensity throughout the work, for the actual intention and techniques (as well as his accounts of them) vary with his changing moods, and some episodes, like Juan's night adventure in the harem, are primarily *risqué* and amusing entertainment, or light satire of the *Beppo* kind. But in spite of these variations in satiric texture, the poem usually combines the *utile* with the *dulce* in a way that justifies Byron's assertion that it is essentially a moral work. It expresses his deep hatred of emotional and intellectual dishonesty or delusion, his contempt for hypocrisy, false sentiment, and cant of every kind; and he sets himself the great satiric task of demonstrating, both in jest and earnest, the reality that lies behind the self-deceptions, the pretences, the illusions, which we normally accept so readily as the whole truth.

In describing Donna Inez, for example, he shows that this "perfect" wife and mother has grave faults concealed by a *façade* of holiness—conceit, Pharisaical self-righteousness, and a lack of Christian charity; while in her educational programme we see her hypocrisy, and the prurience that underlies her prudery —perceptions which prepare us for the hint that even the spotless Inez may have had a past—a love affair with Don Alfonso which affects her attitude to Julia and Juan. This glimpse of disreputable murky motives in respectable Society is typical of Byron's satire, which while casually chatting probes beneath the surface of appearances, and combines a close analysis of individual cases with a general awareness of the kind of thing that usually goes on—an inside knowledge of the workings of Society and of recurring patterns in human behaviour, which adds force to his treatment of particular examples:

> A real husband always is suspicious,
>   But still no less suspects in the wrong place,
> Jealous of some one who had no such wishes,
>   Or pandering blindly to his own disgrace,
> By harbouring some dear friend extremely vicious ;
>   The last indeed's infallibly the case :
> And when the spouse and friend are gone off wholly,
> He wonders at their vice, and not his folly.

Thus parents also are at times short-sighted :
 Though watchful as the lynx, they ne'er discover,
The while the wicked world beholds delighted,
 Young Hopeful's mistress, or Miss Fanny's lover,
Till some confounded escapade has blighted
 The plan of twenty years, and all is over ;
And then the mother cries, the father swears,
And wonders why the devil he got heirs.

But Inez was so anxious, and so clear
 Of sight, that I must think, on this occasion,
She had some other motive much more near
 For leaving Juan to this new temptation,
But what that motive was, I sha'n't say here ;
 Perhaps to finish Juan's education,
Perhaps to open Don Alfonso's eyes,
In case he thought his wife too great a prize.[10]

This kind of psychological realism and worldly wisdom govern the portrayal of young love in Juan's first affair, for Canto I is largely concerned with the deflation of romantic sentiment, insisting on its basis in sexual desire, and on the improper or embarrassing conclusions towards which it can tend.   This idea is embodied in the whole development of the story from the first delicate yearnings to the final bedroom comedy, but it is also presented locally through the style and structure of individual stanzas, where the *naïveté* of the lovers is contrasted with the man of the world's knowing cynicism:

Then there were sighs, the deeper for suppression,
 And stolen glances, sweeter for the theft,
And burning blushes, though for no transgression,
 Tremblings when met, and restlessness when left ;
All these are little preludes to possession,
 Of which young Passion cannot be bereft,
And merely tend to show how greatly Love is
Embarrassed at first starting with a novice.[11]

In the same way Byron points to the difference between conscious and unconscious (or admitted and unadmitted) motives at this stage of the affair—Julia's self-deception is exposed in stanzas which create for us the conflict of her mind

[10] *P.W.*, VI. 42.   [11] *P.W.*, VI. 35.

and feelings, and which use the conventional language of
sentiment with a full awareness of its conventionality and its
falseness to the facts of human nature:

> She now determined that a virtuous woman
> 　　Should rather face and overcome temptation,
> That flight was base and dastardly, and no man
> 　　Should ever give her heart the least sensation,
> That is to say, a thought beyond the common
> 　　Preference, that we must feel, upon occasion,
> For people who are pleasanter than others,
> But then they only seem so many brothers. . . .
>
> And, then, there are such things as Love divine,
> 　　Bright and immaculate, unmixed and pure,
> Such as the angels think so very fine,
> 　　And matrons, who would be no less secure,
> Platonic, perfect, "just such love as mine ;"
> 　　Thus Julia said—and thought so, to be sure ;
> And so I'd have her think, were *I* the man
> On whom her reveries celestial ran.[12]

In stanzas such as these Byron was stripping off what he called
"the tinsel of *Sentiment*"[13] to show the true nature of love
relationships; and this, he was later to declare, was why
Teresa did not like the poem. "She . . . thinks it a detestable
production," he told Hobhouse:

> This will not seem strange even in Italian morality, because
> women all over the world always retain their freemasonry, and
> as that consists in the illusion of the sentiment which constitutes
> their sole empire (all owing to chivalry and the Goths—the
> Greeks knew better), all works which refer to the *comedy* of the
> passions, and laugh at sentimentalism, of course are proscribed
> by the whole *sect*. I never knew a woman who did not admire
> Rousseau, and hate Gil Blas, and de Grammont and the like,
> for the same reason. And I never met with a woman, English
> or foreign, who did not do as much by D. J.[14]

---

[12] *P.W.*, VI. 36.　　　[13] *L.J.*, V. 97.

[14] *Corr.*, II. 176 : cp. *L.J.*, V. 321. See also Dr Henry Muir's *Notes on Byron's
Conversations in Cephalonia* : "That women did not like [*Don Juan*] he was not
surprised ; he knew they could not bear it because it *took off the veil* ; it showed
that all their d—d sentiment was only an excuse to cover passions of grosser
nature ; that all platonism only tended to *that*, and they hated it because it showed
and exposed their hypocrisy." (*L.J.*, VI. 429-30).

The satire is not confined, however, to the illusions and deceptions of the female sex, for Juan's romantic, lovesick melancholy is presented in an exuberant parody of Byron's own earliest manner, and then subjected to open ridicule:

> Silent and pensive, idle, restless, slow,
>> His home deserted for the lonely wood,
> Tormented with a wound he could not know,
>> His, like all deep grief, plunged in solitude :
> I'm fond myself of solitude or so,
>> But then, I beg it may be understood,
> By solitude I mean a Sultan's (not
> A Hermit's), with a haram for a grot.[15]

Here the deflation is less witty, yet it makes a real satiric point —that Juan's mood is basically one of sexual frustration which harem girls could soon cure, but which will only be intensified by solitary brooding; and this is followed by a series of stanzas in which the hero's lack of self-knowledge, his melancholy, pensiveness, and pseudo-profundity, are viewed in the light of the same derisive common sense:

> Young Juan wandered by the glassy brooks,
>> Thinking unutterable things ; he threw
> Himself at length within the leafy nooks
>> Where the wild branch of the cork forest grew ;
> There poets find materials for their books,
>> And every now and then we read them through,
> So that their plan and prosody are eligible,
> Unless, like Wordsworth, they prove unintelligible. . . .

> He thought about himself, and the whole earth,
>> Of man the wonderful, and of the stars,
> And how the deuce they ever could have birth;
>> And then he thought of earthquakes, and of wars,
> How many miles the moon might have in girth,
>> Of air-balloons, and of the many bars
> To perfect knowledge of the boundless skies ;—
> And then he thought of Donna Julia's eyes.

In thoughts like these true Wisdom may discern
    Longings sublime, and aspirations high,
Which some are born with, but the most part learn
    To plague themselves withal, they know not why :
'T was strange that one so young should thus concern
    His brain about the action of the sky ;
If you think 't was Philosophy that this did,
I can't help thinking puberty assisted.[16]

This comes as a valid comment not only on Juan's adolescent musings, but also on the emotional immaturity of Byron's own romantic posturings and meditations. He was by now in conscious reaction from the self-dramatising and self-pitying moods of his former poetry, which he came to see as being "in the false exaggerated style of youth and the times in which we live";[17] and he deliberately set out to discredit attitudes in which he had himself indulged not long before. "Does the cant of sentiment still continue in England?" he asked Lady Blessington in 1823: " 'Childe Harold' called it forth; but my 'Juan' was well calculated to cast it into shade, and had that merit, if it had no other."[18] He never carried out his intention of transforming Juan into "a Sentimental 'Werther-faced man'"[19]—a caricature of the Byronic hero—but he ridicules Byronic modes of feeling in other ways—by the tone which he adopts in Canto X, for example, when describing Juan's passage through the country over which Childe Harold had once stalked in gloomy meditation:

And thence through Berlin, Dresden, and the like,
    Until he reached the castellated Rhine :—
Ye glorious Gothic scenes ! how much ye strike
    All phantasies, not even excepting mine !
A grey wall, a green ruin, rusty pike,
    Make my soul pass the equinoctial line
Between the present and past worlds, and hover
Upon their airy confines, half-seas-over.

---

[16] *P.W.*, vi. 39-40.   [17] *L.J.*, vi. 88.
[18] Lady Blessington, *Conversations*, p. 376.
[19] See above, Chapter VIII, p. 134. The reference is to Moore's amusing description of a Byronic hero as :
    "A fine, sallow, sublime, sort of Werther-faced man,
      With mustachios that gave (what we read of so oft)
      The dear Corsair expression, half savage, half soft."

But Juan posted on through Mannheim, Bonn,
  Which Drachenfels frowns over like a spectre
Of the good feudal times for ever gone,
  On which I have not time just now to lecture.
From thence he was drawn onwards to Cologne,
  A city which presents to the inspector
Eleven thousand maiden heads of bone.
The greatest number flesh hath ever known.[20]

Or there is the deliberate contrast between Harold's dramatic departures from his native land and Juan's sorrowful-ridiculous farewell to Spain and Julia. Byron had himself been sea-sick on leaving England in 1809, and again in 1816, but these facts were carefully excluded from *Childe Harold,* Cantos I and III. Harsh realities of this kind were, however, just what Byron wanted in *Don Juan,* and he now revels in the incongruity between his hero's passionate grief and uncontrollable nausea:

"Farewell, my Spain ! a long farewell !" he cried,
  "Perhaps I may revisit thee no more,
But die, as many an exiled heart hath died,
  Of its own thirst to see again thy shore :
Farewell, where Guadalquivir's waters glide !
  Farewell, my mother ! and, since all is o'er,
Farewell, too, dearest Julia !—(here he drew
Her letter out again, and read it through.)

"And oh ! if e'er I should forget, I swear—
  But that's impossible, and cannot be—
Sooner shall this blue Ocean melt to air,
  Sooner shall Earth resolve itself to sea,
Than I resign thine image, oh, my fair !
  Or think of anything, excepting thee ;
A mind diseased no remedy can physic—
(Here the ship gave a lurch, and he grew sea-sick.)

"Sooner shall Heaven kiss earth—(here he fell sicker)
  Oh, Julia ! what is every other woe ? —
(For God's sake let me have a glass of liquor ;
  Pedro, Battista, help me down below.)

---

[20] *P.W.,* vi. 418-19.

Julia, my love !—(you rascal, Pedro, quicker)—
   Oh, Julia !—(this curst vessel pitches so)—
Belovéd Julia, hear me still beseeching !"
(Here he grew inarticulate with retching.) [21]

Here the humour, although lively, is cruder than usual, but a single blemish should not count for much in one's final judgment on a long poem like *Don Juan*. Yet this passage, taken with some others I have quoted, may suggest a fundamental criticism of Byron's satire as a whole : when a writer tries to strip the veil from our illusions it is obviously important that he himself should have an adequate conception of the truth, and it may well be asked whether Byron's is not superficial—whether he does not merely offer us the cynic's version of reality, an elementary debunking of all generous emotion.

Such an accusation has a certain plausibility, but it is unjust, for the satire in *Don Juan* is more complex and more "adult" than this formula implies. To take the case of Juan's grief on leaving Spain : Byron does not deny the existence and validity of such emotions—on the contrary, he speaks with strong but controlled feeling of his own experience of them; and when he goes on to deflate Juan's soliloquy, it is not because its emotions are essentially false or absurd, but because Juan overstates them, claiming for his love a permanence and a supreme importance which events will easily disprove. Byron is concerned not with attacking love and grief as such, but with showing how his hero, in all sincerity, exaggerates and therefore

---

[21] *P.W.*, vi. 85-6. It is interesting to compare the verses Byron wrote at Falmouth in 1809—like some of his juvenilia they show how certain attitudes usually associated with *Don Juan* existed in embryo at a much earlier period, though they did not then figure in his more ambitious works :

      "Hobhouse muttering fearful curses,
        As the hatchway down he rolls,
     Now his breakfast, now his verses,
        Vomits forth—and damns our souls.
        'Here's a stanza
         On Braganza—
    Help !'—'A couplet ?'—'No, a cup
        Of warm water—'
      'What's the matter ?'
  'Zounds ! my liver's coming up . . .'" etc.
                (*P.W.*, vii. 6).

falsifies his feelings, and how those feelings (whatever senti-
mentalists may say) can soon be dissipated by sea-sickness,
bowel complaints, and other vulgar illnesses. The theme of
this broad comedy, in fact, is the inadequacy of Man's state
to his conceptions[22]—the discrepancy between his high ideals
and noble sentiments and the inevitable limitations imposed
on him by his nature. Byron views these limitations not with
the "rage and fury" he was later to portray in Cain, but with
amusement; in the same way he had been amused to trace
the source of sentiment in sexual desire; and in both cases the
amusement springs essentially from a recognition of the truth—
from the man of the world's seeing further and more clearly
than the lover. This, however, does not prevent his sym-
pathising with Juan and Julia, especially when their cant of
sentiment is laid aside—one of the finest passages in Canto I
is a series of stanzas which show Byron's rich vital responsive-
ness, now humorous, now serious, to things of ordinary life,
and which culminate in an acknowledgement of the quintes-
sential sweetness of young love (although it is no doubt significant that for Byron passion has to have the additional spice
of sinfulness):

> . . . 'T is sweet to hear the watch-dog's honest bark
>   Bay deep-mouthed welcome as we draw near home ;
> 'T is sweet to know there is an eye will mark
>   Our coming, and look brighter when we come ;
> 'T is sweet to be awakened by the lark,
>   Or lulled by falling waters ; sweet the hum
> Of bees, the voice of girls, the song of birds,
> The lisp of children, and their earliest words. . . .
>
> 'T is sweet to win, no matter how, one's laurels,
>   By blood or ink ; 't is sweet to put an end
> To strife ; 't is sometimes sweet to have our quarrels,
>   Particularly with a tiresome friend :
> Sweet is old wine in bottles, ale in barrels ;
>   Dear is the helpless creature we defend
> Against the world ; and dear the schoolboy spot
> We ne'er forget, though there we are forgot.

---

[22] For Byron's use of this phrase in a discussion of *Cain*, see *L.J.*, v. 470.

But sweeter still than this, than these, than all,
    Is first and passionate Love—it stands alone,
Like Adam's recollection of his fall ;
    The Tree of Knowledge has been plucked—all's known—
And Life yields nothing further to recall
    Worthy of this ambrosial sin, so shown,
No doubt in fable, as the unforgiven
Fire which Prometheus filched for us from Heaven.[23]

Byron passes from this rhapsody to the outrageous comedy of the bedroom scene, but the one does not invalidate the other, for they are both aspects of the truth—love, as he knows, can easily become funny or disreputable as well as sweet. And although this episode is treated so light-heartedly, the insertion (towards the end of Canto I) of "Julia's letter" extended the poem's emotional range still further, by showing—or trying to show—the genuine passion which had motivated her complete surrender and ruined her life. Here Byron passes far beyond his man-of-the-world cynicism, for although he sees adulterous intrigue as comedy (as he had done in *Beppo*) he can also see the element of tragedy it may involve, and instead of treating this case merely as a joke, he shows what it had meant for the victim.

This more serious approach to love governs his presentation of the hero's next affair. Juan's terrible experiences in the shipwreck serve to obliterate from his mind and from ours the memory of Julia—it is almost as if he had died and been reborn—so that we see no infidelity, no promiscuity, in his loving Haidée; and Byron's description of their love is not cynical but deeply sympathetic. He is ready, of course, to reveal the little self-deceptions and incongruities of its early stages,[24] or

[23] *P.W.*, VI. 48-9. The whole passage is of considerable technical interest. Six stanzas are linked by the figure of anaphora and by parallelism of thought so as to form a single rhetorical movement, culminating in the praise of first love. But in spite of the close formal and conceptual resemblances between his stanzas Byron skilfully avoids any monotonous sameness in their structure—a regular deflation in the final couplet, for example, or a standardised relation of the speech units to the metrical pattern. So that here we see at once his mastery of the individual *ottava rima* stanza, and his ability to plan beyond its limits and create (as he had not done in deflating Juan's first love-melancholy) larger, even more effective rhetorical units.

[24] *P.W.*, VI. 120, 129.

to remind us gleefully that even two romantic figures on a
romantic island have mundane needs—they must eat and
have their food prepared for them, however wonderful their
feelings:

> And thus like to an Angel o'er the dying
>   Who die in righteousness, she leaned;   and there
> All tranquilly the shipwrecked boy was lying,
>   As o'er him lay the calm and stirless air :
> But Zoe the meantime some eggs was frying,
>   Since, after all, no doubt the youthful pair
> Must breakfast—and, betimes, lest they should ask it,
> She drew out her provision from the basket.[25]

This, however, does not (strictly speaking) operate as deflation
—it serves rather to root the situation and the characters more
firmly in reality by including practical details of a kind often
ignored in poetry.   Indeed the whole love idyll is set in a
context of the actual conditions which might obtain in a remote
Aegean island, and this accuracy helps to make the episode
convincing.   It is important that it should be so, for here we
have one of the main values offered by the poem—Byron is at
pains to insist that the passionate love of Juan and Haidée was
not an illusion based on social or literary conventions, but a
genuine and beautiful experience, perhaps unique, but certainly desirable:

> Young innate feelings all have felt below,
>   Which perish in the rest, but in them were
> Inherent—what we mortals call romantic,
> And always envy, though we deem it frantic.
>
> This is in others a factitious state,
>   An opium dream of too much youth and reading,
> But was in them their nature or their fate :
>   No novels e'er had set their young hearts bleeding,
> For Haidée's knowledge was by no means great,
>   And Juan was a boy of saintly breeding ;
> So that there was no reason for their loves
> More than for those of nightingales or doves.[26]

---

[25] *P.W.*, vi. 123 (cp. 125, 129-30).
[26] *P.W.*, vi. 188.

The comparison in this last couplet is significant and typical, for Byron repeatedly emphasises the *natural* quality of their love, at once intense and unsophisticated:

> Haidée spoke not of scruples, asked no vows,
>   Nor offered any ; she had never heard
> Of plight and promises to be a spouse,
>   Or perils by a loving maid incurred ;
> She was all which pure Ignorance allows,
>   And flew to her young mate like a young bird ;
> And, never having dreamt of falsehood, she
> Had not one word to say of constancy.
>
> She loved, and was belovéd—she adored,
>   And she was worshipped after Nature's fashion. . . .[27]

This love is frankly passionate, but innocent in that it is uncontaminated by hypocrisy, self-deception, or mercenary motives—it is presented as ideal and perfect, in sharp contrast to the institution of marriage and the normal course of sexual relationships in civilised society, which Byron now views not with amusement but with distaste—what seemed funny in a context of normality and habit becomes sordid when contrasted with the ideal:

> Oh beautiful ! and rare as beautiful !
>   But theirs was Love in which the Mind delights
> To lose itself, when the old world grows dull,
>   And we are sick of its hack sounds and sights,
> Intrigues, adventures of the common school,
>   Its petty passions, marriages, and flights,
> Where Hymen's torch but brands one strumpet more,
> Whose husband only knows her not a whore.[28]

We are made to feel the pathos, as well as the passion and the beauty, of their love—it will bring them to damnation, if the harsh religious moralists are to be believed;[29] and it is doomed to end disastrously—the passage of time could only spoil it, and the return of Lambro cuts it short, by ending the magic isolation in which it could flourish. Yet though Byron knows

---

[27] *P.W.*, vi. 135. (Steffan and Pratt, ii. 257 : ". . . worshipp'd ; after nature's fashion . . .").

[28] *P.W.*, vi. 188 (cp. 137-8.)

[29] *P.W.*, vi. 135-6.

it could not last for ever in complete perfection, he looks forward with anguish to its sad conclusion:

> Mixed in each other's arms, and heart in heart,
>   Why did they not then die ?—they had lived too long
> Should an hour come to bid them breathe apart ;
>   Years could but bring them cruel things or wrong ;
> The World was not for them—nor the World's art
>   For beings passionate as Sappho's song ;
> Love was born *with* them, *in* them, so intense,
> It was their very Spirit—not a sense.
>
> They should have lived together deep in woods,
>   Unseen as sings the nightingale ; they were
> Unfit to mix in these thick solitudes
>   Called social, haunts of Hate, and Vice, and Care :
> How lonely every freeborn creature broods !
>   The sweetest song-birds nestle in a pair ;
> The eagle soars alone ; the gull and crow
> Flock o'er their carrion, just like men below.[30]

This strikes a very different note from anything in Canto I, for in the Julia story we had Byron the man of the world's delighted presentation of the actual, while in the Haidée idyll we have his tribute to the ideal. And his response to the ideal is so intense that it modifies—for a time at any rate—his delight in the actual; but at the same time his awareness of the actual is so strong that his ideal must be portrayed outside the world of fashion, far outside society, in a context of Nature and solitude. Or to put it in a different way: Byron was both attracted and repelled by "Sentiment"—his romantic poems and *Beppo* show the two extremes to which he tended—but in *Don Juan* he was aiming at a greater inclusiveness, for the "medley" quality of Italian poetry in *ottava rima* suggested the possibility of combining contrasting elements in the same work, and of expressing his whole personality instead of isolated parts of it. There was, however, a continual danger that, because of his "mobility"[31] of temperament, he might simply alternate

---

[30] *P.W.*, VI. 190-1 (cp. 185-7).

[31] For Byron's use of this term see *P.W.*, VI. 600. See also Lady Blessington, *Conversations*, p. 110 : "Byron is a perfect chameleon . . . . He is conscious of this, and says it is owing to the extreme *mobilité* of his nature, which yields to present impressions." (Cp. *op. cit.*, p. 67).

between indulging and deflating his romantic feelings, and that the variations of mood sanctioned by his models might result in mere emotional and intellectual incoherence. He avoids these pitfalls in the first few cantos by organising his opposing impulses on a framework of ideas: his full sympathy and yearning for young love are reserved for the idealised passion of Don Juan and the child of Nature, which provides a standard by which other amours can be judged; while his urge to deflate and sneer is directed towards the unconscious self-deception, the conscious hypocrisy, and the debased dishonesty of love and marriage in Society. The ideal is contrasted with the actual, and these are equated with the Natural and Social, in a stock romantic opposition which suggests the author of *Childe Harold* rather than of *Beppo*: Byron has deepened his satiric vision by drawing on some emotions and ideas he had used in his earlier poetry, though they are no longer vitiated by his former modes of feeling and expression. One might say, indeed, that the success of this whole episode—its combination of strength, humour, realism and intensity of feeling—is the result of a remarkable integration of Byron the man-of-the-world satirist with Byron the romantic poet.

It must be recognised, however, that this integration is not quite complete, for some discordant, rather irritating notes occur throughout the poem, and point to an occasional confusion in the writer's feelings. Here, for example, are two stanzas which describe Haidée and Juan on the morning after she had found him lying unconscious on the beach:

> For still he lay, and on his thin worn cheek
> A purple hectic played like dying day
> On the snow-tops of distant hills ; the streak
> Of sufferance yet upon his forehead lay,
> Where the blue veins looked shadowy, shrunk, and weak ;
> And his black curls were dewy with the spray,
> Which weighed upon them yet, all damp and salt,
> Mixed with the stony vapours of the vault.
>
> And she bent o'er him, and he lay beneath,
> Hushed as the babe upon its mother's breast,
> Drooped as the willow when no winds can breathe,
> Lulled like the depth of Ocean when at rest,

Fair as the crowning rose of the whole wreath,
    Soft as the callow cygnet in its nest ;
In short he was a very pretty fellow,
Although his woes had turned him rather yellow.[32]

The deflation in this final couplet is undoubtedly amusing, for the reader has been betrayed into responding to the poetry in a way that is suddenly and disconcertingly repudiated; but the satiric point of this is not clear. The description and the similes, and the mood which they induce, are not attributed to Haidée—they are Byron's own. So that the change of tone suggests, not a probing of lovers' delusions, but an instability in his own feelings—it is as if the man of the world had suddenly reasserted himself, and rejected both the style and the emotions of the poet.

In this case Byron is deliberately exploiting the dichotomy in order to produce an immediately comic although basically non-significant effect. Often, however, similar abrupt changes of tone seem to occur almost involuntarily, as if he were afraid or ashamed of the emotion that he has himself evoked. Thus after telling how Juan was cut down in Haidée's sight and dragged off to a galley, Byron switches from the tragic melodrama to a cynical detachment, and takes refuge in a humorous digression on his own drinking habits and their consequences:

Here I must leave him, for I grow pathetic,
    Moved by the Chinese nymph of tears, green tea !
Than whom Cassandra was not more prophetic ;
    For if my pure libations exceed three,
I feel my heart become so sympathetic,
    That I must have recourse to black Bohea :
'T is pity wine should be so deleterious,
For tea and coffee leave us much more serious,

Unless when qualified with thee, Cogniac !
    Sweet Naïad of the Phlegethontic rill !
Ah ! why the liver wilt thou thus attack,
    And make, like other nymphs, thy lovers ill ? . . .[33]

He then returns to Haidée, and describes her broken-hearted swoon, madness, and death, with the final pathetic detail of

[32] *P.W.*, VI. 123-4.   [33] *P.W.*, VI. 197.

her having been with child; but the pathos is made tolerable
by three brilliant stanzas which suggest some consolation and
then distance the whole episode, removing it from its disturbing
immediacy to the remoteness of past legend. It comes, therefore, as a rude shock when he passes from the tact and perfectly
controlled tone of this passage to a casual, flippant dismissal of
the very subject he has treated with such feeling and such care:

> But let me change this theme, which grows too sad,
>   And lay this sheet of sorrows on the shelf ;
> I don't much like describing people mad,
>   For fear of seeming rather touched myself—
> Besides, I've no more on this head to add ;
>   And as my Muse is a capricious elf,
> We'll put about, and try another tack
> With Juan, left half-killed some stanzas back.[34]

Many of Byron's original readers were puzzled and repelled
by these rapid transitions from seriousness to frivolity, and
although he sometimes comments on his practice, he never
wholly succeeds in justifying it in cases like these. ". . . I will
answer your friend C[ohen]," he once wrote to Murray, "who
objects to the quick succession of fun and gravity, as if in that
case the gravity did not (in intention, at least) heighten the
fun."[35] But this is very far from being an adequate account
even of the opening cantos—it implies that all emotion (not
merely the factitious or corrupt) is there only to be deflated,
which is to falsify the whole imaginative impact of the Haidée
episode.

> His metaphor [Byron goes on] is, that 'we are never scorched
> and drenched at the same time.' Blessings on his experience !
> Ask him these questions about 'scorching and drenching'.
> Did he never play at Cricket, or walk a mile in hot weather ?
> Did he never spill a dish of tea over his testicles in handing a
> cup to his charmer, to the great shame of his nankeen breeches ?
> Did he never swim in the sea at Noonday with the Sun in his
> eyes and on his head, which all the foam of Ocean could not
> cool ? Did he never draw his foot out of a tub of too hot water,
> damning his eyes and his valet's ?[36]

---

[34] *P.W.*, VI. 203.   [35] *L.J.*, IV. 341.
[36] Marchand, *Byron*, II. 807 ; *L.J.*, IV. 341-2.

Like Dr Johnson's famous defence of Shakespeare's blending comedy with tragedy, this is essentially an appeal to the facts of experience—to the coexistence in real life of discordant elements—and this certainly points to the nature of *Don Juan's* greatness. In the present case, however, it seems unsatisfactory as a defence of his technique, for in the passages just quoted it is not a question of Byron's portraying serious and frivolous events in quick succession, but of his evoking first a serious and then a frivolous response to the same event, without having any apparent satiric purpose in so doing. The contrasts thus seem to derive not from a view of human life as complex and perhaps chaotic in its sheer variety, but from some kind of conflict or confusion in the writer's own attitude to particular aspects of that life.

Such conflicts and confusions did exist in Byron's mind, and bewildering alternations of mood were a constantly recurring feature of his conversation:

> Byron seems [wrote Lady Blessington] to take a peculiar pleasure in ridiculing sentiment and romantic feelings ; and yet the day after will betray both, to an extent that appears impossible to be sincere, to those who had heard his previous sarcasms : that he is sincere, is evident, as his eyes fill with tears, his voice becomes tremulous, and his whole manner evinces that he feels what he says. All this appears so inconsistent, that it destroys sympathy, or if it does not quite do that, it makes one angry with oneself for giving way to it for one who is never two days of the same way of thinking, or at least expressing himself.[37]

This description is confirmed by other friends and acquaintances, some of whom suggest that the cynicism was often a kind of defence mechanism—George Finlay gives an interesting account of the way in which Byron often chose to apeak of subjects near his heart:

> Lord Byron uttered this in an unemphatical, and rather affectedly monotonous tone. I afterwards observed, that he adopted this tone not unfrequently, whenever he uttered any thing which diverged from the commonest style of conversation. Whenever he commenced a sentence which showed that the

subject had engaged his mind, and that his thoughts were sublime, he checked himself, and finished a broken sentence, either with an indifferent smile, or with this annoying tone. I thought he had adopted it to conceal his feelings, when he feared to trust his tongue with the sentiments of his heart. Often, it was evident, he did it to avoid betraying the author, or rather the poet.[38]

Stanhope confirms this in a note to the passage: "I have observed Lord Byron act thus. He would often suppress noble sentiments that obtruded on his mind, or vainly attempt to turn them into ridicule."[39] Lady Blessington too, with her usual acuteness, had noted this pattern of behaviour, and his tendency to conceal or falsify his real emotions: she tells how Byron would point out beautiful views, "but with a coldness of expression that was remarkable. . . . 'I suppose,' " he said to her on one occasion, " 'you expected me to explode into some enthusiastic exclamations on the sea, the scenery, &c., such as poets indulge in, or rather are supposed to indulge in; but the truth is, I hate cant of every kind, and the cant of the love of nature as much as any other.' So," she observes, "to avoid the appearance of one affectation, he assumes another, that of *not* admiring."[40]

This reluctance to express emotion or enthusiasm openly was probably a consequence of both psychological and social factors in the poet's life. A psychologist would almost certainly relate it to experiences of Byron's childhood—in particular to what he must have suffered from his mother's deplorable inconsistency of temper, which he has himself described with bitterness:

> . . . though timely Severity [he wrote in 1805] may sometimes be necessary & justifiable, surely a peevish harassing System of Torment is by no means commendable, & when that is interrupted by ridiculous Indulgence, the only purpose answered is to soften the feelings for a moment which are soon after to be doubly wounded by the recal of accustomed Harshness.[41]

---

[38] Stanhope, *Greece*, p. 512 : cp. Moore, *Life*, pp. 396, 422.
[39] Stanhope, *Greece*, p. 512, n.
[40] *The Idler in Italy*, II. 17.   [41] *L.J.*, I. 90.

Such treatment as this would tend to make a child reluctant to respond or show emotion, and Byron certainly thought it had had this effect on him: "I am a very unlucky fellow," he wrote to Augusta, after telling her that he could never forgive his mother, "for I think I had naturally not a bad heart; but it has been so bent, twisted, and trampled on, that it has now become as hard as a Highlander's heelpiece."[42]   Here he was exaggerating with some gusto, but it is none the less quite likely that a sensitive, emotional boy like Byron, with his difficult family relationships and his other grounds for feeling insecure, would develop a *façade* at least of pride and callousness as a protection against being hurt; and he describes this very process in a letter of 1814: "I *could* be very sentimental now," he told Moore after parting from him, "but I won't.   The truth is, that I have been all my life trying to harden my heart, and have not yet quite succeeded. . . ."[43]

Even, however, if this tendency did have its origin in Byron's earliest experiences, it was encouraged by his social ambitions.   He might dream and write about Byronic heroes, but his real life was in London or at country houses, and his aim for much of the time was to be a man of the world, a man about town—which again involved a certain check on his expression of strong feeling.   The eighteenth-century distrust of uncontrolled emotion or enthusiasm was often intensified by the cynicism which Grierson regards as an almost inevitable feature of aristocratic society,[44] and which Byron certainly associated with the ideal of a buck or dandy—an ideal which affected his own actions and behaviour even after he left England, never to return.

> The character he most commonly appeared in [writes Trelawny] was of the free and easy sort, such as had been in vogue when he was in London, and George IV was Regent ; and his talk was seasoned with anecdotes of the great actors on and off the stage, boxers, gamblers, duellists, drunkards, &c., &c., appropriately garnished with the slang and scandal of that day.   Such things had all been in fashion, and were at that

---

[42] *L.J.*, I. 203.
[43] *L.J.*, III. 92.
[44] H. J. C. Grierson, *The Background of English Literature*, p. 178.

time considered accomplishments by gentlemen ; and of this tribe of Mohawks the Prince Regent was the chief, and allowed to be the most perfect specimen. Byron, not knowing the tribe was extinct, still prided himself on having belonged to it. . . .[45]

And Trelawny thought that this social experience explained much of Byron's apparent cynicism:

> Byron's idle talk during the exhumation of Williams's remains [he writes], did not proceed from want of feeling, but from his anxiety to conceal what he felt from others. When confined to his bed and racked by spasms, which threatened his life, I have heard him talk in a much more unorthodox fashion, the instant he could muster breath to banter. He had been taught during his town-life, that any exhibition of sympathy or feeling was maudlin and unmanly, and that the appearance of daring and indifference, denoted blood and high breeding.[46]

Trelawny was not conversant with the tone of good society in London, and he writes as if Byron had lived only with Corinthians, but his account of the poet's conversational habits and of their relation to an aristocratic ideal of one kind is no doubt accurate. In view of this it may seem paradoxical that in the years when he was actually living as a man of fashion Byron wrote and published so many poems of "Sentiment" or passion; but this can be explained by the fact that his poetry was divorced at that time from his ordinary life: the expression of emotion—even violent emotion—was, as it were, permissible and proper in a poet, and he could therefore indulge in it with

---

[45] Trelawny, *Recollections*, p. 24.

[46] *Recollections*, p. 90. (Trelawny was not in fact, as he seems to imply here, present during Byron's final illness, but there is other evidence for the latter's joking when he was seriously ill.) Cp. also William Parry, *The Last Days of Lord Byron*, London 1825, (henceforth cited as Parry, *Last Days*), pp. 260-1 :

"He was not only a poet, but, like other young noblemen, he was, for several years, a man of what is called fashion, and *ton*, and the opinions which he then imbibed, and the habits he then formed, he never afterwards got rid of. He deferred to them in his conversation and his manners, long after he had learned to despise them in his heart . . . . At least, in all our conversations, his Lordship was serious and reflecting, though wonderfully quick, acute, and discerning. With his other companions he was, as I have said, light, volatile, and trifling. He was still the man of fashion. Then the opinions and habits of his former days again obtained all their mastery over his mind. His commanding talents, his noble endowments, and his rare acquirements were then all sacrificed on the altar of fashionable frivolity."

no apparent inhibitions in his works themselves, though afterwards in his role of dandy he might feel a little ashamed of himself, and assume a depreciatory tone when mentioning his compositions or their heroes. In his *ottava rima* satires, on the other hand, his aristocratic and poetic personalities were no longer differentiated in this way: all his everyday humour, wit and common sense appear now in his poems—but so do his everyday inhibitions; and at times one can see Byron's social-personal defence mechanism working in *Don Juan*, as he draws back mockingly from the emotion which he has evoked, not because of any falsity or baseness in the emotion, but because he feels he has revealed too much of his deepest feelings—he has exposed himself to the danger of ridicule, which he forestalls by sneering or laughing himself, and momentarily discrediting the values which he has himself established.

X

Don Juan: War and Realism

BYRON was, for better and for worse, a Regency aristocrat. Yet he had a much greater range of interests and experiences, of ideas and emotions, than the average man-about-town, and the greatness of *Don Juan* is often the result of his combining obviously social qualities like conversational ease and lively wit with deeper feelings and profounder moral insights than one might have expected from "a broken Dandy." This is pre-eminently so in his attack on war, which is probably the most serious portion of his satire and the most impressive of all his attempts to reconcile poetry with truth and wisdom.

His refusal to accept the cant of martial glory had appeared at the very beginning of *Don Juan*, when he rejected military and naval heroes, but it did not then constitute a central theme: his comments on soldiers and battles were incidental, and although he wrote a long attack on Wellington for Canto III, it was not developed in the narrative—indeed it was not even included in his final version. By the summer of 1822, however, the evils of war and despotism had come to the foreground of his consciousness, and he proceeded to treat them much more fully in his satire: in Cantos VII and VIII he turned from love to war, and instead of discussing the psychology of passion or the mutability of Man's affections or the cant of sentiment, he set out to expose the horrible realities that lie behind glib talk about fame, glory, and heroic deeds. In July, therefore, he asked Moore to return the fragment about Wellington,[1] and he wrote again in August explaining what his intentions were in this new section of the poem:

> I have written three more cantos of *Don Juan*, and am hovering on the brink of another (the ninth). The reason I want the stanzas again which I sent you is, that as these cantos contain a full detail (like the storm in Canto Second) of the siege and

---

[1] *L.J.*, VI. 96.

assault of Ismael, with much of sarcasm on those butchers in large business, your mercenary soldiery, it is a good opportunity of gracing the poem with x x x. With these things and these fellows, it is necessary, in the present clash of philosophy and tyranny, to throw away the scabbard. I know it is against fearful odds ; but the battle must be fought ; and it will be eventually for the good of mankind, whatever it may be for the individual who risks himself.[2]

This language might well seem exaggerated if used by some other poets, but we know that Byron had been ready to fight for Italian liberty, as he was later ready to fight tyranny in Greece. His metaphors here serve, therefore, to remind us that he now saw poetry as an alternative mode of *action*, as another means by which he could help humanity—not by diverting men and making them forget their sorrows, but by forcing them to see the truth, and rousing them to indignation and rebellion.

In these cantos Byron's basic attitude is not itself new. He insists on the wrongness and futility of fighting for any cause but that of Liberty, he emphasises the waste, suffering, and cruelty of war—the essential inhumanity of the whole business; and these ideas are much the same as those expressed in the third canto of *Childe Harold*. Now, however, they are presented with new power and cogency, which come from Byron's changed techniques and from the different quality of his poetic thinking. In Childe Harold's thoughts on Waterloo only one episode—the night alarm—was recreated with dramatic vividness, and apart from this often-quoted passage Byron tended, in expressing his feelings about the battle, to rely on generalising meditative statements:

> And Ardennes waves above them her green leaves,
> > Dewy with Nature's tear-drops, as they pass—
> > Grieving, if aught inanimate e'er grieves,
> > Over the unreturning brave,—alas !
> > Ere evening to be trodden like the grass
> > Which now beneath them, but above shall grow
> > In its next verdure, when this fiery mass
> > Of living Valour, rolling on the foe
> And burning with high Hope, shall moulder cold and low.

---

[2] *L.J.*, VI. 101.

Last noon beheld them full of lusty life ;—
    Last eve in Beauty's circle proudly gay ;
    The Midnight brought the signal-sound of strife,
    The Morn the marshalling in arms,—the Day
    Battle's magnificently-stern array !
    The thunder-clouds close o'er it, which when rent
    The earth is covered thick with other clay
    Which her own clay shall cover, heaped and pent,
Rider and horse,—friend,—foe,—in one red burial blent ![3]

In these stanzas Byron does communicate his view of war as a purely destructive force and his sense of the pathos of lives being cut short, but he is concerned here only with the general situation of the brave men doomed to die. There is no attempt to show the manner of their deaths, to penetrate the thunder-clouds and watch the actual events of battle, to see the different reactions and fates of the individuals who composed "this fiery mass of living valour," or to analyse the strategy and tactics which controlled their conflict with "the foe"; and this lack of detailed observation and description, this absence of particularity in the narration, makes for a vagueness of effect just where the stanzas should be strongest. Harold's sentiments on Waterloo, indeed, fail to convince us, partly because of the frequent lapses in his style and rhetoric, but also because his views do not seem to emerge from a first-hand knowledge or full apprehension of the events of which he speaks. The condemnation of war in *Don Juan*, on the other hand, triumphantly escapes this weakness, because Byron now enforces his moral judgments by displaying war as it really is— by giving his readers a vivid and detailed account of an actual campaign—by painting, in his own words, "the true portrait of one battle-field."[4] The poem's strength, here as elsewhere, springs from his intense and indefatigable interest in the actual, and from his consequent desire to give an accurate truthful picture of human life.

He had been interested in truth and accuracy even in his early works—in his Eastern tales, for example;[5] but there it had simply been a question of getting the costumes and manners right, whereas now he made a sustained attempt at realism in

[3] *P.W.*, II. 232-3.   [4] *P.W.*, VI. 334.   [5] See Chapter Two, p. 37.

all aspects of the story. Plot, incident, description, character-portrayal, and the poet's own attitude to his narration, were all to be governed by fidelity to truth—by his knowledge of things as they really are.

This was his aim throughout *Don Juan* as a whole, and his treatment of war is not in this respect essentially different from his treatment of love or Society, but it involves some modification of his usual technique: without abandoning his man-of-the-world *persona* he had now to draw on his own wider interests and experiences, and to supplement them with a good deal of specialist information gathered from his reading. He had already perfected this poetic method in the first half of Canto II, where he tried to give a fully realistic description of a shipwreck, utilising his own personal experience of ships and storms at sea, but also guaranteeing the authenticity of his account by basing it on genuine records of such happenings: he told Murray that "[there] was not a *single circumstance* of it *not* taken from *fact*; not, indeed, from any *single* shipwreck, but all from *actual* facts of different wrecks;"[6] and his editors have shown how heavily he was indebted to his reading of various works about disasters and hardships at sea. The result, however, is no mere cento of borrowed phrases or dull catalogue of technicalities and hazards—Byron is completely in control of his material, and he shows great skill in weaving his accumulated facts and details into a fictitious but absorbing narrative, designed to express and emphasise his own vision of reality. He is, for example, characteristically eager to acknowledge and include unpleasant facts as well as pleasant ones—it is this that gives *Don Juan* its variety and truthfulness—and Nature, which was soon to provide an idyllic setting for Haidée and Juan, is here presented as neither benevolent nor beautiful. In describing the terrors of storm and shipwreck Byron insists (in defiance of current romantic fashions) on her apparent cruelty and malevolence:

> 'T was twilight, and the sunless day went down
> Over the waste of waters ; like a veil,
> Which, if withdrawn, would but disclose the frown
> Of one whose hate is masked but to assail.

---

[6] *L.J.*, v. 346.

Thus to their hopeless eyes the night was shown,
    And grimly darkled o'er the faces pale,
And the dim desolate deep : twelve days had Fear
Been their familiar, and now Death was here.[7]

Throughout this episode the elements figure as Man's enemies, and Byron keeps us aware of them as a sinister background to the vagaries of human behaviour which form his main subject:

There's nought, no doubt, so much the spirit calms
    As rum and true religion : thus it was,
Some plundered, some drank spirits, some sung psalms,
    The high wind made the treble, and as bass
The hoarse harsh waves kept time ; fright cured the qualms
    Of all the luckless landsmen's sea-sick maws :
Strange sounds of wailing, blasphemy, devotion,
Clamoured in chorus to the roaring Ocean.[8]

Quotation can hardly do justice to this remarkable experiment in realism, which depends for its success on the cumulative effect of the whole narrative; but Byron's stanzas on the loss of the cutter may serve to exemplify his concern for truth and accuracy in description, his convincing detailed method of narration, and his perception of the contradictory elements in human nature—its paradoxical, sometimes shocking mixture of emotion and physical appetite, of altruism and selfishness:

'T was a rough night, and blew so stiffly yet,
    That the sail was becalmed between the seas,[9]
Though on the wave's high top too much to set,
    They dared not take it in for all the breeze :

---

[7] *P.W.*, VI. 95. (Steffan and Pratt, II. 182 : ". . . o'er their faces pale".)

[8] *P.W.*, VI. 90.

[9] When this detail was queried Byron defended it with an indignant reference both to authority and to his own experience :

"My good Sir ! when the sea runs very high this is the case, as *I know*, but if *my authority* is not enough, see Bligh's account of his run to Timor, after being cut adrift by the mutineers headed by Christian."

"Pray tell me who was the Lubber who put the query ? surely not *you*, Hobhouse ! We have both of us seen too much of the sea for that. You may rely on my using no nautical word not founded on authority, and no circumstances not grounded in reality." (*P.W.*, VI. 98, n.2).

Each sea curled o'er the stern, and kept them wet,
　　And made them bale without a moment's ease,
So that themselves as well as hopes were damped,
　　And the poor little cutter quickly swamped.

Nine souls more went in her : the long-boat still
　　Kept above water, with an oar for mast,
Two blankets stitched together, answering ill
　　Instead of sail, were to the oar made fast ;
Though every wave rolled menacing to fill,
　　And present peril all before surpassed,
They grieved for those who perished with the cutter,
And also for the biscuit-casks and butter.[10]

Touches like this last couplet horrified some readers, who
thought Byron's feelings and sense of humour were perverted.
Keats, for example, on reading the description of the storm in
Don Juan, is said to have thrown down the book and exclaimed
indignantly,

> . . . this gives me the most horrid idea of human nature, that
> a man like Byron should have exhausted all the pleasures of
> the world so compleatly that there was nothing left for him but
> to laugh & gloat over the most solemn & heart rending
> [scenes] of human misery this storm of his is one of the most
> diabolical attempts ever made upon our sympathies, and I
> have no doubt it will fascenate thousands into extreem obduracy
> of heart—the tendency of Byrons poetry is based on a paltry
> originality, that of being new by making solemn things gay &
> gay things solemn. . . .[11]

This, however, is to misinterpret Byron's tone and purpose in
such passages: he was trying to show—now seriously, now
sardonically, but not flippantly—how men really think, feel,
and behave in crises and in sufferings, and for him this meant
exhibiting the comical, grotesque, and shocking aspects of
behaviour, as well as the pathetic and heroic which were
usually to be found in novels or romances. The incongruities
in his account of the wreck are therefore the result, not of
depravity, but of his recognising the complexity and variety

---

[10] *P.W.,* vi. 98-9.
[11] *The Keats Circle : Letters and Papers 1816-1878,* ed. H. E. Rollins, Cambridge
(Massachusetts) 1948, ii. 134.

of human nature, and rejecting the false principle of selection which makes literature falsify life.[12]

Pleased by the success of this experiment, Byron decided to use the same technique for his attack on war.[13] His own experience was much more limited in this field—he had never been a soldier or fought in an action, though he had seen something of the results of war in Spain and the Low Countries; but he had learned a great deal from his reading, and the success of Cantos VII and VIII is largely due to his intelligent choice and skilful use of source material. He had based his narrative on De Castelnau's account of the Siege of Ismail in his *Essai sur l'histoire ancienne et moderne de la Nouvelle Russie*,[14] and he followed this source very closely to ensure his story's accuracy in all particulars. By this means he contrives (in spite of his inexperience) to give the impression of complete familiarity with matters military—he writes like a man about town who has also been a soldier, and who understands the problems of war as well as he does the usages of good Society. Thus after a brief parenthetical apology such as a gentleman would feel obliged to offer, he makes frequent use of military terms and technicalities, which (though culled mainly from De Castelnau) suggest considerable expertise:

> Within the extent of this fortification
> 　A borough is comprised along the height
> Upon the left, which from its loftier station
> 　Commands the city, and upon its site

---

[12] There is only one stanza in which Byron lapses into a flippant derisive tone which would have been perfectly appropriate in *Beppo*, but which constitutes a blemish, a breach of decorum, in his wonderful description of the wreck:

> "All the rest perished ; near two hundred souls
> 　Had left their bodies ; and what's worse, alas !
> When over Catholics the Ocean rolls,
> 　They must wait several weeks before a mass
> Takes off one peck of purgatorial coals,
> 　Because, till people know what's come to pass,
> They won't lay out their money on the dead—
> It costs three francs for every mass that's said." (*P.W.*, VI. 97).

[13] See *L.J.*, VI. 109 : "There is a deal of war—a siege, and all that, in the style, graphical and technical, of the shipwreck in Canto Second, which 'took', as they say in the Row."

[14] *P.W.*, VI. 264. See also E. F. Boyd, *Byron's 'Don Juan'*, New Brunswick 1945, pp. 148-50.

A Greek had raised around this elevation
    A quantity of palisades *upright*,
So placed as to *impede* the fire of those
Who held the place, and to *assist* the foe's.

This circumstances may serve to give a notion
    Of the high talents of this new Vauban :
But the town ditch below was deep as Ocean,
    The rampart higher than you'd wish to hang :
But then there was a great want of precaution
    (Prithee, excuse this engineering slang),
Nor work advanced, nor covered way was there,
To hint, at least, 'Here is no thoroughfare.'

But a stone bastion, with a narrow gorge,
    And walls as thick as most skulls born as yet ;
Two batteries, cap-à-pie, as our St. George,
    Casemated one, and t'other 'a barbette',
Of Danube's bank took formidable charge ;
    While two-and-twenty cannon duly set
Rose over the town's right side, in bristling tier,
Forty feet high, upon a cavalier.[15]

This almost professional display of military knowledge is
accompanied by an awareness, rare in poets, of the sheer
incompetence which soldiers sometimes show in their own trade,
and this gives scope for Byron's typical sardonic humour, which
is used here with complete propriety to bring out the grim
tragi-comedy of both sides' blunders in field-engineering and
in tactics:

Whether it was their engineer's stupidity,
    Their haste or waste, I neither know nor care,
Or some contractor's personal cupidity,
    Saving his soul by cheating in the ware
Of homicide, but there was no solidity
    In the new batteries erected there ;
They either missed, or they were never missed,
And added greatly to the missing list.

---

[15] *P.W.*, vi. 305-6.

A sad miscalculation about distance
  Made all their naval matters incorrect ;
Three fireships lost their amiable existence
  Before they reached a spot to take effect ;
The match was lit too soon, and no assistance
  Could remedy this lubberly defect ;
They blew up in the middle of the river,
While, though 't was dawn, the Turks slept fast as ever.[16]

This ludicrously bungled attack with its indecisive slaughter on both sides is contrasted with conventional ideas of glory, and Byron returns repeatedly to this difference between popular romanticised or sentimental views of war and the true facts of what happens on a battlefield. He is indeed so interested in the practical problems and psychology of soldiering, that he (rather paradoxically) finds himself admiring Suvarov as a fellow realist, who knows that victory and fame are to be won not by high aspirations only, but by an efficient training programme for the assaulting troops:

And every difficulty being dispelled,
  Glory began to dawn with due sublimity,
While Souvaroff, determined to obtain it,
Was teaching his recruits to use the bayonet.

It is an actual fact, that he, commander
  In chief, in proper person deigned to drill
The awkward squad, and could afford to squander
  His time, a corporal's duty to fulfil ;
Just as you'd break a sucking salamander
  To swallow flame, and never take it ill :
He showed them how to mount a ladder (which
Was not like Jacob's) or to cross a ditch.

Also he dressed up, for the nonce, fascines
  Like men with turbans, scimitars, and dirks,
And made them charge with bayonet these machines,
  By way of lesson against actual Turks ;
And when well practised in these mimic scenes,
  He judged them proper to assail the works,—
(At which your wise men sneered in phrases witty),
He made no answer—but he took the city.[17]

---

   [16] *P.W.*, VI. 310-11.   [17] *P.W.*, VI. 319-20.

The syntactical and rhythmical development of this last stanza works towards a complete endorsement of Suvarov's attitude, which on this point coincides with Byron's own, but usually the general is viewed more critically. His efficiency is too ruthless and his realism too cynically callous, for Suvarov (like History) sees men in the gross,[18] whereas the poet is concerned with individual human beings, and realises what a casualty list means in terms of human suffering. This knowledge is the basis of Byron's attack on "Glory." He claims that this great desideratum is a mere illusion, since most "heroes" are unknown or soon forgotten—a fact easily established by citing a few names, English, French, or Russian, from the Siege of Ismail; but his real indictment is that heroes are too often simply "butchers in large business," that glory is won by murdering your fellow-men, that it is of no value to the soldiers who are killed, or to most of those who survive, and that the only people who profit by it are the generals, whose selfishness and cynicism are analysed with an ironic humour much more telling than Childe Harold's rhetoric.[19] And he attacks not only these commanders who exploit the cant of glory, but the civilians who accept it so uncritically: when French or English citizens delight in bulletins of war, it shows that they have no conception of what war is really like; just as when Wordsworth says that Carnage is God's daughter, he betrays his failure to understand what Carnage really means; and it was to force this understanding on his readers that Byron drew *his* picture—detailed, horrifying, and realistic—of a modern battle.

Byron's realism is, however, realistic in the fullest sense, in that he has the honesty to include the good as well as the bad elements in human nature, and although he is attacking the cant of glory he does not fall into the easy mistake of sneering indiscriminately at soldiers and the military virtues—he recognises that in battle men can show great courage, and he gives them credit for it:

> The troops, already disembarked, pushed on
>   To take a battery on the right : the others,
> Who landed lower down, their landing done,
>   Had set to work as briskly as their brothers :

---

[18] *P.W.*, vi. 326-7, 330.   [19] *P.W.*, vi. 334.

> Being grenadiers, they mounted one by one,
> > Cheerful as children climb the breasts of mothers,
> O'er the intrenchment and the palisade,
> Quite orderly, as if upon parade.

> And this was admirable. . . .[20]

The concession does not weaken his indictment of war, but reinforces it by making us feel the fairness and honesty of his procedure; and in the same way he admits the generous impulses which even hardened soldiers feel, without mitigating his account of the horrors of a sack. In his whole treatment of the siege, in fact, Byron avoids oversimplifying the issues, and shows an ability to represent an action not in simple propagandist terms but in all its real complexity. He presents to us the topography and fortifications of Ismail, the tactics of both attackers and defenders, the blunders, failures and successes on each side, the technicalities of war, the appalling loss of life, and, most important of all, the motives and behaviour of the men themselves, from the *naïve* foolhardiness of Juan to the more cautious valour of Johnson the veteran, and the variable conduct of the ordinary soldiers who may come on bravely, run away, and then return to the attack if they find a new leader. Courage, cowardice, cruelty, incompetence, vainglory, generosity, compassion, greed, determination, lust, fanaticism, ambition—all these play their part in Byron's narrative, which carries complete conviction just because he seems to know and fully understand the kind of men, events, and situations which he is describing. Here again, as in the shipwreck episode, the poem's effect is cumulative, and quotations must inevitably fail to convey its total impact, but almost any passage from these cantos will show something of Byron's remarkable understanding of battle conditions and battle psychology, and his equally remarkable gift for expressing it in racy narrative verse.

This realistic portrayal of war is a unique achievement: there is nothing else like it in English poetry, while in prose one has to go to Tolstoy to find a comparable insight into the true nature of battles, with their heroism and excitement on the one hand, their confusion, waste, and horror on the other. And his success in the representation of war is one of the things that

[20] *P.W.*, VI. 334-5.

makes Byron's condemnation so effective: the whole story is told so as to bring out and enforce his views, yet there is no feeling that the evidence is being rigged, for his description of the siege is authentic and convincing, and his comments emerge naturally from the narrative. But equally important is the sureness of his tone, and his soundness of moral judgment as well as of observation: there is nothing of the crude sensationalism, the ghoulish delight in horrors, which had figured so disastrously in *The Siege of Corinth*.[21] We are constantly aware of his humorous mature intelligence, inspiring confidence as well as evoking sympathy; so that when he passes to some stanzas of explicit denunciation, the rhetoric does not have to do all the work itself—the passage, though good in itself, acquires additional force from the detailed narrative it follows and sums up, and also from the whole impression we have formed of the speaker's personality:

> All that the mind would shrink from of excesses—
>   All that the body perpetrates of bad ;
> All that we read—hear—dream, of man's distresses—
>   All that the Devil would do if run stark mad ;
> All that defies the worst which pen expresses,—
>   All by which Hell is peopled, or as sad
> As Hell—mere mortals who their power abuse—
> Was here (as heretofore and since) let loose.

---

[21] E.g. "And he saw the lean dogs beneath the wall
          Hold o'er the dead their Carnival,
          Gorging and growling o'er carcass and limb ;
          They were too busy to bark at him !
          From a Tartar's skull they had stripped the flesh,
          As ye peel the fig when its fruit is fresh ;
          And their white tusks crunched o'er the whiter skull,
          As it slipped through their jaws, when their edge grew dull,
          As they lazily mumbled the bones of the dead,
          When they scarce could rise from the spot where they fed ;
          So well had they broken a lingering fast,
          With those who had fallen for that night's repast.
          And Alp knew, by the turbans that rolled on the sand,
          The foremost of these were the best of his band . . ."
                                                 (*P.W.*, III. 467-8).
Here too Byron was drawing on "fact" : "This spectacle I have seen," he writes in a note, "such as described, beneath the wall of the Seraglio at Constantinople . . ." The effect, however, is not one of scrupulous regard for truth, but of ludicrous exaggeration and a deliberate exploitation of the gruesome. "Despicable stuff," as Gifford said of a later passage. (*P.W.*, III. 494, n.1).

M

If here and there some transient trait of pity
    Was shown, and some more noble heart broke through
Its bloody bond, and saved, perhaps, some pretty
    Child, or an agéd, helpless man or two—
What's this in one annihilated city,
    Where thousand loves, and ties, and duties grew?
Cockneys of London ! Muscadins of Paris !
Just ponder what a pious pastime War is.[22]

The success of these two cantos is unquestionable—they must rank among the finest things that Byron ever wrote. Yet even they are not entirely free from his habitual weaknesses. The limitations, for example, of his man-of-the-world *persona* become painfully apparent when he passes from this terrible indictment of war to a cynically flippant treatment of the rapes which (properly considered) are the culminating horror of a sack:

Much did they slay, more plunder, and no less
    Might here and there occur some violation
In the other line ;—but not to such excess
    As when the French, that dissipated nation,
Takes towns by storm : no causes can I guess,
    Except cold weather and commiseration ;
But all the ladies, save some twenty score,
Were almost as much virgins as before.

Some odd mistakes, too, happened in the dark,
    Which showed a want of lanterns, or of taste—
Indeed the smoke was such they scarce could mark
    Their friends from foes,—besides such things from haste
Occur, though rarely, when there is a spark
    Of light to save the venerably chaste :
But six old damsels, each of seventy years,
Were all deflowered by different grenadiers.

But on the whole their continence was great ;
    So that some disappointment there ensued
To those who had felt the inconvenient state
    Of 'single blessedness', and thought it good

---

[22] *P.W.*, VI. 367.

(Since it was not their fault, but only fate,
     To bear these crosses) for each waning prude
To make a Roman sort of Sabine wedding,
Without the expense and the suspense of bedding.

Some voices of the buxom middle-aged
     Were also heard to wonder in the din
(Widows of forty were these birds long caged)
     'Wherefore the ravishing did not begin !'
But while the thirst for gore and plunder raged,
     There was small leisure for superfluous sin ;
But whether they escaped or no, lies hid
In darkness—I can only hope they did.[23]

This passage taken by itself is very funny, but in its context it strikes a discordant note of frivolous bad taste: it is an upsurge of rakish cynicism, a repudiation of the feelings Byron has just roused, an abandonment of the standards of morality on which his satire has been based. And it can not be justified, like the grotesque or ridiculous features of the shipwreck or the battle, as truth to life, to the checkered nature of our human lot,[24] because these stanzas actually show a falsification of life—a refusal to face the horror of mass rape, or even indeed of individual cases. Byron attacked Suvarov for callousness, for seeing men in the gross, but here he is himself prepared to think of women in the same way ("all the ladies, save some twenty score,/Were almost as much virgins as before"), and to withhold in treating rape the moral sensitivity that he had shown in treating deaths in battle. It is as if the subject of sex jerked him back immediately to his most cynical mood— to the feeling that a man of the world should not take such things seriously; while the joke also provides him with an

---

[23] *P.W.*, vi. 369. The same joke appears (in a less elaborated form) in *The Devil's Drive*, written in 1813 :

> "Then he gazed on a town by besiegers taken.
>   Nor cared he who were winning ;
> But he saw an old maid, for years forsaken,
>   Get up and leave her spinning ;
> And she looked in her glass, and to one that did pass,
>   She said—'pray are the rapes beginning ?' "
>
> (*P.W.*, vii. 25).

[24] *P.W.*, vi. 357.

escape from his own moral intensity, which was probably beginning to embarrass him, and which he thus repudiates (though only for a moment) with his typical defensive irony.

The opposite weakness of romantic sentimentality also appears at one point, when he tries to give a sharper focus to his satire by contrasting Ismail and its horrors with the life of Daniel Boone, "back-woodsman of Kentucky":

> He was not all alone : around him grew
>   A sylvan tribe of children of the chase,
> Whose young, unwakened world was ever new,
>   Nor sword nor sorrow yet had left a trace
> On her unwrinkled brow, nor could you view
>   A frown on Nature's or on human face ;
> The free-born forest found and kept them free,
> And fresh as is a torrent or a tree. . . .
>
> Motion was in their days, Rest in their slumbers,
>   And Cheerfulness the handmaid of their toil ;
> Nor yet too many nor too few their numbers ;
>   Corruption could not make their hearts her soil ;
> The lust which stings, the splendour which encumbers,
>   With the free foresters divide no spoil ;
> Serene, not sullen, were the solitudes
> Of this unsighing people of the woods.
>
> So much for Nature :—by way of variety,
>   Now back to thy great joys, Civilisation !
> And the sweet consequence of large society,
>   War—pestilence—the despot's desolation,
> The kingly scourge, the lust of notoriety,
>   The millions slain by soldiers for their ration,
> The scenes like Catherine's boudoir at threescore,
> With Ismail's storm to soften it the more.[25]

Here we have in an extreme form the same opposition—of Society and Nature—which Byron had used in writing about Haidée's love, but now it is much less acceptable. His ironic realistic scrutiny is not applied here to his own ideal: there is nothing in these stanzas to compare with his account of Zoe's frying eggs, or of Haidée's little follies, or of Lambro's piracies

[25] *P.W.*, VI. 350-1.

which provided the financial basis for life on the island. In discussing Boone, Byron ignores the practical and moral problems of life on an expanding frontier, and his idealisation of the facts depends on his not looking at them too closely, so that the idyll he describes seems unreal, sentimentalised: while attacking the cant of glory he has lapsed into another equally offensive form of cant.

The weakness is, however, only momentary, for his condemnation of war did not depend on this idea of a life of Nature—it was more firmly based on simple decent feelings of respect for ordinary human life and human happiness; and for a contrast to present conditions he looked less to the forests of America than to changes to be brought about by revolution. For Byron tyranny and militarism were almost inseparable: he believed most wars were caused by the ambition, pride and heartlessness of monarchs, whom he portrayed (in Moscow and Constantinople) as having the weaknesses of other men and women, but no corresponding sympathy for their feelings and their sufferings. He argued, therefore, that if despotisms were abolished there would be an end of sanguinary useless wars, and this is why his description of the Siege of Ismail culminates in a kind of revolutionary manifesto, looking forward to an ideal future when kings, tyrants, and their evil deeds will be forgotten, or remembered only as historical curiosities.[26] Here we have the logical conclusion to his views on war and despotism, and it comes with a satisfying affirmative force lacking in the references to Daniel Boone. Rebellion, not romantic yearnings for life in the woods, is the practical solution Byron offers for the evils which he has exposed; and this is far more characteristic of his true self, for in passages like this the satirist becomes the champion of liberty—the poet and man of action are at one.

[26] *P.W.*, VI. 370-1.

XI

Don Juan: Liberty and Politics

YRON's love of liberty and hatred of oppression are among his most attractive features as a man and as a poet, and we are very much aware of them throughout a great part of *Don Juan*. No complete section of the plot, however, is devoted to presenting and elucidating his political ideas: Byron's plans for a continuation of the poem included cantos on the French Revolution and the Greek rebellion,[1] and in these the theme of liberty would have been central, but in *Don Juan* as it stands it figures only in incidental outbursts. Partly as a result of this his views on liberty do not emerge from the poem with the same clarity and force as his ideas on love and war; but there is also some confusion in his treatment of this subject—a confusion which derives from further contradictions in his own beliefs and feelings.

In the nineteenth century Byron became—particularly in the eyes of continental liberals—a symbol of rebellion and of liberty, and the myth was founded on the facts of his life: he had attacked English Society and England's policies, he had written forcefully in the cause of freedom, and by deeds as well as words he had supported subject peoples in their struggles for independence. Yet this popular idea of Byron as the poet of Liberty involved some over-simplification, for he never wholeheartedly repudiated his nation or his class, but remained extremely proud of being a peer of England; and many of his views and sympathies were fundamentally aristocratic, modifying his attitude to "the people," and to the revolution which he sometimes advocated.

In 1812 he had attacked the Framebreakers Bill, defending the rioters as victims of an unjust social and industrial system; and for a time he was associated with the party of Reform; but as we have seen he soon lost his enthusiasm and became

---

[1] See above Chapter Eight, p. 133. And see below, pp. 198, 239-40.

contemptuous of Parliament and its activities. His professed
opinions in these years, however, were usually republican;
and Scott tells how in conversation Byron "used sometimes to
express a high strain of what is now called Liberalism," though
he himself doubted the younger man's basic sincerity in this,
saying that "at heart, [he] would have termed Byron a patrician
on principle."² The truth is that at this time Byron was trying
to have the best of both worlds—living as a man of fashion and
enjoying to the full the liberty which was a privilege of his
class, while thinking (not very seriously, it would seem) of
extending that same privilege to others less fortunate than
himself.

His aristocratic sympathies, however, had a severe blow
when Society rejected him in 1816, and in his resentment at
the separation scandal he expressed a readiness to join in and
assist the revolution if one should break out in England. "Are
you not near the Luddites?" he wrote to Moore, "By the Lord!
if there's a row, but I'll be among ye! How go on the weavers
—the breakers of frames—the Lutherans of politics—the
reformers?" And he enclosed a deliberately provocative song
for these potential rebels:

> As the Liberty lads o'er the sea
> Bought their freedom, and cheaply, with blood,
>   So we, boys, we
>   Will *die* fighting, or *live* free,
> And down with all kings but King Ludd !³

The idea of an English revolution, in which he could play a
part, was often in his mind in the early months of 1817: he
mentioned it in January,⁴ and again in February in terms which
make it clear that he was thinking of armed conflict;⁵ while
in March he spoke of trying to see Rome "before I return to
democratize in England."⁶ In December 1818 he reverted to
the notion: "You may be assured," he wrote to Hobhouse,
"that if anything *serious* is ever required to be done, in which
my insignificance can add an o to the number, I will come
over. . . ";⁷ and in August of the following year he was

---

² *L.J.*, III. 412 : cp. II. 376, n.2.   ³ *L.J.*, IV. 30.
⁴ *L.J.*, IV. 48.   ⁵ *Corr.*, II. 37.
⁶ *Corr.*, II. 38.   ⁷ *Corr.*, II. 96.

writing to Kinnaird in the same vein.[8] The attraction of these
projects lay, partly at least, in their providing him with a
spectacular revenge on the Society that had rejected him—
like Lara he would lead "the people" against his own class,
and we glimpse his motives when he writes, only half-jokingly,
of heading a revolutionary commission to take over his mother-
in-law's estates.[9]

As time went on, however, his ideas changed. By October
1819 his enthusiasm for revolutions had abated, as he thought
of the harm that must be done on both sides;[10] and in January
1820 his reluctance was even more marked—he told Augusta
that he would return if civil war broke out, but that he dreaded
what he might do, and despised the men involved (adding
characteristically that all he desires is "to preserve what
remains of the fortunes of our house").[11] When he came to
think realistically about English politics instead of dreaming
about simplified dramatic conflicts, he found that his feelings
were more complicated than he had supposed. He believed
in certain principles, for example, but disliked and distrusted
many of the men who represented them. For some time now
he had felt an aristocratic distaste for the leaders of the Radicals:
"I am and have been for *reform* always," he told Hobhouse in
June 1819, "but not for the *reformers*. I saw enough of them at
the Hampden Club; Burdett is the only one of them in whose
company a gentleman would be seen, unless at a public meeting,
or in a public-house."[12] When Hobhouse stood as Radical
candidate for Westminster, after being committed to Newgate
for a breach of parliamentary privilege, Byron voiced these
views even more strongly:

> I am out of all patience to see my friends sacrifice themselves
> for a pack of blackguards, who disgust one with their Cause,
> although I have always been a friend to and a Voter for
> reform. . . . If we must have a tyrant, let him at least be
> a gentleman who has been bred to the business, and let us
> fall by the axe and not by the butcher's cleaver.
>
> No one can be more sick of, or indifferent to, politics than

---

[8] *Corr.*, II. 124.   [9] *Ibid.*   [10] *L.J.*, IV. 358.
[11] *L.J.*, IV. 397-98.   [12] *Corr.*, II. 115-16.

I am, if they let me alone ; but if the time comes when a part must be taken one way or the other, I shall pause before I lend myself to the views of such ruffians, although I cannot but approve of a Constitutional amelioration of long abuses.[13]

This is very different from his earlier desire to see an English revolution, and the discovery of the Cato Street Conspiracy intensified his dislike of the Radicals and distrust of their policies:

. . . really, if these sort of awkward butchers are to get the upper hand, *I* for one will declare *off*. I have always been . . . a well-wisher to, and voter for reform in parliament ; but 'such fellows as these, who will never go to the gallows with any credit,' such infamous scoundrels as Hunt and Cobbett, in short, the whole gang (always excepting you, B. and D.)[14] disgust, and make one doubt of the virtue of any principle or politics which can be embraced by similar ragamuffins.

. . . in short, the Radicals seem to be no better than Jack Cade or Wat Tyler, and to be dealt with accordingly.[15]

Byron might still resent English Society's behaviour towards himself, but he had no desire to see the social structure overthrown by men whom he regarded as mere agitators or conspirators. This is evident in his reaction to the news of Peterloo, for while he was shocked at the attack on "the poor

[13] *L.J.*, IV. 410-11. The malicious ballad that Byron wrote on Hobhouse's political adventures shows his aristocratic disdain for "the people" as well as for their leaders :—

"Who are now the people's men,
    My boy Hobbie O ?
There's I and Burdett—Gentlemen
    And blackguard Hunt and Cobby O . . .

When to the mob you make a speech,
    My boy Hobbie O,
How do you keep without their reach
    The watch within your fobby O ?

But never mind such petty things,
    My boy Hobbie O ;
God save the people—damn all Kings,
    So let us Crown the Mobby O !"
                    (*P.W.*, VII. 68-9).

[14] I.e. Hobhouse, Burdett and Douglas Kinnaird.
[15] *Corr.*, II. 138.

starving populace," he would have been quite pleased if the
yeomanry had cut down Orator Hunt;[16] and in May 1820 he
redefined his views in a typical pronouncement: "And pray
don't *mistake me*; it is not against the pure principle of reform
that I protest, but against low, designing, dirty levellers, who
would pioneer their way to a democratical tyranny. . . ."[17]

Byron's new attitude was due not only to his dislike of the
Radicals, but to an involuntary sympathy with the Society
he knew. *Marino Faliero*, written between April and July of
1820, presents in dramatic form some of the difficulties of the
aristocratic-revolutionary. The hero of this play is a nobleman
who has been honoured by his peers and then insulted and
disgraced, and who in his desire for vengeance leads a popular
rebellion. The subject had caught Byron's attention in
February 1817,[18] when his resentment at the separation
scandal was still strong, and when he was intending to return to
England for a civil war. On coming to treat the story in 1820
he still liked the idea of a prince leading a revolution, but he
now did his best to show the tensions in Marino's mind when
he made common cause with the plebeians against his own
class:

DOGE

And is it then decided ! must they die ?

ISRAEL BERTUCCIO

Who ?

DOGE

My own friends by blood and courtesy,
And many deeds and days—the Senators ?

ISRAEL BERTUCCIO

You passed their sentence, and it is a just one.

DOGE

Aye, so it seems, and so it is to *you* ;
You are a patriot, a plebeian Gracchus—
The rebel's oracle, the people's tribune—
I blame you not—you act in your vocation ;

---

[16] *Corr.*, II. 143.   [17] *Corr.*, II. 148 (cp. 144).   [18] *L.J.*, IV. 58-9.

They smote you, and oppressed you, and despised you ;
So have they *me* : but *you* ne'er spake with them ;
You never broke their bread, nor shared their salt ;
You never had their wine-cup at your lips :
You grew not up with them, nor laughed, nor wept,
Nor held a revel in their company ;
Ne'er smiled to see them smile, nor claimed their smile
In social interchange for yours, nor trusted
Nor wore them in your heart of hearts, as I have :
These hairs of mine are grey, and so are theirs,
The elders of the Council : I remember
When all our locks were like the raven's wing,
As we went forth to take our prey around
The isles wrung from the false Mahometan ;
And can I see them dabbled o'er with blood ?
Each stab to them will seem my suicide.[19]

Marino Faliero is not autobiographical, but it deals with circumstances and ideas of peculiar interest to Byron, and it seems probable that passages like this reflect tensions that he himself had felt, or might have felt in such a situation. The whole question of revolution in England produced a conflict between his professed love of liberty (and a desire for vengeance) on the one hand, and his essentially aristocratic sympathies and outlook on the other.

No such conflict was induced, however, by the spectacle of subject nations struggling for independence; and from early in 1820 he became more deeply involved in movements for national liberation. This was mainly because, living abroad, he found these movements actually going on around him, while he also had the fact of tyranny before his eyes. In *Childe Harold*, Canto IV, he had written bitterly about the Austrian domination of Italy, and now as a result of his close friendship with the Gambas he entered into Carbonari plots against the foreign tyrants. He was prepared to fight in this cause if it came to open war, and indeed he welcomed the prospect of decisive action with immediate and spectacular results, in contrast to the wearisome routine procedures of English politics. "The Spanish business has set all Italy a constitutioning," he wrote to Kinnaird, "and they won't get it without some *fechting*, as

[19] *P.W.*, IV. 407-8 (cp. 366-7, 391-2, 400, 402-3, 408-9).

we Scottish say. Now this being likely, I shall stay to see what turns up, and perhaps take a turn amongst them, instead of coming to hear so much, and to see so little done, as seems to be your Anglo-fashion at present."[20] The sheer impotence of the Opposition in these years of reaction does much to explain Byron's disillusionment with English politics, but he was in any case temperamentally unfitted for a parliamentary career—". . . the tame, ordinary vicissitude of public affairs," as Moore said, "having but little in it to stimulate a mind like his, whose sympathies nothing short of a crisis seemed worthy to interest."[21] He may have been a little envious of Hobhouse's political activity; but plans for an Italian insurrection offered him the chance of playing a more dramatic part, and the whole project caught his imagination as he compared it to other heroic fights for independence:

> If the Neapolitans have but a single Massaniello amongst them, they will beat the bloody butchers of the crown and sabre. Holland, in worse circumstances, beat the Spains and Philips ; America beat the English ; Greece beat Xerxes ; and France beat Europe, till she took a tyrant ; South America beats her old vultures out of their nest ; and, if these men are but firm in themselves, there is nothing to shake them from without.[22]

In Italy, moreover, the political issues were clear-cut—the rights and wrongs were obvious. The people were rebelling against tyrants, the nation was fighting a foreign oppressor, and Byron was wholeheartedly on the Italian side: ". . . the *Powers* mean to war with the peoples," he wrote in his diary for January 13th, 1821: "The intelligence seems positive—let it be so—they will be beaten in the end. The king-times are fast finishing. There will be blood shed like water, and tears like mist; but the peoples will conquer in the end. I shall not live to see it, but I foresee it."[23]

Here he does not distinguish between freedom from a foreign power and freedom from despotic rulers—such distinctions were unnecessary when the Italian people were rebelling

[20] *Corr.*, II. 141.
[22] *L.J.*, v. 188-9 (cp. 185, 205, 206).
[21] Moore, *Life*, p. 467.
[23] *L.J.*, v. 173.

against foreign despots. But in some of his remarks on liberty[24] he fails to distinguish between these two freedoms and the separate problem of freedom for the masses in a country with constitutional government and an hierarchical social structure. The freedom which he wanted for himself, and which he enjoyed to a large extent as an English nobleman, was a complete freedom from restraint, whether democratic or despotic; but he had no clear ideas about the implications of giving this kind of freedom to everybody. Indeed the question did not really interest him—in the last years of his life his main political preoccupations were the Italian and Greek bids for independence, and he paid much less attention to the problems presented by home politics. When he did speak about them his lack of serious thought on the subject gave an instability to his opinions, and one finds him fluctuating between different and opposing views.[25] "It is still more difficult," he wrote in May 1821, "to say which form of Government is the *worst*—all are so bad. As for democracy, it is the worst of the whole; for what is (*in fact*) democracy? an Aristocracy of Blackguards."[26] By October he had come to think a republic inevitable, and he was sorry for it,[27] but sometimes he could write about the idea with enthusiasm: "There is nothing left for Mankind but a Republic, and I think that there are hopes of such. The two Americas (South and North) have it; Spain and Portugal approach it; all thirst for it. Oh Washington!"[28] Yet a republic did not necessarily mean democracy: it could be an oligarchic, even an aristocratic, form of government which kept power in the hands of those best fitted to exercise it, and Byron inclined to this ideal, telling Parry that he would be prepared to fight in defence of his class if it were attacked by any party or faction at home.[29] In English politics, in fact,

---

[24] E.g. *Corr.*, II. 144.

[25] Cp. Lady Blessington, *Conversations*, pp. 343-4 : "I have heard him assert opinions one day, and maintain the most opposite, with equal warmth, the day after : this arises not so much from insincerity, as from being wholly governed by the feeling of the moment : he has no fixed principle of conduct or of thought, and the want of it leads him into errors and inconsistencies. . . ."

[26] *L.J.*, v. 405-6.

[27] *Corr.*, II. 203.

[28] *L.J.*, v. 462.

[29] Parry, *Last Days*, pp. 173-4.

his loyalties were confused and contradictory: "Born an aristocrat," he wrote, "and naturally one by temper, with the greater part of my present property in the funds, what have *I* to gain by a revolution?"[30]   And though he went on to say that revolution is inevitable, it is clear from his letters and conversations that he viewed the prospect with mixed feelings.

It is not surprising, therefore, that his attitude should vary in *Don Juan*.   Sometimes he thinks of the poem as a contribution to the cause of liberty, inspiring oppressed peoples to rebellion; and he speaks of revolutions and republics as the sole alternatives to futile wars and cruel despotisms:

> But never mind ;—'God save the King !' and *Kings* !
> For if *he* don't, I doubt if *men* will longer—
> I think I hear a little bird, who sings
> The people by and by will be the stronger :
> The veriest jade will wince whose harness wrings
> So much into the raw as quite to wrong her
> Beyond the rules of posting,—and the mob
> At last falls sick of imitating Job.
>
> At first it grumbles, then it swears, and then,
> Like David, flings smooth pebbles 'gainst a Giant ;
> At last it takes to weapons such as men
> Snatch when Despair makes human hearts less pliant.
> Then comes 'the tug of war ;'—'t will come again,
> I rather doubt ; and I would fain say 'fie on't,'
> If I had not perceived that Revolution
> Alone can save the earth from Hell's pollution.[31]

These stanzas evoke full emotional assent, occurring as they do in a narrative which brings home to us the horrors of war, and the dreadful fact that wars are often fought only to satisfy a tyrant's whim.   (The hint of reluctance in the third last line has the effect of strengthening the passage, by showing that its liberalism is far from facile—it suggests that Byron knows about all the disadvantages of revolution, but has come in spite of this to see it as the only possible course of action.)

[30] *L.J.*, VI. 388.
[31] *P.W.*, VI. 345-6.

Sometimes, on the other hand, his emphasis is different, and while still asserting his hostility to despotisms, he expresses definite distrust of full democracy or mob-rule:

> . . . I will war, at least in words (and—should
>   My chance so happen—deeds), with all who war
> With Thought ;—and of Thought's foes by far most rude,
>   Tyrants and sycophants have been and are.
> I know not who may conquer : if I could
>   Have such a prescience, it should be no bar
> To this my plain, sworn, downright detestation
> Of every despotism in every nation.

> It is not that I adulate the people :
>   Without *me*, there are demagogues enough,
> And infidels, to pull down every steeple,
>   And set up in their stead some proper stuff.
> Whether they may sow scepticism to reap Hell,
>   As is the Christian dogma rather rough,
> I do not know ;—I wish men to be free
> As much from mobs as kings—from you as me. [32]

This wish is perfectly reasonable—Byron was clearsighted enough to see that individual liberties could be threatened as much by the populace as by a king; but the *effect* of this second stanza is to modify the passionate conviction of the first, and though he goes on to inveigh against slavery, urging the "Peoples" to rebel against their tyrants, this passage leaves us with the impression of an unresolved conflict in the writer's mind.

This appears again when his description of the lights of London makes him think of the French revolutionaries' use of *their* lamp-posts as gallows:

> The line of lights, too, up to Charing Cross,
>   Pall Mall, and so forth, have a coruscation
> Like gold as in comparison to dross,
>   Matched with the Continent's illumination,
> Whose cities Night by no means deigns to gloss.
>   The French were not yet a lamp-lighting nation,
> And when they grew so—on their new-found lantern,
> Instead of wicks, they made a wicked man turn.

---

[32] *P.W.*, VI. 381-2.

A row of Gentlemen along the streets
　　Suspended may illuminate mankind,
As also bonfires made of country seats ;
　　But the old way is best for the purblind :
The other looks like phosphorus on sheets,
　　A sort of *ignis fatuus* to the mind,
Which, though 't is certain to perplex and frighten,
Must burn more mildly ere it can enlighten.[33]

The first three lines of this second stanza seem to imply that the experiment is well worth making, since mankind is infinitely more important than the gentlemen, but the next line shows a curious shift of feeling.　At first one is tempted to read it ironically: if "the purblind" are the aristocracy, the old way is obviously best for them, but not for the people; if "the purblind" are the people, the old way may *seem* best to them, but in fact it is not.　Both these readings are, however, ruled out by what follows, for the next few lines make it clear that "the purblind" *are* the people and that Byron is not being ironical—he is saying that since the people are purblind, the old way is genuinely better, for the French method is likely to do much more harm than good.　The last line is again ambiguous: it might mean that good may come of the harm, or that it would be better if the harm never took place.　So that even in this one stanza we can see Byron at once attracted and repelled by the idea of revolution, with the ambiguity and fluctuations in his feeling mirrored in the verse.

Then in another mood he admits that his republicanism springs from a rebellious temperament, rather than from political convictions:

　　　　. . . I was born for opposition.

But then 't is mostly on the weaker side ;
　　So that I verily believe if they
Who now are basking in their full-blown pride
　　Were shaken down, and 'dogs had had their day,'
Though at the first I might perchance deride
　　Their tumble, I should turn the other way,
And wax an ultra-royalist in Loyalty,
Because I hate even democratic Royalty. [34]

---

[33] *P.W.*, VI. 435.　　　　[34] *P.W.*, VI. 550.

This reminds one of an attitude recorded in Byron's Journal of 1813-14: "As for me," he had written, ". . . I have simplified my politics into an utter detestation of all existing governments; and, as it is the shortest and most agreeable and summary feeling imaginable, the first moment of an universal republic would convert me into an advocate for single and uncontradicted despotism."[35] Childish enough. And yet even here one cannot say that Byron simply liked to be "agin the government," for his very next sentence shows that there were intellectual as well as temperamental reasons for his cynicism: "The fact is," he goes on, "riches are power, and poverty is slavery all over the earth, and one sort of establishment is no better nor worse for a *people* than another."[36] Here his awareness of an economic basis for personal liberty was difficult to reconcile with his simpler political concepts, and similar problems arise in *Don Juan*—he can see, for example, that even the republics and revolutionaries whom he admires are dependent ultimately on the great financiers:

> Who hold the balance of the World? Who reign
> O'er congress, whether royalist or liberal?
> Who rouse the shirtless patriots of Spain?
> (That make old Europe's journals 'squeak and gibber' all)
> Who keep the World, both old and new, in pain
> Or pleasure? Who make politics run glibber all?
> The shade of Buonaparte's noble daring?—
> Jew Rothschild, and his fellow-Christian, Baring.
>
> Those, and the truly liberal Lafitte,
> Are the true Lords of Europe. Every loan
> Is not merely a speculative hit,
> But seats a Nation or upsets a Throne.
> Republics also get involved a bit;
> Columbia's stock hath holders not unknown
> On 'Change; and even thy silver soil, Peru,
> Must get itself discounted by a Jew.[37]

Here we have his characteristic urge to penetrate appearances and see things as they really are, and disconcerting insights of

---

[35] *L.J.*, II. 381.
[36] *Ibid.* Cp. *L.J.*, II. 329 : "I don't know what liberty means,—never having seen it,—but wealth is power all over the world. . . ."
[37] *P.W.*, VI. 456-7 : cp. V. 573-4.

N

this kind are among the best things in *Don Juan*. But though he was capable of such perceptions, Byron presents them incidentally, without fully assimilating them or working out their implications; and he makes no attempt to reconcile this economic realism with his habitual beliefs, although it seems to undermine the values (of liberty etc.) which he has been presenting to us.

Byron had in fact little capacity or inclination for sustained coherent reasoning—"Whenever he reflects, he is a child," said Goethe—and although he was always interested in politics and religion, he never thought out his ideas on either. He writes therefore from his feelings of the moment, rather than from any definite philosophy. As Parry remarked:

> His hatred . . . of any particular form of government, arose not from any deduction of reasoning, but from some palpable evidence of injustice, cruelty, and oppression. His opinions were the results of his feelings, and were what rigid logicians call prejudices. They were formed, as I have often heard him say, though my expressions fall short of his vigorous language, from what he had seen and felt, and not from any theory.[38]

This tends to confirm my diagnosis of his weaknesses, but it also points to compensatory strengths—to the deep emotional conviction Byron felt on many issues that fell within the range of his experience. He had actually seen the effects of tyranny and national subjection, and he *knew* that they were evil, so that he was able to denounce them passionately and wholeheartedly. In "The Isles of Greece," for example, the minstrel expresses an intense love for his country and a patriotic sense of her heroic past, together with hatred of slavery and shame at the degradation of the modern Greeks: it is a moving hymn to Liberty—an example of Byron's "public" poetry at its best. Then he hated despots for their callous delight in war and their indifference to human suffering, and the cantos on the siege of Ismail show his capacity for generous indignation as he calls on the people to rebel against their cruel masters. He was, furthermore, acutely aware of Britain's responsibility for the present state of Europe, and when he came to deal

[38] Parry, *Last Days*, p. 211.

directly with his native country, after his attacks on war and
despotism, his first thoughts were of the part she had played
in recent Continental history—by helping to restore old
dynasties, and by supporting reactionary governments, the
Land of the Free had become the greatest enemy of Freedom,
and Byron reproaches her with genuine regret:

> I've no great cause to love that spot of earth,
>   Which holds what *might have been* the noblest nation ;
> But though I owe it little but my birth,
>   I feel a mixed regret and veneration
> For its decaying fame and former worth.
>   Seven years (the usual term of transportation)
> Of absence lay one's old resentments level,
> When a man's country's going to the devil.
>
> Alas ! could she but fully, truly, know
>   How her great name is now throughout abhorred ;
> How eager all the Earth is for the blow
>   Which shall lay bare her bosom to the sword ;
> How all the nations deem her their worst foe,
>   That worse than *worst of foes*, the once adored
> False friend, who held out Freedom to Mankind,
> And now would chain them—to the very *mind* ;—
>
> Would she be proud, or boast herself the free,
>   Who is but first of slaves ? The nations are
> In prison,—but the gaoler, what is he ?
>   No less a victim to the bolt and bar.
> Is the poor privilege to turn the key
>   Upon the captive, Freedom ? He's as far
> From the enjoyment of the earth and air
> Who watches o'er the chain, as they who wear.[39]

The perception in this last stanza—that oppression limits and
corrupts the oppressor as well as the oppressed—is striking,
original, and true. (One is continually being surprised at the
power of Byron's mind in individual insights, even though it
lacks co-ordinating power.) His repeated attacks on England's
foreign policy are cogent and consistent, for he wholeheartedly
condemns its effect on other countries' hopes of freedom; and

[39] *P.W.*, vi. 420.

he sums up her imperial and colonial record by saying that Englishmen have "butchered half the earth, and bullied t'other."[40] In all these cases Byron figures unmistakably and unambiguously as the poet of liberty, compelling our respect and admiration, and *Don Juan* would be infinitely poorer if it did not have these passages of generous political indignation.

His class loyalties tend most to affect the satire when he comes to discuss England herself, for he shows surprisingly little inclination to attack political and social conditions there. Juan's starry-eyed soliloquy on Shooter's Hill is ludicrously cut short by the footpads, but here Byron is using his deflatory technique to achieve a merely humorous effect, rather than to make a satiric point: the robbers certainly prove England is much less secure a place than Juan thought, but their presence does not necessarily invalidate his rhapsody on the constitution.[41] This rhapsody is perhaps discredited by its very fulsomeness, but Byron goes on to insist that Britain is supremely fortunate in the relation of her monarchy to Parliament and people.

> He saw, however, at the closing session,
> > That noble sight, when *really* free the nation,
> A King in constitutional possession
> > Of such a Throne as is the proudest station,
> Though Despots know it not—till the progression
> > Of Freedom shall complete their education.
> 'T is not mere Splendour makes the show august
> To eye or heart—it is the People's trust.[42]

If this stanza's second line implies that England was not "really" free, Byron makes no attempt to follow up the implication. In a later canto he adopts a very different tone, deriding politicians' cant, and suggesting that Parliament is far from being the institution Juan thought it:

> Lord Henry was a great electioneerer,
> > Burrowing for boroughs like a rat or rabbit.
> But county contests cost him rather dearer,
> > Because the neighbouring Scotch Earl of Giftgrabbit

---

[40] *P.W.*, VI. 424.   [41] *P.W.*, VI. 429-30.   [42] *P.W.*, VI. 478.

Had English influence, in the self-same sphere here ;
   His son, the Honourable Dick Dicedrabbit,
Was member for the 'other interest' (meaning
The same self-interest, with a different leaning).[43]

But the Radical suggestion of this final couplet is never developed. The truth is that home politics were no longer one of Byron's main concerns, and his indifference is reflected in the satire. There are references to the use of cavalry against crowds,[44] to the catching of poachers in steel traps,[45] and so on, but these are incidental details which do not cohere into any major criticism of England's social and political system. He speaks once of having

    seen some nations, like o'erloaded asses,
Kick off their burthens—meaning the high classes,[46]

but on the whole he accepts the hierarchical structure of society without questioning its validity. From the time Don Juan reaches England the main subject is the manners and the morals of the aristocracy—not the aristocracy's relation to "the people." Byron quietly shelves the problem of liberty, and leaves himself free to write, with a unique blend of knowledge, sympathy, detachment, and contempt, of the world in which he had once moved. The deep ambivalence of his attitude towards the English aristocracy finds adequate expression, and produces admirable social comedy, once he abandons the political preoccupations which involved him in such difficulties, both emotional and intellectual.

[43] *P.W.*, vi. 593.   [44] *P.W.*, vi. 453.
[45] *P.W.*, vi. 591.   [46] *P.W.*, vi. 453.

XII

Don Juan: The Poet and Society

IN the later cantos of *Don Juan* Byron's theme is the life led by the English aristocracy. This had figured throughout the poem in satirical digressions and in comments linking the immediate narrative to the Great World Byron knew so well; but now he takes that world as his main subject.

This had been among his plans early in 1821,[1] and he may have been encouraged later in the same year by "John Bull's" advising him to bring the Don to England, so that he could make full use of his unrivalled knowledge of Society.[2] Medwin has a story of Byron's mentioning this project even while Teresa's ban was still in force:

> I shall next draw a town and country life at home, which will give me room for life, manners, scenery, &c. I will make him neither a dandy in town, nor a fox-hunter in the country. He shall get into all sorts of scrapes, and at length end his career in France. Poor Juan shall be guillotined in the French Revolution![3]

Yet although he had been toying with this idea for some time now, Byron had probably not planned these cantos even in outline; and when he did embark on them he seems to have

---

[1] See Chapter Eight, pp. 133-4.

[2] "Scotland . . . is and will remain Sir Walter's. And what, you will say, is mine ? I will tell you, Lord Byron : England is yours, if you choose to make it so.—I do not speak of the England of days past, or of the England of days to come, but of the England of the day that now is . . . . There is nobody but yourself who has any chance of conveying to posterity a true idea of the *spirit* of England in the days of his Majesty George IV. Mr. Wordsworth may write fifty years about his 'dalesmen' ; if he paints them truly, it is very well ; if untruly, it is no matter : but you know what neither Mr. Wordsworth nor any Cumberland stamp-master ever can know. You know the society of England,—you know what English gentlemen are made of, and you very well know what English ladies are made of ; and . . . that *knowledge* is a much more precious thing . . . than any *notion* you or any other Englishman ever can acquire either of Italians, or Spaniards, or Greeks." *John Bull's 'Letter to Lord Byron'*, ed. A. L. Strout, pp. 95-6 (cp. pp. 98-9).

[3] Medwin, *Conversations*, pp. 250-1.

found himself with an unforeseen wealth of material, for the scale and pace of the poem are drastically altered—no fewer than six of its sixteen cantos are devoted to the English episode, which even then is far from being complete. This more extended treatment is not altogether an improvement, for these cantos were written very hurriedly, and brilliant as they undoubtedly are, they show the poem's increasing tendency to formlessness. The story loses its former impetus and languishes, while Byron deals discursively with the world in which he had once moved like Juan; and in spite of his own critical allegiances, there are times when he seems guilty of what Arnold calls "the modern English habit (too much encouraged by Wordsworth) of using poetry as a channel for thinking aloud, instead of making anything."[4] His creative powers are strong as ever; his style is a constant though varied delight; and *Don Juan* never ceases to exhilarate and entertain the reader; yet one often feels the absence of the *shaping* spirit of Byron's imagination, and the lack of a controlling sense of purpose. This results not only in formal and architectural weaknesses, but in a reduction of the poem's satiric force, for Byron often fails to recognise basic confusions in his feelings towards Society, and he therefore shows some uncertainty about his own intention in these cantos.

Sometimes he thought of himself as a satirist of the traditional kind, writing with a serious didactic purpose: "*Don Juan*," he declared on one occasion, "will be known by and bye, for what it is intended,—a *Satire* on *abuses* of the present states of Society, and not an eulogy of vice";[5] and he told Dr Kennedy that his object was

'To remove the cloke, which the manners and maxims of society . . . throw over their secret sins, and shew them to the world as they really are. You have not,' added he, 'been so much in high and noble life as I have been ; but if you had fully entered into it, and seen what was going on, you would have felt convinced that it was time to unmask the specious hypocrisy, and shew it in its native colours . . . .
It is impossible you can believe the higher classes of society

---

[4] *Unpublished Letters of Matthew Arnold*, ed. Arnold Whitridge, New Haven 1923, p. 17.   [5] *L.J.*, VI. 155.

worse than they are in England, France, and Italy, for no
language can sufficiently paint them.'[6]

Pronouncements similar in tone occur from time to time in
the poem itself, with Byron threatening to expose and castigate
vice like another Juvenal:

> He paused—and so will I ; as doth a crew
>   Before they give their broadside. By and by,
> My gentle countrymen, we will renew
>   Our old acquaintance ; and at least I'll try
> To tell you truths *you* will not take as true,
>   Because they are so ;—a male Mrs. Fry,
> With a soft besom will I sweep your halls,
> And brush a web or two from off the walls.
>
> Oh Mrs. Fry ! Why go to Newgate ? Why
>   Preach to *poor* rogues ? And wherefore not begin
> With Carlton, or with other houses ? Try
>   Your hand at hardened and imperial Sin.[7]

Or again, with a slight change of emphasis:

> But now I'm going to be immoral ; now
>   I mean to show things really as they are,
> Not as they ought to be : for I avow,
>   That till we see what's what in fact, we're far
> From much improvement with that virtuous plough
>   Which skims the surface, leaving scarce a scar
> Upon the black loam long manured by Vice,
> Only to keep its corn at the old price.[8]

Such statements of intention are, however, unreliable as
pointers to his actual achievement in these cantos. Certainly
he tries, very successfully, "to show things really as they are,"
but his attitude is for the most part less severely moralistic than
these passages suggest. The vices, follies and absurdities which
he exposes do not rouse in him the *saeva indignatio* he showed in
his attack on war, and the satire here is in a fundamental sense
less serious—because less morally intense—than it was in
Cantos VII and VIII:

---

[6] Kennedy, *Conversations on Religion*, pp. 163-4.
[7] *P.W.*, VI. 425.   [8] *P.W.*, VI. 466.

My Muse, the butterfly hath but her wings,
    Nor stings, but flits through ether without aim,
Alighting rarely :—were she but a hornet,
Perhaps there might be vices which would mourn it.[9]

But usually she isn't, and they don't.   The satire is thus curiously unstable, based as it is not on any firm belief or principle, but on Byron's fluctuating feelings, partly critical and hostile, partly tolerant and sympathetic, towards English aristocratic life: as a reformed rake, but not altogether a repentant one, he obviously found it difficult to decide on any definite satiric attitude.   In this respect he differed radically from Pope, in spite of his great admiration for the latter: the Augustan, without any trace of inconsistency, was at once a member and a critic of Society—he identified himself with the best traditions, social, intellectual, moral, and religious, of his age, and he attacked vice, folly, and bad taste as aberrations from the standards these provided.   Byron sometimes seems— and claims—to be doing just the same, but his moral values are less firmly held than Pope's, and he often betrays by his tone and comments an affinity with not the best but the most raffish elements in *his* Society.   In his reflexions on Blue-stockings, for example, he appears less as a satirist of the classic type than as a cynical dandy, a sexual opportunist, a man wholly of the world which he so frequently professes to despise:

I don't mean that they are passionless, but quite
    The contrary ; but then 't is in the head ;
Yet as the consequences are as bright
    As if they acted with the heart instead,
What after all can signify the site
    Of ladies' lucubrations ? So they lead
In safety to the place for which you start,
What matters if the road be head or heart ?[10]

This stanza is, of course, amusing, but it is also symptomatic of his failure to maintain a serious satiric role for any length of time—a failure which appears again in his treatment of Aurora Raby.

[9] *P.W.*, VI. 509.   [10] *P.W.*, VI. 437-8.

Aurora is exceptionally interesting, not as a successful character creation, but as an attempt on Byron's part to establish a religious-moral ideal of the kind we find in Pope, in place of the "romantic" values of some of the former cantos. His use of the Nature-Society antithesis was poetically convincing in the Haidée episode, but much less so in the references to Daniel Boone, and it comes to seem incongruous in a satirist whose very idiom and characteristic modes of feeling derive mainly from his social experience. Sometimes he is remarkably successful in combining his "aristocratic" qualities with less extreme romantic attitudes:

> The London winter and the country summer
>   Were well nigh over. 'T is perhaps a pity,
> When Nature wears the gown that doth become her,
>   To lose those best months in a sweaty city,
> And wait until the nightingale grows dumber,
>   Listening debates not very wise or witty,
> Ere patriots their true *country* can remember ;—
> But there's no shooting (save grouse) till September.[11]

But this contrast between town and country is very different from the absolute opposition of Nature and Civilisation. The latter antithesis could be preserved, and the bad firmly equated with the social or the civilised, only by his averting his gaze from everything that was good in society and civilisation; and while Byron might do this occasionally, he had too intelligent and questioning a mind to rest content for long with such an over-simplifying "literary" convention. He did use it again in *The Island* (that rag-bag of old Byronic themes),[12] but he thought very little of this poem—in it he was pandering to some extent to "the reigning stupidity" of public taste, and he wrote contemptuously about the South Sea Paradise he had portrayed, with its idyll of natural love: "You think higher of readers than I do," he told Leigh Hunt, "but I will bet you a flask of Falernum that the most stilted parts of the political *Age of Bronze*, and the most pamby portions of the Toobonai Islanders, will be the most agreeable to the enlightened public. . . . "[13] This awareness of his own poetic faults (as well as of

---

[11] *P.W.*, VI. 493.   [12] E.g. *P.W.*, V. 611.   [13] *L.J.*, VI. 164-5.

his readers' weaknesses) was probably responsible for Byron's
now abandoning his Nature ideal, and going on to delineate in
the last two cantos of *Don Juan* an ideal of womanhood attain-
able *within* society, though free from all its vices and illusions.
Aurora Raby is different from Haidée, but as perfect in her
own way:[14] she is a product not of Nature, but of the best in
her civilisation—having been brought up a strict Catholic she
is deeply virtuous and quite unworldly, looking with detachment on the follies and the vanities of the *beau monde*. She
provides a standard, higher and finer than the man of the
world's, by which Adeline and her circle can be judged, and
we are made to see their affairs, their flirtations, their malicious
gossip, through her eyes; while by her purity and beauty she
revives Juan's nobler emotions, which had been overlaid by
his varied sexual adventures.[15]

These ideal feelings are aroused, however, only to be once
again deflated. Juan passes from sublime musings about
Aurora to an involvement with the Duchess of Fitz-Fulke, and
this is perfectly in keeping with Byron's view of human nature
—Juan's inconsistency, his inability to resist temptation, is
another case of the inadequacy of man's state to his conceptions.
Yet there is a deeper, less defensible inconsistency in Byron's
own attitude to these events: he has been at pains to present
Aurora as the embodiment of virtues which he seems to
reverence, yet he shows no grief or disapproval at the hero's
suddenly abandoning them—he views Juan's latest fall from
grace with the same tolerance that he had shown for the affair
with Dudu in the harem. Life, he seems to say, is like this,
and he personally finds the spectacle amusing. So that
although *Don Juan* ends before Aurora Raby has had time to
play much part, it looks as if she represents not any profoundly
apprehended values, but another sentimentalised ideal—an
ideal which does not affect his basic attitudes to life, or which
affects them only for brief moments. Byron really wants to
have it both ways—to be both a moral satirist and an amusingly
cynical man of the world; and the poem reflects this
fundamental ambiguity of outlook.

Its greatness in these later cantos really lies, not as he

[14] *P.W.*, VI. 560.   [15] *P.W.*, VI. 603.

sometimes claimed, in its denunciation of sin and hypocrisy, but in its brilliantly witty survey of Society, and in the presentation of his own mixed feelings towards it.

Here we can profitably return to the comparison with Pope, who in *The Rape of the Lock* (his most light-hearted satire) had had somewhat similar intentions. In that poem he used the mock-heroic primarily for its normative potentialities: he was trying to make people see an incident in its true proportions, and he therefore chose a mode of satire which deliberately falsifies proportions but keeps us aware of the distortion—since these Catholic families were intent on making a mountain out of a molehill, he would write a poem the formula for which would be "the molehill seen as mountain." But he also uses the mock-heroic to express his feelings (of mixed admiration and amusement) for Belinda and her circle. Their life is trivial and foolish, and Pope is fully aware of this, but it is also elegant, gracious, luxurious, civilised, so that it seems at once attractive and absurd; and to do justice to the delicate poise of his reactions to it, Pope adopts the mock-heroic style, which demands a double level of response by simultaneously elevating the subject and implying that the elevation is exaggerated—by praising and implying a reservation in the praise.

Byron probably did not think of *The Rape of the Lock* as a model for his own satiric task, but he admired it, and he sometimes uses this style to achieve effects not unlike Pope's—to convey, for example, his sense of both the glitter and the shoddiness, the intoxicating bustle and the foolish pretentiousness of a London evening in the *beau monde*:

> Then dress, then dinner, then awakes the world !
>   Then glare the lamps, then whirl the wheels, then roar
> Through street and square fast flashing chariots hurled
>   Like harnessed meteors ; then along the floor
> Chalk mimics painting ; then festoons are twirled ;
>   Then roll the brazen thunders of the door,
> Which opens to the thousand happy few
> An earthly Paradise of *Or Molu*.[16]

The feature of mock-heroic most congenial to Byron was its bathetic contrasts, and some of his best effects are gained by

[16] *P.W.*, vi. 447-8.

passing from the innocuous, the literary, the conventional, to the unexpected or malicious, as in

> Fair virgins blushed upon him ; wedded dames
> Bloomed also in less transitory hues. . . .[17]

While often the incongruous juxtapositions are so neat, so pregnant, and so witty, that in detailed effects he seems to rival Pope on his own ground—in lines like these, for example:

> Preserving partridges and pretty wenches
> Are puzzles to the most precautious benches.[18]

This couplet operates in exactly the same way as

> Whether the Nymph shall break *Diana's* Law,
> Or some frail *China* Jar receive a Flaw,
> Or stain her Honour, or her new Brocade. . . .[19]

"Partridges and pretty wenches" pleases us by the incongruity, which is intensified by the terms being linked so closely by their juxtaposition, by alliteration, and by syntax.[20] But beneath the surface incongruity we perceive resemblances: just as virginity *can* be compared to a frail china jar, or honour to a new brocade—the one is flawed and the other stained so easily, and the damage once done can never be repaired—so pretty wenches *are* like partridges in their plumpness and desirability, and both are game which men pursue. The major ironies, again, are similar in nature: Pope implies that Belinda's honour and her new brocade, her virginity and a frail china jar, are of equal value in the eyes of Ariel (and perhaps of Belinda herself); Byron implies that partridges and pretty wenches are equally difficult to preserve, and that to a magistrate they are on exactly the same footing. The fundamental difference between Pope and Byron can be seen again, however, in the former's adhering firmly, even in this light-hearted satire,

---

[17] *P.W.*, vi. 441.
[18] *P.W.*, vi. 591.
[19] *The Poems of Alexander Pope*, Twickenham Edn, London 1939, ii. 164.
[20] Cp. "Puffs, Powders, Patches, Bibles, Billet-doux" (*op. cit.*, ii. 155). Pope's use of alliteration here is more tactful than Byron's—he has always a more delicate sensitivity to words and their effects. Yet it is none the less remarkable that Byron, who shows so little aptitude for the sustained use of heroic couplets, should be able to write such admirable couplets at the close of his *ottava rima* stanzas.

to his moral principles, so that the humour of his lines lies partly in the deliberate contrast between Ariel's view and Pope's own. The humour of Byron's couplet depends on a similar contrast between the magisterial and moral viewpoints, but here there is some doubt about the writer's own position: the preceding lines and stanzas with their joking tone suggest that he regards the pretty wenches as fair game; the stanzas which follow, with their show of sympathy and social-moral indignation, suggest just the opposite; and this typical uncertainty about his own satiric standpoint prevents his ever making Pope's full use of the mock-heroic's normative potentialities and *controlled* ambiguities of feeling.

Byron, of course, never even attempts to make any sustained use of this one satiric mode—he lacked the artistic self-discipline it would have required, and he preferred the flexibility of his own *ottava rima* manner, in which he could vary his technique and tone from stanza to stanza, or from line to line, in accordance with the fluctuations of his mood. At worst, this means that parts of the poem simply reflect his mental and emotional confusions; but it can at best result in the clear recognition and precise expression of a whole complex of ideas and feelings, as in his "Ubi Sunt" meditation on the changes he has seen in the *beau monde*:

'Where is the World ?' cries Young, 'at *eighty*'—'Where
    The World in which a man was born ?' Alas !
Where is the world of *eight* years past ? '*T was there*—
    I look for it—'t is gone, a globe of glass !
Cracked, shivered, vanished, scarcely gazed on, ere
    A silent change dissolves the glittering mass.
Statesmen, Chiefs, Orators, Queens, Patriots, Kings,
And Dandies—all are gone on the Wind's wings.

Where is Napoleon the Grand ? God knows !
    Where little Castlereagh ? The devil can tell !
Where Grattan, Curran, Sheridan—all those
    Who bound the Bar or Senate in their spell ?
Where is the unhappy Queen, with all her woes ?
    And where the Daughter, whom the Isles loved well ?
Where are those martyred saints the Five per Cents ?
And where—oh, where the devil are the Rents ?

Where's Brummell? Dished. Where's Long Pole Wellesley?
   Diddled.
   Where's Whitbread? Romilly? Where's George the Third?
Where is his will? (That's not so soon unriddled.)
   And where is 'Fum' the Fourth, our 'royal bird?'
Gone down, it seems, to Scotland to be fiddled
   Unto by Sawney's violin, we have heard :
'Caw me, caw thee'—for six months hath been hatching
This scene of royal itch and loyal scratching.

Where is Lord This? And where my Lady That?
   The Honourable Mistresses and Misses?
Some laid aside like an old Opera hat,
   Married, unmarried, and remarried : (this is
An evolution oft performed of late).
   Where are the Dublin shouts—and London hisses?
Where are the Grenvilles? Turned as usual. Where
My friends the Whigs? Exactly where they were. . . .[21]

The variations of tone in this passage make it much more
complex than, say, Villon's *Ballade*

> Dictes moy ou, n'en quel pays,
> Est Flora la belle Rommaine. . . .

Byron's opening stanza, dignified and solemn in its diction,
imagery and cadences, expresses his sorrowful wonder at the
transience of worldly things, and this first statement of his
theme is moving, though not startling or unconventional. The
second stanza opens on the same note ("ou est le preux Charle-
maigne?"), but the colloquial "God knows!" shows Byron
breaking with tradition—it suggests a humorous devil-may-care
irreverence, which becomes unmistakable in the next line. It
is also immediately apparent that this catalogue of names is
not going to be homogeneous like its literary prototypes: in
the contrast between "Napoleon the Grand" and "little
Castlereagh", between "God knows" and "the devil can tell,"
we see Byron modulating his lament to satire. Yet the quality
of true lament is present in the next four lines, and they are
not deflated by the satirical mock-lament of the concluding
couplet, in which he switches suddenly from death to economic

[21] *P.W.*, VI. 450-1.

changes. Both its lines display a characteristically clever use of bathos. "Where are those martyred saints?" might seem on a first reading to continue the Queen-Daughter topic; certainly it shows a momentary heightening of style; so that the next phrase, mundane and commercial, comes as a surprise, and the contrast is intensified by the near-homophony of "saints" and "cents." We naturally expect the last line to develop this idea, so that it does not surprise us in the same way, but there is again a piquant element of contrast—the opening words have a touch of the literary-elegiac, which blends almost immediately into the colloquial-satiric. The third stanza sees a return to the fully elegiac mood: the contemporary slang words "dished" and "diddled" give the first line a wry humour —Byron is using the dandies' own vocabulary—but there is real regret and nostalgia in his voice as he speaks of all these men, both friends and enemies, who have vanished from the London scene to death, exile, or ruin. George IV, on the other hand, has vanished only to Scotland on a state visit, and Byron's tone changes completely in discussing this—the nicknames (one quite recent, one traditional) of "Fum" and "Sawney," the raucous Scots proverb and the itching-scratching metaphor serve to express intense, contemptuous dislike for King and subjects. His tone alters again in the fourth stanza, and we realise that he is concerned not only with the transience but with the recurrence or continuance of some phenomena: the Great World changes—it consists indeed of things ephemeral—but, in some ways, *plus ça change, plus c'est la même chose*, and this too is a cause for melancholy mirth. Yet he keeps returning, sadly or ironically, to the changes of these years— changes which, varied in themselves, evoke varied responses, all of which Byron acknowledges and weaves into his meditation, so that the passage gives an honest and inclusive record of his mood—a record that is poignant and amusing, gay and melancholy, without any inconsistency or incoherence.

This adaptation of the "Ubi Sunt" convention to express more complicated thoughts and feelings shows the fertility of Byron's invention, which is responsible for the astonishing vitality and varied excellence of his style throughout the poem. This can be seen in almost every passage quoted, and one could easily multiply examples of his ingenious rhyming, witty phrases, exuberant word-play, and amusingly urbane indecency. And the lively sense of language which enabled him to write like this was accompanied by an acute critical intelligence, which made him scrutinise his own technique, so that he often comments in the poem itself on aspects of its style and meaning. To take imagery, for example, Byron was still capable of perpetrating vague pretentious metaphors and similes, but usually he makes fun of the conventional and shoddy here as readily as in the fields of sentiment and diction. Sometimes he extracts new life from an old simile by giving it a new, unexpected twist:

> But first of little Leila we'll dispose,
>> For like a day-dawn she was young and pure—
> Or like the old comparison of snows,
>> (Which are more pure than pleasant, to be sure,
> Like many people everybody knows). . . .[22]

Or in the following passage he checks himself when he embarks on a stale literary image, and substitutes an entirely new one drawn—very appropriately—from the Society life he is describing:

> But Adeline was not indifferent : for
>> (*Now* for a common-place !) beneath the snow,
> As a Volcano holds the lava more
>> Within—*et caetera*. Shall I go on ?—No !
> I hate to hunt down a tired metaphor,
>> So let the often-used Volcano go.
> Poor thing ! How frequently, by me and others,
> It hath been stirred up till its smoke quite smothers !
>
> I'll have another figure in a trice :—
>> What say you to a bottle of champagne ?
> Frozen into a very vinous ice,
>> Which leaves few drops of that immortal rain,
> Yet in the very centre, past all price,
>> About a liquid glassful will remain ;
> And this is stronger than the strongest grape
> Could e'er express in its expanded shape :

---

[22] *P.W.*, vi. 466-7.

O

> 'T is the whole spirit brought to a quintessence ;
>> And thus the chilliest aspects may concentre
> A hidden nectar under a cold presence.
>> And such are many—though I only meant her
> From whom I now deduce these moral lessons,
>> On which the Muse has always sought to enter.
> And your cold people are beyond all price,
> When once you've broken their confounded ice.[23]

The element of self-parody and self-criticism here reminds us that in *Don Juan* Byron is often correcting his own errors of the past,[24] and part of our pleasure in the poem lies in the recognition of his increased maturity. He attacks the cant of sentiment he had himself encouraged in *Childe Harold*, and his account of the Siege of Ismail can be seen as a retelling, from a saner and more sensitive moral standpoint, of *The Siege of Corinth*. Then the ghost episode in Canto XVI is in effect a parody of his own mystery-mongering in *Lara*[25]—a discrediting of the Gothic supernatural which had once appealed to him; while the description of the portraits at "Norman Abbey" ridicules (by implication) his own former sentimentalising of his family history:[26]

> Steel Barons, molten the next generation
>> To silken rows of gay and gartered Earls,
> Glanced from the walls in goodly preservation :
>> And Lady Marys blooming into girls,
> With fair long locks, had also kept their station :
>> And Countesses mature in robes and pearls :
> Also some beauties of Sir Peter Lely,
> Whose drapery hints we may admire them freely.
>
> Judges in very formidable ermine
>> Were there, with brows that did not much invite
> The accused to think their lordships would determine
>> His cause by leaning much from might to right :
> Bishops, who had not left a single sermon ;
>> Attorneys-general, awful to the sight,
> As hinting more (unless our judgments warp us)
> Of the 'Star Chamber' than of 'Habeas Corpus'.

---

[23] *P.W.*, VI. 490-1.

[24] He is, of course, still ready to correct the faults of others too, even those of his "*buon camerado* Scott"—see *P.W.*, VI. 458-9.

[25] See *P.W.*, III. 331-2.   [26] See Chapter Two, p. 16.

> Generals, some all in armour, of the old
>   And iron time, ere lead had ta'en the lead ;
> Others in wigs of Marlborough's martial fold,
>   Huger than twelve of our degenerate breed :
> Lordlings, with staves of white or keys of gold :
>   Nimrods, whose canvas scarce contained the steed ;
> And, here and there, some stern high patriot stood,
> Who could not get the place for which he sued.[27]

This new sense of the past, with its gay deflation of romantic sentiment and aristocratic family pride, is matched by Byron's comic-realistic vision of the present. He seizes with delight on the more absurd features of fashionable life—on the songs, for example, inflicted on company by musical young ladies:

> Oh ! the long evenings of duets and trios !
>   The admirations and the speculations ;
> The "Mamma Mia's !" and the "Amor Mio's !"
>   The "Tanti palpiti's" on such occasions :
> The "Lasciami's", and quavering "Addio's",
>   Amongst our own most musical of nations !
> With "Tu mi chamas's" from Portingale,
> To soothe our ears, lest Italy should fail.[28]

These Italian titles and their rhyming terminations convey perfectly the affectation and monotony of such performances; and here again the satire has a personal as well as a public application, since Byron himself had written two translations of the Portuguese song "Tu mi chamas."[29] Then the reactions of the house-party to the Duchess's flirtatiousness are described with a comic observation as malicious and amusing as that of *Beppo*; and there is a brilliant account of Lord Henry's entertainment of the squires whose votes he wanted to secure.[30] Byron's tone here is, however, more astringent as he touches on the subjects of class-consciousness and hypocrisy, and indeed his excellent light comedy can often modulate into

[27] *P.W.*, vi. 501.

[28] *P.W.*, vi. 586.

[29] *P.W.*, iii. 71-2.

[30] E.g. *P.W.*, vi. 595. Yet another ambivalence appears in Byron's presentation of the squirearchy : he exposes the snobbery and malice which the aristocracy shows towards them, but he has himself a good share of the same feelings, and he too laughs at the squires as dunces and unfashionable boors.

more serious, though no less witty, criticisms of Society. He sometimes speaks of its pretensions with dry disillusion:

> In the great world,—which, being interpreted,
>   Meaneth the West or worst end of a city,
> And about twice two thousand people bred
>   By no means to be very wise or witty,
> But to sit up while others lie in bed,
>   And look down on the Universe with pity,—
> Juan, as an inveterate patrician,
> Was well received by persons of condition.[31]

Or he gives a bitterly sardonic summary of the lives lived by young noblemen:

> They are young, but know not Youth—it is anticipated,
>   Handsome but wasted, rich without a sou ;
> Their vigour in a thousand arms is dissipated ;
>   Their cash comes *from*, their wealth goes *to* a Jew ;
> Both senates see their nightly votes participated
>   Between the Tyrant's and the Tribunes' crew ;
> And having voted, dined, drunk, gamed, and whored,
> The family vault receives another Lord.[32]

While probably his deepest insight, conveyed to us in the authentic accents of experience, is not into the immorality or hypocrisy of aristocratic life, but into its sheer futility and boredom:

> Doubtless it is a brilliant masquerade :
>   But when of the first sight you have had your fill,
> It palls—at least it did so upon me,
> This paradise of Pleasure and *Ennui*.
>
> When we have made our love, and gamed our gaming,
>   Dressed, voted, shone, and, may be, something more—
> With dandies dined—heard senators declaiming—
>   Seen beauties brought to market by the score,
> Sad rakes to sadder husbands chastely taming—
>   There's little left but to be bored or bore.
> Witness those *ci-devant jeunes hommes* who stem
> The stream, nor leave the world which leaveth them. . . .[33]

---

[31] *P.W.*, VI. 440-1.   [32] *P.W.*, VI. 449-50.   [33] *P.W.*, VI. 520 (cp. 510).

And hence high life is oft a dreary void,
    A rack of pleasures, where we must invent
A something wherewithal to be annoyed.
    Bards may sing what they please about *Content* ;
Contented, when translated, means but cloyed ;
    And hence arise the woes of Sentiment,
Blue-devils—and Blue-stockings—and Romances
Reduced to practice, and performed like dances.[34]

The tone of this carries complete conviction: it is satire of a kind which could be written only by an aristocrat who had savoured and exhausted all the pleasures of Society, and in the same way he describes the boredom of a country-house party with an intimate detailed knowledge which could come only from personal experience:

The gentlemen got up betimes to shoot,
    Or hunt : the young, because they liked the sport—
The first thing boys like after play and fruit ;
    The middle-aged, to make the day more short ;
For *ennui* is a growth of English root,
    Though nameless in our language :—we retort
The fact for words, and let the French translate
That awful yawn which sleep can not abate.

The elderly walked through the library,
    And tumbled books, or criticised the pictures,
Or sauntered through the gardens piteously,
    And made upon the hot-house several strictures,
Or rode a nag which trotted not too high,
    Or on the morning papers read their lectures,
Or on the watch their longing eyes would fix,
Longing at sixty for the hour of six.[35]

Yet Byron, paradoxically, finds delight and inspiration in this life which he condemns as tedious. He obviously feels the satirist's characteristic pleasure in handling a congenial (even if detested) subject; but over and above this he continually shows a greater capacity for enjoyment than his "disillusioned" stanzas might suggest. The follies and the vanities which he describes cause him far more amusement than disgust; even

[34] *P.W.*, VI. 536-7.   [35] *P.W.*, VI. 512.

after deploring Society romances bred in idleness, he goes on to portray one in a mood of comic tolerance and sympathy; while sometimes he can write appreciatively—even enthusiastically—about English country life and London pleasures.[36] "England was, after all I may say against it, very delightful in my day," he admitted once to Lady Blessington,[37] and while in his exile he had a keen sense of the boring, ridiculous and unpleasant aspects of Society, he also felt a certain nostalgia for it, so that he re-creates for us its fun as well as its futility, and his own mood in these later cantos varies like that of the onlooker—a symbol of himself—whom he imagines at a London ball:

> Thrice happy he who, after a survey
>   Of the good company, can win a corner,
> A door that's *in* or boudoir *out* of the way,
>   Where he may fix himself like small 'Jack Horner,'
> And let the Babel round run as it may,
>   And look on as a mourner, or a scorner,
> Or an approver, or a mere spectator,
> Yawning a little as the night grows later.[38]

---

[36] E.g. *P.W.*, VI. 503-4, 429.
[37] Lady Blessington, *Conversations*, p. 226.
[38] *P.W.*, VI. 448.

XIII

The Vision of Judgment

IN the preceding chapters I have tried to indicate the nature of *Don Juan's* excellence—and limitations; but the poem is so long and varied, and its stylistic quality so high throughout, that even an extended commentary cannot really do it justice, and still less can its achievement be summed up in a single neat concluding paragraph. Before passing to *The Vision of Judgment*, however, it is worth while emphasising the extent to which *Don Juan's* strengths and weaknesses are both related to the poem's inclusiveness. Byron's popular romantic works had nearly all depended on the exclusion of some of his finest qualities—his lively intelligence, his robust common sense, his understanding of human nature in its real complexity, his zest for life, his sense of humour, and his ironical, deflatory wit. All these appear, however, in his *ottava rima* satires, contributing greatly to their success; while in *Don Juan* they are combined in a new exciting synthesis with elements from his romantic personality—with the love of liberty, the hatred of oppression and of war, the respect for courage and for passionate love, which he now disengages from the more factitious attitudes of the Byronic hero. The work's satiric power derives in great part from this new poetic personality, with its astringent, witty, flexible modes of expression, and its new or strengthened positive beliefs, which include (as well as those just mentioned) an insistence on fidelity to truth, and a detestation of all forms of cant. These values help to determine the objects and the methods of Byron's attack, and they also lead him to reject or ridicule his former attitudinising, for *Don Juan* is at once a presentation of the author's comic-realistic view of human life, and a record of his own increased self-knowledge and maturity.

Even now, however, this self-knowledge and maturity were not complete, and Byron's complex personality was not entirely "integrated." Hence the poem's inclusiveness, its tendency to register all his responses, all his passing thoughts and feelings, was not wholly beneficial: it means that though *Don Juan* gives a wonderfully accurate picture of the kind of man that Byron was, in doing so it reflects his intellectual and psychological confusions. Such confusions in a writer's mind do not, however, necessarily issue in confused art—*Beppo* is a striking instance to the contrary—and when they do occur in this poem the immediate cause must be a failure on Byron's part to define his satirical intentions clearly, and to treat his material in accordance with them. This is in point of fact the greatest weakness that results from his casual extemporising way of writing: Byron has throughout the general intention of deflating cant and showing things as they really are, but his attitude to the reality which he reveals varies according to his mood, so that the poem reflects the movements and the inconsistencies of his own mind. This often results in a blurring of the satiric focus; and while *Don Juan* is always witty, always penetrating, always entertaining, it sometimes seems to lack coherence—formal, emotional, and intellectual. It is thus a very great poem, but a flawed one.

The Vision of Judgment, on the other hand, has all *Don Juan's* strengths and none of its weaknesses.

To understand the reasons for this difference we must look to the occasion of the work, and to Byron's motives and intention in writing it. George III died on January 29th, 1820, and the poet's reaction to the news (surprisingly enough) was one of kindly pity qualified only by his habitual irony: "I see the good old King is gone to his place," he wrote to Murray: "one can't help being sorry, though blindness, and age, and insanity, are supposed to be drawbacks on human felicity; but I am not at all sure that the latter, at least, might not render him happier than any of his subjects."[1] Here there is no real bitterness against George III—no disposition to attack him; and *The Vision of Judgment* was in fact provoked not by the King's death, but by a semi-official poem about it, published more than a year later. On April 11th, 1821, there appeared "*A Vision of Judgement.* By Robert Southey, Esq., Ll.D. Poet Laureate; . . . &c."[2] This work was divided into twelve

---

[1] *L.J.*, IV. 406.

[2] Robert Southey, *A Vision of Judgement*, London 1821, (henceforth cited as Southey, *Vision*), p. iii.

sections: "The Trance; The Vault; The Awakening; The Gate of Heaven; The Accusers; The Absolvers; The Beatification; The Sovereigns; The Elder Worthies; The Worthies of the Georgian Age; The Young Spirits; The Meeting." It tells how Southey, when listening to the bell tolling for George III's death, fell into a trance, and was conducted by an angel to the vault where the King lay; how he saw the dead man's spirit rise to Heaven's gate, where it faced its accusers (Wilkes and Junius) and shamed them into silence; how the Devil and all the damned were then hurled down to Hell, while the King was absolved of blame by those of the blessed (including Washington) who had once opposed him but had now come to see his true worth; how he was welcomed to Heaven by the monarchs of England from Alfred onwards, and by the Elder Worthies—an extraordinary collection including the Venerable Bede, Shakespeare, and Milton (who, we are told, was "no longer here to Kings and to Hierarchs hostile"); how he was met by the Worthies of the Georgian Age, including those who had died in youth with their promise unfulfilled; how finally he was reunited to Parents, Children, and Consort. As the King entered Heaven with this retinue, Southey pressed forward too, but found himself falling, and awoke once more on the shores of Derwentwater, hearing the bell tolling for King George's passing. This work was published on April 11th: Byron began his *Vision* on May 7th. And although he left off the same day, this poem—which was to be his masterpiece— was "resumed about the 20th of September," and completed by October 4th.[3]

It is easy to see why Southey's volume should have roused Byron to a rejoinder. He already had a grudge against the Laureate for having (as he thought) spread scandalous rumours about his life in Switzerland, and the *Vision* gave him further cause for personal resentment, since a whole section of the Preface was devoted to a thinly-veiled attack on *Don Juan* and its author. Southey deplores

> those monstrous combinations of horrors and mockery, lewdness and impiety, with which English poetry has, in our days,

---

[3] *P.W.*, IV. 525, n.3. And see above, Chapter Eight, pp. 134-5.

first been polluted ! For more than half a century [he writes], English literature had been distinguished by its moral purity, the effect, and in its turn, the cause of an improvement in national manners. A father might, without apprehension of evil, have put into the hands of his children any book which issued from the press, if it did not bear, either in its title-page or frontispiece, manifest signs that it was intended as furniture for the brothel. There was no danger in any work which bore the name of a respectable publisher, or was to be procured at any respectable booksellers. This was particularly the case with regard to our poetry. It is now no longer so ; and woe to those by whom the offence cometh !⁴

With obvious reference to Byron, Southey then goes on to attack "the men" responsible for this:

Men of diseased hearts and depraved imaginations, who, forming a system of opinions to suit their own unhappy course of conduct, have rebelled against the holiest ordinances of human society, and hating that revealed religion which, with all their efforts and bravadoes, they are unable entirely to disbelieve, labour to make others as miserable as themselves, by infecting them with a moral virus that eats into the soul ! The school which they have set up may properly be called the Satanic school ; for though their productions breathe the spirit of Belial in their lascivious parts, and the spirit of Moloch in those loathsome images of atrocities and horrors which they delight to represent, they are more especially characterized by a Satanic spirit of pride and audacious impiety, which still betrays the wretched feeling of hopelessness wherewith it is allied.⁵

There can be no doubt of Byron's resentment at this onslaught or of his desire for vengeance—he met Southey's next attack by challenging him to a duel⁶—but the anger that he felt on reading the *Vision* had other less narrowly personal grounds too. Byron had come to feel a serious concern for the present state of English poetry, and to despise the Lake Poets as producers of bad poetry, disseminators of bad theories of poetry, and corrupters of the public taste, especially with regard

⁴ Southey, *Vision*, pp. xvii-xviii.
⁵ *Op. cit.*, pp. xix-xxi. (Moore is also glanced at in this Preface—see p. xix.)
⁶ *L.J.*, VI. 392 ; *Self-Portrait*, II. 687-8.

to poetry of the eighteenth century. Southey (with less genius than any of the group) had now published in his official capacity as Poet Laureate a work feeble in itself, a work which in listing great poets among England's Elder Worthies made no mention of Dryden or Pope, a work, finally, in which he had followed the Lake Poets' unfortunate practice of constructing some half-baked theory, and then writing in accordance with it. The greater part of his Preface consisted of an explanation and defence of the poem as a technical experiment—an adaptation to the English language of the classical unrhymed hexameter; but Byron disliked metrical innovations and poetry written on a "system,"[7] and he could see that Southey's verse was not in fact successful, so that on every ground, both practical and theoretical, the *Vision* seemed to him to call for critical attack and merciless deflation.

His political objections to the poem, however, were even more important than this critical distaste. Byron despised the Lake Poets as a set of renegades, and Southey, with the Laureateship as a reward for his apostasy, seemed the very type of a successful turncoat. His early play *Wat Tyler* had been published piratically by some Radicals in 1817, to show what revolutionary views Southey had once held; but his *Vision* demonstrated unashamedly how conservative and loyalist he had now become. The dedication is addressed in terms of fulsome flattery to George IV, congratulating him on the glories, military, political, and cultural, of his reign and regency:

> We owe much to the House of Brunswick ; but to none of that illustrious House more than to Your Majesty, under whose government the military renown of Great Britain has been carried to the highest point of glory. From that pure glory there has been nothing to detract ; the success was not more splendid than the cause was good ; and the event was deserved by the generosity, the justice, the wisdom, and the magnanimity of the counsels which prepared it. The same perfect integrity has been manifested in the whole administration of public affairs. More has been done than was ever before attempted, for mitigating the evils incident to our stage of society ; for imbuing the rising race with those sound principles of religion

---

on which the welfare of states has its only secure foundation ;
and for opening new regions to the redundant enterprize and
industry of the people.   Under Your Majesty's government,
the Metropolis is rivalling in beauty those cities which it has
long surpassed in greatness : sciences, arts, and letters are
flourishing beyond all former example . . . . The brightest
portion of British history will be that which records the im-
provements, the works, and the achievements of the Georgian
Age.

That Your Majesty may long continue to reign over a free
and prosperous people, and that the blessings of the happiest
form of government which has ever been raised by human
wisdom under the favour of Divine Providence may, under
Your Majesty's protection, be transmitted unimpaired to
posterity, is the prayer of

Your MAJESTY'S
Most dutiful Subject and Servant,
ROBERT SOUTHEY.[8]

Byron found this peculiarly offensive, coming from a man who
had once been both a revolutionary and a pacifist, and the
poem itself was just as bad, with its vilification of men who had
worked or fought for Liberty.   It gave, moreover, a completely
false impression of George III's reign, and of George III
himself: it was an outrageous attempt to whitewash him, or in
the words of Byron's Preface, "to canonise a monarch, who,
whatever were his household virtues, was neither a successful
nor a patriot king,—inasmuch as several years of his reign
passed in war with America and Ireland, to say nothing of the
aggression upon France. . . ."[9]   Byron set out then to correct
this false historical estimate, as well as to expose the author as
a renegade and bad poet: ". . . it is my intent," he wrote to
Moore, "to put the said George's Apotheosis in a Whig point
of view, not forgetting the Poet Laureate for his preface and
his other demerits."[10]

The words "canonise" and "apotheosis" point to the final
reason for his dislike of Southey's *Vision*—its use of religion.
Byron, as we have seen, was no philosopher, and he had no
clear system of beliefs, whether Christian or deistic, atheistic

[8] Southey, *Vision*, pp. vi-viii.   [9] *P.W.*, IV. 483.
[10] *L.J.*, v. 385 (cp. 387).

or agnostic—his opinions, as he admitted to Dr Kennedy, were "unsettled," "unsteady and unfixed";[11] but this did not prevent his holding strong views on particular issues. Thus he reacted violently against certain aspects of the Calvinism he had known in his youth, and the idea of perpetual damnation was especially repugnant to him. Dr Kennedy found, indeed, that this was the greatest obstacle to Byron's acceptance of Christianity:

> "But why are you," said his lordship, "so anxious to maintain and prove the eternity of hell punishments ? It is certainly not a humane doctrine, and appears very inconsistent with the mild and benevolent doctrines of Christ." . . . "I cannot decide the point," said his lordship. "But, to my present apprehension, it would be a most desirable thing, could it be proved, that ultimately all created beings were to be happy. This would appear to be most consistent with the nature of God, whose power is omnipotent, and whose principal attribute is love. I cannot yield to your doctrine of the eternal duration of punishment. . . ."[12]

Holding these humane views, he disliked all those who complacently accepted doctrines of damnation, and he condemned, from the standpoint of a superior morality, the narrow sectarian zeal of the "unco guid" (of whatever denomination) who were prepared to consign their fellow mortals to an everlasting bonfire.[13] And Southey's poem had done exactly this: not only did it smugly usher George III into Heaven, but it banished his main opponents (except Washington) to Hell. The mere fact that they had dared to criticise the established order constituted, in the eyes of the ex-revolutionary Laureate,

---

[11] Kennedy, *Conversations on Religion*, pp. 134-5, 46.

[12] *Op. cit.*, pp. 227, 228 (cp. 219 ff., 235, 259).

[13] See, for example, *P.W.*, vi. 106 :

> "And their baked lips, with many a bloody crack,
> Sucked in the moisture, which like nectar streamed ;
> Their throats were ovens, their swoln tongues were black,
> As the rich man's in Hell, who vainly screamed
> To beg the beggar, who could not rain back
> A drop of dew, when every drop had seemed
> To taste of Heaven—If this be true, indeed,
> Some Christians have a comfortable creed."

a major sin. So that his *Vision*, for all its parade of reverence and awe, seemed to Byron a smug, irreligious tract, in which Southey arrogated to himself the functions of the Deity, attributing to God and the whole celestial hierarchy the views of political conservatives in the early nineteenth century, and savagely condemning champions of liberty to Hell forever. "There is something at once ludicrous and blasphemous," he wrote, "in this arrogant scribbler of all work sitting down to deal damnation and destruction upon his fellow creatures, with Wat Tyler, the Apotheosis of George the Third, and the Elegy on Martin the regicide, all shuffled together in his writing desk."[14] Or again: "The way in which that poor insane creature, the Laureate, deals about his judgments in the next world, is like his own judgment in this. If it was not completely ludicrous, it would be something worse."[15]

For all these reasons, then, the work roused Byron's anger and contempt. "The gross flattery," he wrote "the dull impudence, the renegado intolerance, and impious cant, of the poem by the author of 'Wat Tyler,' are something so stupendous as to form the sublime of himself—containing the quintessence of his own attributes."[16] And for Byron, Southey himself had by now acquired a representative status, so that the poem seemed the quintessence not only of the Laureate's faults, but of those of his age and country. "The truth is," Byron had written in February 1821, "that in these days the grand *'primum mobile'* of England is *cant*; cant political, cant poetical, cant religious, cant moral";[17] and Southey's *Vision* seemed to him to combine all these varieties of cant. It was the very embodiment or epitome of the tendencies he disliked most in modern England, and in attacking it he was not only wreaking his revenge on Southey, but asserting some of his own most firmly held and deeply felt beliefs.[18]

Byron chose now to return to his *ottava rima* style, and *The Vision of Judgment* shows his complete mastery of this medium.

[14] *L.J.*, vi. 389.
[15] *P.W.*, iv. 483.
[16] *P.W.*, iv. 481.
[17] *L.J.*, v. 542.
[18] Cp. Lady Blessington, *Conversations*, p. 390 : " 'There are but two sentiments to which I am constant,—a strong love of liberty, and a detestation of cant. . . .' "

In the first fifteen stanzas he uses it with great economy and
flexibility to get the story under way and to suggest the values
on which his satire will be based; and though his style is just
as lively and varied as it was throughout *Don Juan*, it is now
consistently subordinated to the poem's satiric purpose.   He
begins with a brief, amusing sketch of the state of affairs in
Heaven:

> Saint Peter sat by the celestial gate :
>   His keys were rusty, and the lock was dull,
> So little trouble had been given of late ;
>   Not that the place by any means was full,
> But since the Gallic era 'eighty-eight'
>   The Devils had ta'en a longer, stronger pull,
> And 'a pull altogether,' as they say
> At sea—which drew most souls another way.
>
> The Angels all were singing out of tune,
>   And hoarse with having little else to do,
> Excepting to wind up the sun and moon,
>   Or curb a runaway young star or two,
> Or wild colt of a comet, which too soon
>   Broke out of bounds o'er the ethereal blue,
> Splitting some planet with its playful tail,
> As boats are sometimes by a wanton whale.[19]

The tone here is humorous and flippant, but the humour and
the flippancy have a definite satiric function: by expressing
gay irreverence and aristocratic scepticism they imply that the
author and the reader are both sophisticated men of the world
who cannot take this Christian mythology very seriously—it
may serve its turn in a poem, perhaps, but for us there can be
no question of literal belief in it.   Byron's poetic manner thus
establishes at the very outset a mood of patronising, amused
indulgence towards the machinery of Southey's Heaven.

Almost immediately, however, he proceeds to modulate
the tone to express his horror at events on earth, and we pass
from the ludicrous predicament of the overworked Recording
Angel to a completely serious indictment of war—an expression
of violent disgust at the crime and suffering which culminated

[19] *P.W.*, IV. 487.

in the battle Southey saw as the highest point of Britain's military glory:

> This was a handsome board—at least for Heaven ;
>   And yet they had even then enough to do,
> So many Conquerors' cars were daily driven,
>   So many kingdoms fitted up anew ;
> Each day, too, slew its thousands six or seven,
>   Till at the crowning carnage, Waterloo,
> They threw their pens down in divine disgust—
> The page was so besmeared with blood and dust.[20]

Then come the old king's death and funeral:

> In the first year of Freedom's second dawn
>   Died George the Third ; although no tyrant, one
> Who shielded tyrants, till each sense withdrawn
>   Left him nor mental nor external sun:
> A better farmer ne'er brushed dew from lawn,
>   A worse king never left a realm undone !
> He died—but left his subjects still behind,
> One half as mad—and t'other no less blind.
>
> He died ! his death made no great stir on earth :
>   His burial made some pomp ; there was profusion
> Of velvet—gilding—brass—and no great dearth
>   Of aught but tears—save those shed by collusion :
> For these things may be bought at their true worth ;
>   Of elegy there was the due infusion—
> Bought also ; and the torches, cloaks and banners,
> Heralds, and relics of old Gothic manners,
>
> Formed a sepulchral melodrame. Of all
>   The fools who flocked to swell or see the show,
> Who cared about the corpse ? The funeral
>   Made the attraction, and the black the woe,
> There throbbed not there a thought which pierced the pall ;
>   And when the gorgeous coffin was laid low,
> It seemed the mockery of hell to fold
> The rottenness of eighty years in gold.[21]

In the first of these stanzas Byron's harsh antitheses give the effect of just but inexorable judgment. In the second and third,

---

[20] *P.W.*, IV. 488.   [21] *P.W.*, IV. 489-90.

where he makes particularly skilful use of phrasing in relation to the verse pattern, he exploits to the full the deflatory potentialities of this style, but without showing any flippancy or cynicism. The anomalies he now describes are not ridiculous but horrible, and his tone is grimly ironic as he exposes the discrepancies between appearance and reality in the royal funeral—the appearance of public concern and grief, the reality of vulgar curiosity or indifference; the appearance of glory and riches, the reality of death and bodily decay.

It is a natural enough transition to pass from this to speculations on the fate of the king's soul, and these lead to a more informal, conversational verse-meditation, which at first sight seems a casual digression, but which is really of central thematic importance.

> "God save the king !" It is a large economy
>   In God to save the like ; but if he will
> Be saving, all the better ; for not one am I
>   Of those who think damnation better still :
> I hardly know too if not quite alone am I
>   In this small hope of bettering future ill
> By circumscribing, with some slight restriction,
> The eternity of Hell's hot jurisdiction.
>
> I know this is unpopular ; I know
>   'Tis blasphemous ; I know one may be damned
> For hoping no one else may e'er be so ;
>   I know my catechism ; I know we're crammed
> With the best doctrines till we quite o'erflow ;
>   I know that all save England's Church have shammed,
> And that the other twice two hundred churches
> And synagogues have made a *damned* bad purchase.
>
> God help us all ! God help me too ! I am,
>   God knows, as helpless as the Devil can wish,
> And not a whit more difficult to damn,
>   Than is to bring to land a late-hooked fish,
> Or to the butcher to purvey the lamb ;
>   Not that I'm fit for such a noble dish,
> As one day will be that immortal fry
> Of almost every body born to die.[22]

---

[22] *P.W.*, IV. 492.

After the superbly insolent opening the pervasive tone of this passage condemns intolerance and bigotry, implying that the most humane and gentlemanly thing to do is to hope for other men's salvation—not for their damnation. By his rueful, self-depreciatory comments Byron ranges himself with erring humanity as opposed to the religious Pharisees; and his references to fish and lambs (traditional types of the helpless victim) introduce the idea of food as well as sacrifice, and thus lead up (through "noble dish") to the startling, grotesquely horrible conception of

> that immortal fry
> Of almost every body born to die

—a conception which throws discredit on the Moloch God who would relish such a holocaust, as well as on the self-righteous sadists who are willing to defend it.

Having thus established his own gentlemanly ethic of tolerance, good humour and good sense, Byron takes up the story, and in stanzas xvi-lxxxiv he bases his narrative on the sequence of events in Southey's poem, or rather in "The Gate of Heaven" and "The Accusers" sections of that poem. His technique is not, strictly speaking, that of parody, but of travesty: he does not attempt to imitate the Laureate's style, but makes his plot appear ridiculous by presenting it in a completely different style, transforming the whole tone, feeling, and significance of the original work. The arrival of George III at Heaven's gate was announced in Southey's poem with great formality and ceremony:

> O'er the adamantine gates an Angel stood on the summit.
> Ho ! he exclaim'd, King George of England cometh to judgement !
> Hear Heaven ! Ye Angels hear ! Souls of the Good and the
> > Wicked
> Whom it concerns, attend !²³

In Byron's *Vision* St Peter, roused from his slumbers to receive the king, reacts like any other irritable, crotchety old man:

> . . . "Well, what's the matter ?
> Is Lucifer come back with all this clatter ?"

---

²³ Southey, *Vision*, p. 13.

> "No," quoth the cherub : "George the Third is dead."
>   "And who *is* George the Third ?" replied the apostle :
> "*What George ? what Third ?*"   "The King of England," said
>   The angel. "Well ! he won't find Kings to jostle
> Him on his way. . . ."[24]

There was an amusing *naïveté* in Southey's presentation of this
whole episode. No doubt he believed that all souls were equal
in the sight of God, but his poem seems to suggest that a royal
soul is peculiarly precious, and that the arrival of the King of
England is a supremely important occasion in Heaven, calling
as it does for the attendance of God Himself, Archangels,
Angels, Principalities, Cherubim, Seraphim, Thrones, Domina-
tions, Virtues, and Powers. All this fuss seemed to Byron a case
of Southey's carrying his loyal sycophancy into the next world:
hence the deflation of it in *his* poem is a blow at the corrupt
distorted values it implied; and this is a representative example
of the way in which his comedy and ridicule (however light-
hearted) are used in this work to enforce his moral judgements.

It is worth noticing, moreover, that he sets bounds to his
ridicule: while he is merciless in poking fun at Southey's
Heaven and its machinery, Byron says nothing about God,
Christ, or the central mysteries of the faith. "The reader
is . . . requested to observe," he wrote in his Preface, "that
no doctrinal tenets are insisted upon or discussed; that the
person of the Deity is carefully withheld from sight, which is
more than can be said for the Laureate. . . ."[25] He thought
it blasphemous bad taste on Southey's part to drag God and
the Cross into his propagandist poem, and for all his own
apparent irreverence Byron shows more real respect for
Christian susceptibilities by confining himself to semi-
mythological characters, like Michael and Satan.

His treatment of these characters is not always deflatory.
Sometimes instead of ridiculing what Southey presented in all
seriousness, Byron does just the opposite and transforms the
ridiculous or contemptible into something great and impressive.
Southey's Devil was a grotesque semi-allegorical figure,
representing the Spirit of Rebellion and Unrest by which
George III's reign had been troubled—he was impudent and

uncouth, "many-headed and monstrous," with "numberless
bestial ears erect to all rumours" and "numberless mouths . . .
fill'd with lies."[26]   Byron's Satan is conceived of in completely
different terms, as this first description of him shows:

> But bringing up the rear of this bright host
>   A Spirit of a different aspect waved
> His wings, like thunder-clouds above some coast
>   Whose barren beach with frequent wrecks is paved ;
> His brow was like the deep when tempest-tossed ;
>   Fierce and unfathomable thoughts engraved
> Eternal wrath on his immortal face,
> And *where* he gazed a gloom pervaded space.[27]

This Devil is clearly related to Milton's heroic Satan in the
early books of *Paradise Lost*;   he also has the pride, the dignity,
and power (but none of the absurdity) of Byron's own romantic
heroes;   and our sense of his greatness is increased by the
account of Michael's meeting with him:

> He and the sombre, silent Spirit met—
>   They knew each other both for good and ill ;
> Such was their power, that neither could forget
>   His former friend and future foe ; but still
> There was a high, immortal, proud regret
>   In either's eye, as if 'twere less their will
> Than destiny to make the eternal years
> Their date of war, and their 'Champs Clos' the spheres.[28]

These are fit adversaries, great and dignified, and if they are
sometimes more familiar in manner than their Miltonic
prototypes, it is with the familiarity of great aristocrats—the
description of their first guarded civilities shows Byron
applying his social knowledge to the supernatural, or
presenting the supernatural in social terms:

> And therefore Michael and the other wore
>   A civil aspect : though they did not kiss,
> Yet still between his Darkness and his Brightness
>   There passed a mutual glance of great politeness.

---

[26] Southey, *Vision*, pp. 16-17.   [27] *P.W.*, IV. 495.   [28] *P.W.*, IV. 498.

> The Archangel bowed, not like a modern beau,
>   But with a graceful oriental bend,
> Pressing one radiant arm just where below
>   The heart in good men is supposed to tend ;
> He turned as to an equal, not too low,
>   But kindly ; Satan met his ancient friend
> With more hauteur, as might an old Castilian
> Poor Noble meet a mushroom rich civilian.[29]

It is perfectly in accordance with this mode of characterisation that Michael should feel obliged at one point to reprove St Peter and apologise to Satan for the saint's "vulgar" display of temper;[30] while in another speech of Michael's the Devil and he are related even more closely to the contemporary social scene:

> Then he addressed himself to Satan : "Why—
>   My good old friend, for such I deem you, though
> Our different parties make us fight so shy,
>   I ne'er mistake you for a *personal* foe ;
> Our difference is *political*, and I
>   Trust that, whatever may occur below,
> You know my great respect for you : and this
> Makes me regret whate'er you do amiss—"[31]

This comic view of their relationship replaces the tragic one of the stanza quoted previously, but the effect is not to make them seem ridiculous: it is rather to make us see the Devil as a great aristocratic politician—no longer a lost Archangel, certainly, but the leader, as it were, of His Celestial Majesty's Opposition. In this role he impeaches George III (just as, for example, Burke did Warren Hastings), and this provides us with the explanation for his metamorphosis: Byron is writing as a gentleman, with a gentleman's assumptions and beliefs, and his Devil must be something of a gentleman too, since it is the Devil who must deliver Byron's own indictment of the King.

This indictment is extremely formidable. Satan's first insistence on the unimportance to him of George III's soul is a counter to Southey's inflated treatment of the trial; but the issues raised in Satan's speech are far from unimportant,

[29] *P.W.*, IV. 499.　　[30] *P.W.*, IV. 503-4.　　[31] *P.W.*, IV. 507.

and his charges are, the poem implies, both serious and unanswerable :

> "He came to his sceptre young ; he leaves it old :
>   Look to the state in which he found his realm,
> And left it ; and his annals too behold,
>   How to a minion first he gave the helm ;
> How grew upon his heart a thirst for gold,
>   The beggar's vice, which can but overwhelm
> The meanest hearts ; and for the rest, but glance
> Thine eye along America and France.
>
> 'Tis true, he was a tool from first to last
>   (I have the workmen safe) ; but as a tool
> So let him be consumed.   From out the past
>   Of ages, since mankind have known the rule
> Of monarchs—from the bloody rolls amassed
>   Of Sin and Slaughter—from the Caesars' school,
> Take the worst pupil ; and produce a reign
> More drenched with gore, more cumbered with the slain.
>
> He ever warred with freedom and the free :
>   Nations as men, home subjects, foreign foes,
> So that they uttered the word 'Liberty !'
>   Found George the Third their first opponent.   Whose
> History was ever stained as his will be
>   With national and individual woes ?
> I grant his household abstinence ; I grant
> His neutral virtues, which most monarchs want ;
>
> I know he was a constant consort ; own
>   He was a decent sire, and middling lord.
> All this is much, and most upon a throne ;
>   As temperance, if at Apicius' board,
> Is more than at an anchorite's supper shown.
>   I grant him all the kindest can accord ;
> And this was well for him, but not for those
> Millions who found him what Oppression chose."[32]

Here Byron-Satan shows forensic skill by anticipating and discounting the most probable defence, in order to secure a conviction.   In admitting the King's private virtues he is

[32] *P.W.*, IV. 501-2.

following Dryden's precept about "rebating the Satyre (where Justice would allow it) from carrying too sharp an Edge"; but he does this only to render his real attack the more effective. Even in making his concessions and doing them full justice he contrives to make them seem comparatively unimportant, partly by his very readiness to admit them, partly by the dryness of his tone ("*neutral* virtues," "*decent* sire," "*middling* lord*,*" etc.), and partly by the casual introduction of this topic at the end of a stanza, after a climax of denunciation. So that we are made to feel, with Satan, that such virtues cannot count for much against the King's great public faults. With galling insolence Satan suggests that even these were largely the work of cleverer men—

> " 'Tis true, he was a tool from first to last
> (I have the workmen safe) . . ."

—but he insists that George III still bears some responsibility for the crimes committed in his name, with his approval—for the terrible slaughter in his wars, for the fact that these were fought in evil causes (to maintain his tyranny over America, to restore a tyranny to revolutionary France), and for the denial of basic liberties to men at home and abroad. The whole indictment has the power that comes from strong conviction and deep feeling, and Byron's use of Satan as a mouthpiece saves him from any embarrassment at having to reveal what he believes, so that his views are firmly, forcefully asserted without any hesitations or ironical disclaimers. Nor is there any of the intellectual confusion which sometimes figures in *Don Juan*, for Byron is now thinking mainly as a Whig aristocrat, to whom freedom and liberty are simple (admittedly) but vitally important concepts. They mean freedom from foreign rule, freedom from despots, freedom of speech, freedom of political action, freedom, finally, to worship God as one pleases without suffering civil disabilities;[33] and these are noble ideals which Byron does not question or deflate. Their

---

[33] The end of Satan's speech and his comic by-play with St Peter emphasise the penalties incurred by Catholics in Christian England ; and it is worth remembering that Byron's second major speech in the House of Lords had been in favour of Catholic Emancipation.

universal validity is suggested by their being held by Government as well as Opposition in the heavens: in Southey's poem "the angels all were Tories," but Byron reverses this and makes them Whigs, so that even Michael does not query the assumption that a foe to Liberty deserves damnation—he merely asks the devil for proof of the accusation.

And so the Devil calls his witnesses. In the original *Vision* John Wilkes and Junius had both appeared, but they failed to testify because they dared not utter at Heaven's gate the lies they had told on earth:

> Wretched and guilty souls, where now their audacity ? Where now
> Are the insolent tongues so ready of old at rejoinder ?
> Where the lofty pretences of public virtue and freedom ?
> Where the gibe, and the jeer, and the threat, the envenom'd invective,
> Calumny, falsehood, fraud, and the whole ammunition of malice ?
> Wretched and guilty souls, they stood in the face of their Sovereign,
> Conscious and self-condemn'd ; confronted with him they had injured,
> At the Judgement-seat they stood.[34]

And Southey tells with gloating satisfaction how the thwarted Devil hurled them down to Hell:

> Seizing the guilty pair, he swung them aloft, and in vengeance
> Hurl'd them all abroad, far into the sulphurous darkness.
> Sons of Faction, be warn'd ! And ye, ye Slanderers ! learn ye
> Justice, and bear in mind that after death there is judgement.[35]

Byron, in one of the cleverest touches in his poem, retains Wilkes's refusal to speak out but completely changes its motivation. Wilkes, though a demagogue, has the instincts of a gentleman, and having said his say on earth he is reluctant to carry his political quarrels beyond the grave—unlike the Christian Laureate he is prepared to forgive opponents who are now dead:

[34] Southey, *Vision*, pp. 17-18.   [35] *Op. cit.*, p. 20.

"*Above* the sun repeat, then, what thou hast
    To urge against him," said the Archangel. "Why,"
Replied the spirit, "since old scores are past,
    Must I turn evidence ? In faith, not I.
Besides, I beat him hollow at the last,
    With all his Lords and Commons : in the sky
I don't like ripping up old stories, since
His conduct was but natural in a prince.

Foolish, no doubt, and wicked, to oppress
    A poor unlucky devil without a shilling ;
But then I blame the man himself much less
    Than Bute and Grafton, and shall be unwilling
To see him punished here for their excess,
    Since they were both damned long ago, and still in
Their place below : for me, I have forgiven,
And vote his *habeas corpus* into Heaven."[36]

Junius, on the other hand, is prepared to let his former
accusations stand—we are thus reminded that George III is
guilty, in spite of Wilkes's generosity; and Satan is going on to
call witnesses to the King's American policy, when suddenly
the trial is interrupted by the arrival of Southey himself, not
conducted by an angel, but snatched up from the Lake District
by the devil Asmodeus, who had found him working on his
Vision.

    At this point Byron abandons Southey's plot, and switches
to open ridicule of the Laureate and his poem:

Now the bard, glad to get an audience, which
    By no means often was his case below,
Began to cough, and hawk, and hem, and pitch
    His voice into that awful note of woe
To all unhappy hearers within reach
    Of poets when the tide of rhyme's in flow ;
But stuck fast with his first hexameter,
Not one of all whose gouty feet would stir.

But ere the spavined dactyls could be spurred
    Into recitative, in great dismay
Both Cherubim and Seraphim were heard
    To murmur loudly through their long array ;

---

[36] *P.W.*, IV. 510-11.

> And Michael rose ere he could get a word
>> Of all his foundered verses under way,
> And cried, "For God's sake stop, my friend ! 'twere best—
>> '*Non Di, non homines*'—you know the rest."[37]

Here Byron achieves his effect mainly by comic narrative, but one also notes the cutting precision of "recitative" as a description of Southey's verse, and the sustained metaphor of "spavined," "spurred" and "foundered," which suggests that the Laureate's Pegasus is a broken-down old nag; while the Horatian tag "*Non Di, non homines*," invokes a whole tradition of critical discrimination and concern for literary standards. Then comes an attack on Southey as a renegade as well as a bad poet:

> He said—(I only give the heads)—he said,
>> He meant no harm in scribbling ; 'twas his way
> Upon all topics ; 'twas, besides, his bread,
>> Of which he buttered both sides ; 'twould delay
> Too long the assembly (he was pleased to dread),
>> And take up rather more time than a day,
> To name his works—he would but cite a few—
> 'Wat Tyler'—'Rhymes on Blenheim'—'Waterloo.'
>
> He had written praises of a Regicide ;
>> He had written praises of all kings whatever ;
> He had written for republics far and wide,
>> And then against them bitterer than ever ;
> For pantisocracy he once had cried
>> Aloud, a scheme less moral than 'twas clever ;
> Then grew a hearty anti-jacobin—
> Had turned his coat—and would have turned his skin.
>
> He had sung against all battles, and again
>> In their high praise and glory ; he had called
> Reviewing 'the ungentle craft,' and then
>> Became as base a critic as e'er crawled—
> Fed, paid, and pampered by the very men
>> By whom his muse and morals had been mauled :
> He had written much blank verse, and blanker prose,
> And more of both than any body knows.[38]

---

[37] *P.W.*, IV. 518.   [38] *P.W.*, IV. 520-22.

In the first of these stanzas Byron tries to catch the ingratiating sycophantic note he thought appropriate to Southey, but after the list of titles—with their evidence of the Laureate's lack of integrity—he passes to the open scorn and indignation of the satirist, insisting through his savagely contemptuous antitheses that the turncoat's life itself has been "one vile antithesis." Southey then speaks again in his own person, offering to write Satan's life—or Michael's, so that we see him as a low professional hack, ready to turn his hand to anything that might be profitable; and when he insists on reading his *Vision*, his arrogant assumption of the right to judge men's souls is ridiculed by being made ludicrously explicit:

> "But talking about trumpets, here's my 'Vision' !
>   Now you shall judge, all people—yes—you shall
> Judge with my judgment ! and by my decision
>   Be guided who shall enter heaven or fall.
> I settle all these things by intuition,
>   Times present, past, to come—Heaven—Hell—and all,
> Like King Alfonso.   When I thus see double,
> I save the Deity some worlds of trouble."[39]

Then in a final piece of admirable fooling his attempt to read the poem puts the whole assembly to immediate flight, so that we dismiss his *Vision* with a gust of laughter, while he himself is thrown down to the Lakes, where we contemptuously leave him.

In this section Byron has contrived to revenge himself on Southey by exposing and deriding his most blatant faults as a man and as a poet; but he has also solved the very difficult problem of how to end his own poem.   Satan's indictment, after all, had been a true one, and George III *was* guilty, so that it would have been impossible for Byron to find him innocent and let him pass triumphantly into Heaven.   Yet he could not, on the other hand, have let George III be found guilty and packed off to Hell, because this would have been to

---

[39] *P.W.*, IV. 522-3.   Byron explains his reference in a note to the poem : "King Alfonso, speaking of the Ptolomean system, said, that 'had he been consulted at the creation of the world, he would have spared the Maker some absurdities.' " (*P.W.*, IV. 523, n.1).

lapse into the very fault which he condemned in Southey—
the arrogant vindictive dooming of one's political opponents
to damnation. Byron escapes from this dilemma by not
allowing the trial to finish—the interruption is carefully timed,
and the subsequent ridicule of Southey is an integral part of
the poem's narrative structure, for in the moments of chaos
caused by the Laureate's intolerable verses, the old king slips
unobtrusively into Heaven, where Byron with gentlemanly
tolerance and a final touch of amused irreverence is well
content to let him stay:

> As for the rest, to come to the conclusion
>   Of this true dream, the telescope is gone
> Which kept my optics free from all delusion,
>   And showed me what I in my turn have shown ;
> All I saw farther, in the last confusion,
>   Was, that King George slipped into Heaven for one ;
> And when the tumult dwindled to a calm,
> I left him practising the hundredth psalm.[40]

Southey's poem, then, was at once the occasion of Byron's
answer and a cause of its success, for it provided him with what
he lacked in some parts of *Don Juan*—a single major target and
a clearly defined satiric purpose: his *Vision*, he told Hobhouse,
was "by way of reversing rogue Southey's,"[41] and this object
was always before his eyes. In this poem, therefore, as in
Beppo, all his detailed effects contribute to the total meaning
of the work, for while the local excellence of Byron's style is
as high as ever, it is now the instrument, precise and perfectly
controlled, of his artistic-moral purpose. Although he runs
through the whole gamut of his moods, from flippant irreverence
to solemn denunciation, they do not result in any inconsistency
or confusion, for he now shows the great satirist's complete
control of tone, manipulating it according to the poem's needs.
(His cynical humour and urge to deflate, which sometimes run
riot in *Don Juan*, are never allowed to weaken his own beliefs or
feelings in the *Vision*—they are used instead to discredit
Southey's work in all its aspects.) And he speaks himself of
the poem's being written in his "finest . . . Caravaggio style,"[42]

---

[40] *P.W.*, IV. 525.   [41] *Corr.*, II. 203.   [42] *Ibid.*

meaning presumably that the light and the dark—or in this case the humorous and the serious—are united in a pattern of deliberate contrasts, all of which contribute to the composition as a whole. The structure of the *Vision* is as admirable as the style: Southey's plot provided a framework for the poem, but Byron shows brilliant originality and artistic skill in his adaptation of the Laureate's work—in his selection of some parts of it for detailed treatment, in his reversal of its values, and in his abandoning its sequence of events at exactly the right moment, so as to achieve his own superb conclusion. The result is a narrative-meditative poem in which the narrative is extremely entertaining but also completely functional, being designed to ridicule one set of values and to assert another, while the comments and digressions are designed to reinforce the narrative and bring out its full implications. Hence the poem is as coherent and compact, as economical, as aesthetically satisfying, as *Beppo*—and it is fully as amusing. Yet its implications are as profound as those of the best cantos of *Don Juan*: Southey's poem embodied so many corrupt values in small compass that an attack on it involved the assertion of Byron's political, moral, and critical beliefs, and the whole poem is directed to this end. Sometimes the *ottava rima* style seems to act as a mirror, reflecting all the casual and contradictory elements in Byron's mind, but *The Vision of Judgment* (like the best parts of *Don Juan*) is more like a burning-glass, which focusses all his relevant ideas and feelings on the subject, and presents them with maximum effectiveness. It has, in fact, the characteristic excellences of *Don Juan*, with none of the longer poem's faults, just as it has the artistic perfection of *Beppo* without any of its triviality. *The Vision of Judgment* is Byron's masterpiece, aesthetically perfect, intellectually consistent, highly entertaining, and morally profound—the supreme example of satire as it could be written by an English poet-aristocrat.

APPENDIX

Byron's Plans for Further Cantos of *Don Juan*

Although Byron never returned to *Don Juan* after May 8th, 1823, he had some ideas for a continuation of the poem.

In spite of the leisurely progress of the plot in the later cantos, he almost certainly had a definite catastrophe in mind for the conclusion of the English episode—he seems to be working (however slowly) towards some climax, possibly a scandal over Juan and Lady Adeline,[1] and it has been plausibly suggested that the hero might have left England in rage and disillusion, as Byron himself had done in 1816.[2]

He had not decided definitely on Juan's subsequent adventures, but he had various possibilities in mind. Leigh Hunt, who since July 1822 had been a member—though an unwelcome one—of Byron's circle, maintains that he was still uncertain about the future conduct of his satire: "Speaking of 'Don Juan,' I will here observe that he had no plan with regard to that poem; that he did not know how long he should make it, nor what to do with his hero. He had a great mind to make him die a Methodist—a catastrophe which he sometimes anticipated for himself."[3] This idea was mentioned also to Lady Blessington, who recorded in her journal Byron's own statement:

> that as people have chosen to identify him with his heroes, and make him responsible for their sins, he will make Don Juan end by becoming a methodist; a metamorphosis that cannot, he thinks, fail to conciliate the good opinion of the religious persons in England, who have vilified its author.[4]

He told Hamilton Browne, too, that he expected to die a miser and a Methodist, "which he said he intended should also be

---

[1] See, for example, *P.W.*, vi. 484, 541-2.
[2] E. F. Boyd, *Byron's 'Don Juan'*, pp. 69-70.
[3] *Lord Byron and Some of His Contemporaries*, 1st edn, London 1828, p. 75.
[4] *The Idler in Italy*, ii. 57 (entry for May 1st, 1823) : cp. *Conversations*, p. 206.

the *denouément* of Don Juan";[5] and though the discussions on religion which he held with Dr Kennedy were no doubt sincere up to a point—they accord with what we know of Byron's interests and reading—there may have been some grounds for the belief that he was gathering material for his satire:

> The wits of the garrison [Dr Kennedy himself wrote] made themselves merry with what was going on, and passed many jokes on the subject. Some of them affected to believe,—I know not on what ground,—that Lord B.'s wish to hear me proceeded from his desire to have an accurate idea of the opinions and manners of the Methodists, in order that he might make Don Juan become one for a time, and thus paint their conduct with the greater accuracy and fidelity : some of them did not hesitate to tell me that this was the case, and that, if I were wise, I should let his lordship alone.[6]

This, however, was only one of Byron's ideas for the poem, and fully as important was his notion of drawing on his Greek adventures. Before leaving Italy he told Lady Blessington that he would write two poems about the expedition, "one an epic, and the other a burlesque,"[7] and the latter was soon identified with his existing satire: "If things are farcical," he told Trelawny at Cephalonia, "they will do for *Don Juan*; if heroical, you shall have another canto of *Childe Harold*."[8] "He said," notes Dr Kennedy, "he would give his travels in the Morea to the world; but laughing, added, it would depend on the reception he met with, whether they should be written in the Childe Harold or the Don Juan style."[9] After spending some time in Missolonghi, he decided that he *would* make use of his experiences there for further cantos, and his irritation at Stanhope's Benthamite procedures suggested one object for his satire. After complaining to Parry about the slackness of the Greek Committee in London, he went on:

> Well, well, I'll have my revenge : talk of subjects for Don Juan, this Greek business, its disasters and mismanagement,

---

[5] *Blackwood's Edinburgh Magazine*, XXXV .(Jan. 1834), 64.

[6] Kennedy, *Conversations on Religion*, p. 211.

[7] Lady Blessington, *Conversations*, p. 319.

[8] Trelawny, *Recollections*, p. 142 : cp. Trelawny's letter of September 2nd, 1823, quoted by Marchand, *Byron*, III. 1118.

[9] Kennedy, *Conversations on Religion*, p. 296.

have furnished me with matter for a hundred cantos. Jeremy Bentham and his scholar, Colonel Stanhope, shall be two of my heroes.[10]

I do not intend to write till next winter; then I may possibly finish another Canto. There will be both comedy and tragedy; my good countrymen supply the former, and Greece the latter. In one week, I have been in a fit : the troops mutinied—a Turkish brig burned—Sass killed—an earthquake—thunder, lightning, and torrents of rain—such a week I never witnessed. I shall tire them all with Juan's pranks.[11]

The end which he had previously contemplated—Juan's death in the French Revolution—has been abandoned or postponed indefinitely, and Byron seems prepared to extend his poem almost without limit. His early references to twelve or twenty-four books—the traditional numbers for epic—had already been superseded by more ambitious although humorous statements of intention:

> But now I will begin my poem. 'T is
>   Perhaps a little strange, if not quite new,
> That from the first of Cantos up to this
>   I've not begun what we have to go through.
> These first twelve books are merely flourishes,
>   *Preludios*, trying just a string or two
> Upon my lyre, or making the pegs sure ;
>   And when so, you shall have the overture. . . .
>
> I thought, at setting off, about two dozen
>   Cantos would do ; but at Apollo's pleading,
> If that my Pegasus should not be foundered,
> I think to canter gently through a hundred.[12]

Similar pronouncements now appear in Byron's conversation. In Cephalonia in October 1823 he said to Dr Henry Muir that "he would write a hundred Cantos of *Don Juan* at least, now that they had attacked him. He had not yet begun the work; the sixteen Cantos already written were only a kind

---

[10] Cp. Julius Millingen, *Memoirs of the Affairs of Greece*, London 1831, p. 117.
[11] Parry, *Last Days*, pp. 192-3.
[12] *P.W.*, VI. 470.

of introduction";[13] while he had told Hamilton Browne that "he would continue Don Juan to one hundred and fifty cantos, if the public would have patience,"[14] and he returned to this figure in a conversation with Colonel Napier in October.[15]

Byron had in fact found this poem so congenial that he now intended to prolong it more or less indefinitely, just as Sterne had come to say that he would write another volume of his novel each year of his life; and if he had lived to continue it, *Don Juan* would probably have become still less of an organic unity, and more of a comparatively unshaped running commentary on Byron's own experiences.

[13] *L.J.*, VI. 429.
[14] Stanhope, *Greece*, p. 505.
[15] *His Very Self and Voice : Collected Conversations of Lord Byron*, ed. E. J. Lovell, New York 1954, p. 428.

Selected Bibliography

I. BYRON'S WORKS AND LETTERS

Byron. A Self-Portrait. Letters and Diaries, 1798 to 1824, ed. PETER QUENNELL, 2 vols., London 1950.

Byron's "Don Juan", edd. T. G. STEFFAN and W. W. PRATT, 4 vols., Austin (Texas) 1957.

Lord Byron's Correspondence, ed. JOHN MURRAY, 2 vols., London 1922.

The Works of Lord Byron: Letters and Journals, ed. R. E. PROTHERO, 6 vols., London 1898-1901.

The Works of Lord Byron: Poetry, ed. E. H. COLERIDGE, 2nd edn, 7 vols., London 1904-5.

II. WORKS BY BYRON'S CONTEMPORARIES

BLESSINGTON, LADY: *Conversations of Lord Byron with the Countess of Blessington,* London 1834.

———: *The Idler in Italy*, 3 vols., London 1839-40.

BROUGHTON, [JOHN CAM HOBHOUSE], LORD: *Italy: Remarks made in several Visits from the Year 1816 to 1854*, 2 vols., London 1859.

———: *A Journey through Albania and other Provinces of Turkey . . . during the Years 1809 and 1810*, 2nd edn, 2 vols., London 1813.

———: *Recollections of a Long Life*, ed. Lady Dorchester, 6 vols., London 1909-11.

BROWNE, J. HAMILTON: " Voyage from Leghorn to Cephalonia with Lord Byron, and a Narrative of a Visit, in 1823, to the Seat of War in Greece", in *Blackwood's Edinburgh Magazine*, XXXV (Jan. 1834), pp. 56 ff., and XXXVI (Sep. 1834), pp. 392 ff.

DALLAS, R. C.: *Recollections of the Life of Lord Byron, from the Year 1808 to the End of 1814 . . .*, London 1824.

FRERE, J. HOOKHAM: *The Monks and the Giants*, ed. R. D. Waller, Manchester 1926.

GALT, JOHN: *The Life of Lord Byron*, 3rd edn, London 1830.

GAMBA, PIETRO: *A Narrative of Lord Byron's Last Journey to Greece . . .*, London 1825.

GINGUENÉ, P. L.: *Histoire littéraire d'Italie*, 14 vols., Paris 1811-35.

GUICCIOLI, TERESA: *My Recollections of Lord Byron; and those of Eye-witnesses of his Life*, tr. H. E. H. Jerningham, 2 vols., London 1869.

His Very Self and Voice: Collected Conversations of Lord Byron, ed. E. J. LOVELL, New York 1954.

HOBHOUSE, J. C.: see BROUGHTON.

HUNT, J. H. LEIGH: *The Autobiography of Leigh Hunt*, ed. J. E. Morpurgo, London 1949.

——: *Lord Byron and some of his Contemporaries . . .*, 1st edn, London 1828.

John Bull's "Letter to Lord Byron," ed. A. L. STROUT, Norman (Oklahoma) 1947.

KENNEDY, JAMES: *Conversations on Religion, with Lord Byron and others, held in Cephalonia . . .*, London 1830.

MEDWIN, THOMAS: *Conversations of Lord Byron: Noted during a Residence with His Lordship at Pisa, in the Years 1821 and 1822*, 2nd edn, London 1824.

MILLINGEN, JULIUS: *Memoirs of the Affairs of Greece . . .*, London 1831.

MOORE, THOMAS: *The Life, Letters and Journals of Lord Byron*, new and complete edn, repr., London 1932.

——: *Memoirs, Journal and Correspondence of Thomas Moore*, ed. Lord John Russell, 8 vols., London 1853-6.

PARRY, WILLIAM: *The Last Days of Lord Byron . . .*, London 1825.

POLIDORI, J. W.: *The Diary of Dr John William Polidori, 1816*, ed. W. M. Rossetti, London 1911.

ROGERS, SAMUEL: *Recollections of the Table-talk of Samuel Rogers*, ed. A. Dyce, London 1887.

SHELLEY, P. B.: *The Letters of Percy Bysshe Shelley*, ed. R. Ingpen, 2 vols., London 1914.

STANHOPE, LEICESTER: *Greece, in 1823, 1824 & 1825; Being Documents on the Greek Revolution. . . . To which are added Reminiscences of Lord Byron*, London 1828.

TRELAWNY, E. J.: *Recollections of the Last Days of Shelley and Byron*, ed. E. Dowden, London 1923.

——: *Records of Shelley, Byron, and the Author*, 2 vols., London 1878.

III. MODERN STUDIES, CRITICAL AND BIOGRAPHICAL

ARNOLD, MATTHEW: "Byron," in *Essays in Criticism, Second Series*, London 1888.

BEWLEY, MARIUS: "The Colloquial Mode of Byron," in *Scrutiny*, XVI (1949), pp. 8 ff.

BORST, W. A.: *Lord Byron's First Pilgrimage*, New Haven (Conn.) 1948.

BOTTRALL, RONALD: "Byron and the Colloquial Tradition in English Poetry," in *The Criterion*, XVIII (1938-9), pp. 204 ff.

BOWRA, C. M.: "Don Juan," in *The Romantic Imagination*, London 1950.

BOYD, ELIZABETH F.: *Byron's "Don Juan"*. *A Critical Study*, New Brunswick 1945.

BROWN, W. C.: "Byron and English Interest in the Near East," in *Studie^s in Philology*, XXXIV (1937), pp. 55 ff.

BUTLER, E. M.: *Byron and Goethe*, London 1956.

CALVERT, W. J.: *Byron: Romantic Paradox*, Chapel Hill (N. Carolina) 1935.

CECIL, LORD DAVID: *The Young Melbourne* . . ., London 1939.

CHEW, S. C.: "Byron," in *The English Romantic Poets*. *A Review of Research*, ed. T. M. Raysor, New York 1950.

——: *Byron in England. His Fame and After-Fame*, London 1924.

——: *The Dramas of Lord Byron. A Critical Study*, Göttingen 1915.

CLINE, C. L.: *Byron, Shelley and their Pisan Circle*, London 1952.

DU BOS, CHARLES: *Byron and the Need of Fatality*, tr. E. C. Mayne, London 1932.

ELIOT, T. S.: "Byron," in *On Poetry and Poets*, London 1957.

ELTON, OLIVER: "Byron," in *A Survey of English Literature 1780-1830*, London 1912.

ERDMAN, D. V.: "Byron and Revolt in England," in *Science and Society*, XI (1947), pp. 234 ff.

——: "Lord Byron and the Genteel Reformers," in *P.M.L.A.*, LVI (1941), pp. 1065 ff.

——: "Lord Byron as Rinaldo," in *P.M.L.A.*, LVII (1942), pp. 189 ff.

ESTÈVE, EDMOND: *Byron et le romantisme français*, Paris 1907.

EVANS, BERTRAND: "Manfred's Remorse and Dramatic Tradition," in *P.M.L.A.*, LXII (1947), pp. 752 ff.

FUESS, C. M.: *Lord Byron as a Satirist in Verse*, New York 1912.

GENDARME DE BÉVOTTE, GEORGES: *La Légende de Don Juan*, 2 vols., Paris 1911.

GRIERSON, H. J. C.: "Byron and English Society," in *The Background of English Literature*, London 1925.

JACK, IAN: *Augustan Satire*, Oxford 1952.

JOHNSON, E. D. H.: "*Don Juan* in England," in *ELH (A Journal of English Literary History)*, XI (1944), pp. 135 ff.

KNIGHT, G. WILSON: *Lord Byron. Christian Virtues*, London 1952.

LEAVIS, F. R.: "Byron's Satire," in *Revaluation*, London 1936.

LOVELACE, RICHARD MILBANKE, LORD: *Astarte: A Fragment of Truth concerning . . . Lord Byron*, rev. edn, London 1929.

MARCHAND, L. A.: *Byron: A Biography*, London 1957.

MAYNE, ETHEL C.: *Byron*, 2nd edn, London 1924.

——: *The Life and Letters of Anne Isabella, Lady Noel Byron*, London 1929.

MAZZINI, GIUSEPPE: "Byron and Goethe," in *Essays*, ed. W. Clarke, London 1887.

MILBANKE, R.: see LOVELACE.

NICOLSON, HAROLD: *Byron. The Last Journey*, rev. edn, London 1940.

ORIGO, IRIS: *The Last Attachment*, London 1949.

PRATT, W. W.: *Byron at Southwell*, Austin (Texas) 1948.

PRAZ, MARIO: *The Romantic Agony*, tr. Angus Davidson, 2nd edn, London 1951.

RAYMOND, DORA NEILL: *The Political Career of Lord Byron*, New York 1924.

ROBSON, W. W.: "Byron as Poet," in *Proceedings of the British Academy*, XLIII (1957), pp. 25 ff.

RUSSELL, BERTRAND A. W.: "Byron," in *History of Western Philosophy*, London 1946.

SMILES, SAMUEL: *A Publisher and His Friends. Memoir and Correspondence of the Late John Murray . . .*, London 1891.

STEFFAN, GUY: "The Devil a Bit of Our Beppo," in *Philological Quarterly*, XXXII (1953), pp. 154 ff.

WARD, W. S.: "Byron's 'Hours of Idleness' and Other than Scotch Reviewers," in *Modern Language Notes*, LIX (1944), pp. 547 ff.

WIENER, H. S. L.: "Byron and the East: Literary Sources of the 'Turkish Tales'," in *Nineteenth Century Studies*, ed. Herbert Davis, W. C. De Vane, and R. C. Bald, Ithaca (New York) 1940.

Index

PRINTED IN GREAT BRITAIN BY
OLIVER AND BOYD LTD
EDINBURGH